Entrepreneur Magazine
Guide to Integrated Marketing

The *Entrepreneur* Magazine Small-Business Series

ENTREPRENEUR MAGAZINE
Guide to Integrated Marketing

Jeanette Smith

John Wiley & Sons, Inc.

New York • Chichester • Brisbane • Toronto • Singapore

This text is printed on acid-free paper.

Copyright © 1996 by Jeanette Smith
Published by John Wiley & Sons, Inc.

This publication is designed to provide accurate and authoritative information in regard to the subject matter covered. It is
said with the understanding that the publisher is not engaged
in rendering legal, accounting, or other professional services.
If legal advice or other expert assistance is required, the services of a competent professional person should be sought.

Library of Congress Cataloging-in-Publication Data:

Smith, Jeanette.
    Entrepreneur magazine : guide to integrated marketing /
Jeanette Smith.
        p.   cm. — (Entrepreneur magazine small business series)
    Includes bibliographical references.
    ISBN 0-471-12439-7 (cloth : alk. paper). — ISBN 0-471-12441-9
(pbk. : alk. paper)
    1. Advertising media planning—Handbooks, manuals, etc.   2. Direct
marketing—Handbooks, manuals, etc.   I. Title.   II. Series.
HF5826.5.S64   1996
658.8′4—dc20   96-530
                                                                      CIP

Printed in the United States of America

10   9   8   7   6   5   4   3   2   1

CONTENTS

PREFACE

There is a John McPherson "Close to Home" cartoon that shows a patient on the operating table with his two doctors off to the side studying a how-to book, *Bypass Surgery Made Easy!*

Imagine for a moment that your company is the patient and you're a doctor about to set in motion your company's marketing "operation." The operation won't be as successful if you use old marketing methods and books, because there's a totally new marketing technique, explained in this book, that's virtually guaranteed to be successful. It's a process that marketing pros have pretty much kept within their closed-door fraternity.

This hot new technique is simply *integrating* a single marketing message throughout advertising, direct marketing, promotion, and publicity, by way of mixed media. It's recognizing that all these marketing entities can sleep under the same blanket—and the more they cuddle, the warmer each is.

Businesses of all sizes with all sizes of pockets deserve to know about this technique. That's what this book is here for—to get you a much higher degree of marketing success. Using the book is a lot like going to college on a sports scholarship: All you want to do is play the sport, but learning what's in the play book must come before you get the coaching you need to jump into the fun of the game.

The first couple of chapters describe and explain "plays" for this marketing technique, and it's important that you read them to be able to perform in this sport. *Then* comes the *fun*. You can then jump to the chapters that let you play the game the best way to benefit your team—your business—and get you in shape for the big money contracts that happen when you become a top-rated player.

It's probably a safe assumption that every businessperson in this country knows the word *marketing*. But marketing isn't the subject here. The subject is *marketing communications* throughout an almost unlimited media mix that is changing so fast you don't dare blink for fear you'll miss something!

The purposes for the book are: first, to let you in on this little-known, little-understood, but effective moneymaking strategy; second, to explain it in an "edutaining"—easy, informative, and sometimes fun-to-read—style, rather than in a scholarly, technical text; and finally, to provide a combat manual that shows you how to use this strategy to deal with the marketing warfare that exists in this high-tech, electronic age.

As an added value, you'll get "copycatting" guidance. After the overview chapters and each of the sections on advertising, direct marketing, promotion, and publicity, you're invited to sit down with a businessperson and four professional marketers to copycat from their knowledge, tips, and techniques, along with their examples of various ads, promotions, marketing strategies, and publicity releases that have proved enormously effective and productive.

Perhaps the biggest edge this book gives you is to show you that, yes, although big agencies are called on to design and construct programs for megacorps, you can do it yourself for your own business, whatever size it is. Or, if you don't have time, you'll learn that there are *affordable* ways to get the job done—*if* you know *how* it should be done, so you can be its guide and evaluator.

•

One last word about the book. It's meant to be marked up with pen and highlighter. As you walk through the processes and notice something that you want to come back to, make a note on the page and tag the place with a sticky note so you can easily return to the information.

PART I

MIXED MEDIA MARKETING COMMUNICATIONS

1

Traditional Marketing versus Mixed Media Marketing Communications

Traditional marketing did it one way; Mixed Media
Marketing Communications works entirely differently.
New tech caused the change. There are differences be-
tween marketing and marketing communications. How
MMMC works. Five MMMC principles. Copycat—it's
the way to go.

Marketing insiders call it Integrated Marketing Communications—IMC.
We prefer to call it Mixed Media Marketing Communications—MMMC.
And we believe it is time businesses of all sizes not only hear about this
technique that large corporations have kept so quiet but are shown how it
works and how to make it work for them.

Whatever it's called, MMMC consolidates *all* communications to
present an individual, focused marketing, sales, or image message. In
contrast, traditional marketing communication uses an assortment of
communications forms to deliver a variety of messages about the product,
service, or company, and these forms of communication seem to take off
in all directions. For example, the package might pitch one thing, perhaps
an image, while ads peddle price and value. The envelope and contents of
a direct-mail piece might say something else in a hard-sell fashion, while
the kinds and looks of signs you use on and off your property to identify
and promote your company or service tend to give a feeling of soft-sell
dignity and status. And the publicity and public relations messages you
send out give yet another impression.

That is *not* the way MMMC works. Probably the simplest explanation of MMMC is that it correlates, combines, blends, and consolidates *all* marketing communication that you want the public—not the *mass* public but specific segments of the public—to perceive and accept. In the past, marketing has focused on a different strategy, a different message, for each entity. When a corporation wished to make the public aware of its presence, it hired an advertising agency, a public relations or publicity agency, a sales promotion agency, and perhaps even a company that specializes in so-called direct response marketing. Each of these separate entities developed goals, objectives, and individual plans, usually without consulting one another. Even when all the programs were handled in-house, there was little or no consolidation.

Finally there is recognition among a few of the most successful megacorporations that there must be a coalition of these marketing entities. These corporations have come up with customized mixes of advertising *and* direct marketing *and* promotion *and* publicity. As never before, they've coordinated and *integrated* this mixed-media marketing effort, and it's working beyond anyone's expectations.

NEW TECHNOLOGIES CAUSED THE CHANGE

MMMC is the best thing that has happened for business in a long time, and it came about as a result of the explosion of new technologies that has effectively killed mass marketing. More importantly, new technologies such as high-tech databases permit an intimate knowledge of consumers so that marketers are able to get a clear idea who they're talking to and what their audience wants to know.

New technologies have built a bridge across what recently have been some very rough waters. And that bridge will sooner or later force *all* businesses to make one of three choices: They can turn back to the old ways because new ways tend to be intimidating, they can just stand there and watch others cross over to find immense success, or they can cross the bridge and discover a previously little-known but beautifully paved road that big corporations are using to get to their marketing goals.

MARKETING AND MARKETING COMMUNICATIONS AREN'T THE SAME

To avoid any confusion about what marketing is, let it be said that it's an intricate, sometimes tangled, group of operations that often are wrongly and unceremoniously lumped into the single activity of advertising or sales. The word *marketing* itself is a hot button for many businesspeople—they know it's necessary, but they wish it would go away. Some even call it "the M word."

In *The Marketing Glossary* (Amacom/American Management Association), Mark N. Clemente describes marketing as four distinct processes:

1. Developing a product or service
2. Establishing a price for it
3. Communicating information about it through various direct and indirect communications channels
4. Coordinating its distribution to ensure product accessibility by target buyers

Marketing communications, then, is only that distinctly separate third process. It is almost every form of communication a business presents to the public.

Among the closed-door brotherhood of professional marketers and a few university professors, MMMC is often spoken of as Integrated Marketing Communications (IMC). Stan Rapp and Tom Collins, in their book *The Great Marketing Turnaround* (Prentice Hall), call it "individualized marketing" and define it as

> . . . any integrated program of sales communications directly from the advertiser to selected members of the public, whether by means of letters, brochures, audiocassettes, videocassettes, telephone messages, computer disks, advertiser-sponsored events, or any other means of direct contact.

Consumers have always called the shots—by deciding whether to line up at the cash register or walk out without buying. Now technology lets them say what they think, what they like, and what they want. A good portion of today's consumers have visited cyberspace and realize that there are *two directions* to this new highway that runs through it. (By the way, the word *cyberspace* came from a science fiction novel by William Gibson, *Neuromancer.* It's a "place" out there where communication and interaction between computers occurs.)

Today's consumers know they can sit down at their computers and, instead of having to accept only the information a business deigns to deliver to them, they can get the information *they* desire about products and services they want or are considering. They can even place orders from their offices or homes without any sales pressures.

High tech is the most obvious reason the new kid—MMMC—came to town.

A MYSTERIOUS, SOMETIMES WEIRD, WIRED WORLD

> For some who think a hard drive is a long road trip, a 486SX is a sports car, an icon is a religious statue, and software is snuggly clothing, . . . [this] is going to be an out of this world experience, reminiscent of *2001: A Space Odyssey.* You know the movie—the one where the computer takes over from the humans.

Lynn Bulmahn's words in the *Waco Tribune-Herald* indicate how difficult it can be to live in prehistoric technological times—like last year! We're talking Star Wars here, where terms such as *gigabyte* (one billion bits of information) and *terrabyte* (one trillion bits of information) are already being bandied about. "We're in the equivalent of the industrial revolution," says Robert Kavner, head of AT&T's rapidly expanding multimedia efforts.

HOW MMMC WORKS

Let's say you own a restaurant and you understand how MMMC works. Here is a way you might put it to use.

First, your chef comes up with a new item—a fat-free, sinfully tasty, low-calorie coconut cream pie. Naturally, you want to alert your regular customers beyond just listing the pie on the menu, so you create a tabletop promotion piece. At the same time, you watch for reactions from customers, which you recognize are outstanding: "How on earth do you get a pie that tastes so good to be fat-free and have only seventy calories?"

You decide to turn such reactions into a news story—a publicity story—so you write a press release and send it to the "Dining Out" editor at the local newspaper. You attach a note saying that you will be happy to set up an interview with the restaurant's chef, who created the recipe, to do a feature story about him and his creation. The editor takes you up on the offer, and as soon as the piece appears in the paper, you use it as a means to attract new customers with a direct-mail piece that includes a reproduction of the newspaper story and send it to a mailing list of people in your immediate geographic area.

But you also know you can use this same story to expand your coverage area—to reach people across town—so you take the same information and build a newspaper ad and a radio spot around it. The newspaper ad and the direct-mail piece each include a coupon that invites recipients to enjoy free servings of the pie when they come in for dinner. That way, you open up the direct-response avenue that transforms your one-way communication—with promotion, advertising, publicity, and direct mail doing the communicating—into a two-way, customer-participation connection.

With this plan, you've consolidated a convincing message into an in-store promotion piece and then into publicity, a direct-mail piece, and advertising in two appropriate media. You've circled the mixed media field. The vehicle you used to carry that single, consolidated marketing message to your present and future customers is MMMC.

It's not always necessary, however, to use all forms of communication media in order to accomplish an objective. Following is an example of a more limited MMMC plan.

A MORE COMPACT PLAN

Let's say you own a company that manufactures on-site signage for both local and national businesses and you would like to gain new customers as well as build remembrance among businesses you have already researched and know are likely customers.

- First, you prepare a convincing message that can be integrated into direct-response pieces to be sent to a list of businesses you believe will soon be in the market for new signs (businesses whose signage is old and needs replacement, as well as businesses that have announced plans for new locations or buildings).
- You also create an informational brochure with photos of completed projects and testimonial-type quotes from previous customers. This promotion piece is enclosed with the direct-mail piece and can also be used as a handout.
- Next you compile a list of trade publications that are read by potential customers (banking journals if banks are on your list, restaurant publications if restaurants are included, and so on). Then you create an advertisement with the same message as the mailing piece and place it in the trade publications.

The MMMC program for the sign company is ongoing—a constant drip-drip-drip reminder that builds name recognition and remembrance while it develops an image of reliability and experience, thereby producing new clients.

FIVE PRINCIPLES OF AN MMMC PROGRAM

Carole M. Howard, writing in *Public Relations Quarterly,* narrowed down to five the principles she believes are necessary for conducting an MMMC plan or program.

1st Principle: When any good idea is brainstormed and adopted for one of your target audiences, we need to immediately think of how [the same idea] also can be used to reach other priority audiences of the product or the company.

2nd Principle: Think broadly when you're brainstorming [mixed] media.

3rd Principle: Whenever you create materials for one audience, consider their value for [other targeted groups] as well.

4th Principle: To facilitate the sharing and exchange of information across functions that are essential to [mixed media] marketing, your marketing and PR should be a regular item on editorial and business meeting agendas.

THE FIFTH PRINCIPLE: COPYCATTING

Now you understand the concept but perhaps you still feel that MMMC is something you're not quite qualified to undertake for your company. Before you turn that feeling into a final decision, there are some people you should meet—a businessperson (very much like you) and some highly trained, experienced marketing professionals who have already accomplished this mission. At various points in this book, they will walk you through the processes involved in MMMC.

In Chapters 3, 8, 12, 16, and 21, these people will first explain, and then demonstrate with real-life examples, how they used MMMC to achieve success. Each case is meant to show you a way you can adapt and apply it to your own situation. Using the knowledge and experience of these experts, you will hitchhike to your own successful strategy and end result. They all take different routes to reach their goals, one of which may be a route you can take.

Start building a sample file of newspaper publicity stories, ads, promotion pieces, and direct response materials that might apply to your needs. Pay particular attention to any items that you react strongly to—either positively or negatively. Attach a note to each item telling what it was about that particular piece that caught your attention. Was it the wording, the layout, the teaser on the envelope? Was it something you could possibly adapt for your own use? How? Jot down your reaction immediately because the intensity of your response will fade with time. Different circumstances will elicit a different, less intense response.

2

Marketing as a Search and Rescue Function

> Conducting research to locate the right market. Where to find it and the kinds of ways to do it. Learn from and about the competition. Databases are everywhere.

Okay. Now that you know why MMMC is important, let's look at some facts and findings that reveal why you need it. After that, we'll learn where to locate the information that is the foundation of an MMMC program.

According to *Advertising Age*, although there is growing recognition of the need for it, "implementation remains low despite high interest in the concept of integrated marketing communications.

"Integrated marketing communications [we call it mixed media marketing communications] is the buzz in today's business world. Unfortunately, it usually ends there—buzz lacking a bite," complained *Ad Age* in February 1995. The headline reads, "Few wed market communications," and the article goes on to cite a survey of business marketers by Tucker Chicago (Schaumburg, Illinois), Elrick and Lavidge (a Westchester market research company), and *Ad Age's* Business Marketing.

The figures show that "less than one-third (26 percent) of the 263 responding companies developed an annual marketing communications plan, and only 15 percent took database marketing to a level of sophistication higher than developing a mailing list, which about 70 percent do on a regular basis."

The report goes on to show that the top reasons companies don't implement MMMC are lack of expertise (58%) and lack of budget (48%).

This book is dedicated to reducing that first figure, to helping the 58 percent who lack expertise to not only determine how to implement MMMC but also recognize that it's actually easier than other methods, and it can in fact soften the attack on the budget.

SEARCH IS A BETTER WORD THAN *RESEARCH*

In marketing, research might better be called "search and rescue." You will benefit greatly from the research you do. It will play across the entire mixed-media field. You'll use your research to determine how to write the message—what benefits to indicate and what kind of language to use. And your research will dictate which media to use, which types of direct-response and direct-mail pieces will attract consumers, which kinds of promotion *your* targeted audience actually will respond to, and ultimately, which publicity message will be the most convincing. The degree of the necessity for research is expressed in a single sentence by William M. Luther in his book *The Marketing Plan* (Amacom/American Management Association).

> Even if your communications budget is only $10,000, it is wiser to spend $1,000 in research to get a fix on whether the other $9,000 is working than to waste the entire $10,000.

Every ad or ad campaign starts as an answer to a problem. It's the same way we used to treat sunburn: We'd put the salve on *after* the problem had occurred. Now we eliminate the problem of sunburn by putting a lotion on *first*. It's the same with all types of marketing, and it's imperative with MMMC: To accomplish a goal, do the research first.

Because marketing embraces far more than advertising, businesses of all sizes must not only have a clear picture of their consumers both present and potential—but they must also know the public's perception of their own company, product, or service. Of equal importance is the need to identify what the competition is up to. This knowledge is the equivalent of applying a lotion *before* going out in the sun.

FINDING THE RIGHT MARKET

It only makes sense that, before you go after new customers or bring a product or service to market, you should make sure the product or service *has* a market. Likewise, you should know *who* has a desire or need for your product or service. This means digging up all the information you can—about present and potential customers, about the competition, and about the image people have of your company, product, or service. This brings us to three highly important words in marketing—*demographics, psychographics,* and *geographics.*

Demographics provides the most frequently used information because it focuses on consumer *behavior.* This is also the most easily located information. Demographics includes data about age, sex, occupation, income, family size, level of education, race, religion, and nationality.

Psychographics gets personal: It gives psychological characteristics. It zeroes in on the behavior that reveals people's personal values, self-concepts, interests, opinions, and lifestyles. It tells, for instance, why people buy certain products over those of the competition, how often they make such purchases, and whether they are impulse buys or planned purchases.

Geographics is particularly useful for direct-mail programs. With geographics, a target market is defined by its location—a neighborhood, city, or state, or sometimes according to population density (urban, suburban, or rural markets, for example).

REDUCING THE MUMBO JUMBO

In his book *The Marketing Plan: How to Prepare and Implement It* (Amacom/American Management Association), William M. Luther has reduced all this "marketese" to five questions. Answer them and you can forget about words like *psychographics* and *demographics.*

1. Who is the target audience?
2. What do the customers want?
3. What does the competition offer them?
4. What can we offer them?
5. What do they think we offer them?

Now, isn't that simple? But if you hire an agency, you'll have to remember the marketese. Agency people speak it, and these questions may be a little too simple for them.

For example, let's say you are marketing a new vitamin supplement. Basic research shows that a good portion of your potential market is the so-called mature market. Common knowledge tells you that some older people have sizable retirement incomes, and others can barely meet their monthly bills. Some travel regularly, and some seldom venture away from the TV set. Some live in their own homes, and others live in community homes.

The information you need includes age segmentation, health status, work status, marital status, level of education, housing situation, discretionary income, and spending patterns. And perhaps the most important factor is gender: Are your potential customers mainly men or women?

ROPING IN NEW RIDERS

Haggar Apparel, the leader in all-cotton, no-iron pants, and more recently a contender in the men's blue jean market with a product called Mustang jeans, determined through demographic searches that their customers are men between twenty and forty years old who shop at discount stores.

Although Haggar is not a do-it-yourself marketer (the Richards Group is their agency), they follow the cross-media, MMMC concept to get their message to the proper groups. They use in-store signage, revitalized packaging and logos, outdoor billboards, and ads in *People* magazine. So when the competition, Lee jeans, pulled out of discount stores and moved into department stores, Haggar was poised to fill in the gap. "It left an opening that we felt really presented an opportunity for another top-of-the-line denim product to enter into that market," says Milton Hickman, senior VP and general manager of The Horizon Group, a division of Haggar.

The results? Mustang jeans today account for "a pretty substantial part of the total Haggar mix"—sales of which were reported to be upwards of $394 million in 1993, according to Hickman. Having a well-defined portrait of their customers and being able to move immediately because they knew what their competition was doing made success a reality for Haggar.

COLLECTING INFORMATION

So how do you go about locating the information you need without wasting time? It isn't that difficult. Really.

Demographic data is probably the easiest kind to locate. Much of it is available in census reports, from chambers of commerce, and from the most convenient resource of all—the reference section of your local library.

The federal government is the largest resource, with studies and reports available from the departments of Education, Labor, Commerce, and Agriculture. Certain university and public libraries are designated as government repositories, so if your local library doesn't have the information you need, they can no doubt tell you where the nearest government repository is.

If there is a trade association for your business or industry, contact it. Such organizations are often gold mines of data. The same is also true of trade journals: They often conduct surveys to assess consumer opinions and attitudes and to gauge product or service satisfaction.

It sometimes seems as if research librarians are genetically predisposed toward curiosity, diligence, and an honest desire to help. But before you lean too heavily on them, try the library's InfoTrac computer system. In just minutes, you can search literally thousands of magazine articles on a specific topic.

And for those of you whose personal computers are connected to online services, you may be able to find the information you need via that route.

Start with Your Own Files

Check out your own customers. More and more, businesspeople are realizing that they sometimes neglect their regular customers when they go after new ones. It's a fact that shouldn't be forgotten: Getting a new customer will cost four to six times more than keeping a regular one.

The information you want about who buys your product is often right within your own company records. And if you have a toll-free number you may be sitting on a direct-mail list that is about as focused as you could ask for. Your 800-number telephone statement contains the telephone numbers of people who are interested enough in your product or service to make a call, and you can use reverse number directories to find addresses for these telephone numbers.

Surveys

Market research has been around for a long time. A Bill Whitehead cartoon in *Advertising Age* shows a prehistoric surveyer making notes at his rock desk, and the person on whom the product has been tested is lying unconscious on the ground. The third person—the person being questioned—is holding a huge rock club, and saying, "It's sturdy, easy to grip, and makes a solid 'thunk' sound when you hit someone. . . . Yeah, I'd buy it."

That's pretty much the way it's done today, too. The most widely used approach to collecting primary marketing data is the survey method. There are basically four ways to survey:

1. By mail
2. Interviews (one-on-one or in groups)
3. By telephone
4. With focus groups

Mail surveys are probably the easiest and perhaps the least expensive, depending upon the extent of the geographic area covered. They do not have a high response rate, however, and they often reflect bias because of the high percentage of nonrespondents.

Personal interviews are on average the best means for gathering detailed information. People are most likely to respond to someone they perceive as friendly, honest, and sincere. Another advantage is that the interviewer can show or demonstrate an object, something that can't be done by telephone or mail.

Personal interviews can be costly when professionals are employed, but costs can be eliminated or lowered considerably when college students or older high school students are enlisted. Instructors in business, marketing, or advertising often welcome such projects so that students can learn survey techniques and their benefits. There's another plus: When students introduce themselves and mention they're conducting a survey as part of a course assignment, they receive more objective answers, and respondents are more receptive to being questioned.

If students are enlisted, though, make sure to work out with the instructor in advance how the students will be compensated. Sometimes class credit is sufficient, but if compensation will be coming from you, agree in advance about the form and amount.

You've seen those TV shows where the cops interrogate a suspect behind a one-way window? Focus sessions let you watch a group of 8 to 12 carefully chosen individuals and hear their remarks without affecting their attitudes—usually without them even knowing that they are being observed. It's a valuable means to get immediate, frank, sincere feedback. It's a valuable way to learn not only how individuals feel about your product, service, or company, but *why* they feel that way.

If there is a public perception that your company and its people are cold and uncaring, or that you don't offer as much value as your competitors, focus sessions are a good way to find out about such attitudes so that your MMMC plan can make provisions for reversing negative opinions.

THE QUESTIONNAIRE

No matter which method you use to solicit information, you'll need a questionnaire. Only you know the precise information you require, but the following list indicates items that most often are important. Use it to draft a basic questionnaire that you can adapt for different methods.

Age bracket
Gender
Geographic location
Income level
Education level

Marital status
Size of household
Occupation
Ethnic background
Owns, rents house, apartment
Type and number of vehicles
Use of public transportation
Distance from home to workplace
History and frequency of purchasing your product
Usual payment method
Route of product knowledge (recommendation, direct mail, news-
    paper, TV, etc.), including name or call letters of medium

Lifestyle Information

If you need more personal information, add any of the following questions that fit your research needs.

Travel habits (local, national, international; car, train, bus, air, boat)
Attendance at school events, PTA meetings
Attendance at civic meetings
Hobbies
Political activity
Charity work
Memberships (fraternal groups, civic organizations)
Dining out habits
Purchase frequency (your product or service and the competition's)
Reasons for purchase decisions
Attraction (package, company image, service, warranty, price, etc.)

LEARNING FROM AND ABOUT THE COMPETITION

Competition doesn't always mean rivalry, contention, conflict, or strife.
Sometimes the competition can be very useful to your organization.

Knowing why your competitors' customers buy products or services, or why *your* customers have switched to your competitors' products can help you not only shore up your own fort but also learn how to
attract new customers. The most important reason to check out the competition is that if you don't know what the competition is doing, you'll
know less than your customers do.

Knowing what the competition is up to and defining its market segments will save you time, money, and effort in attempts to invade their

undisputed territories. Common sense tells us that it's much easier to attract prospects who have no loyalty or allegiance to a particular competitor.

What You Need to Find Out

Some of the questions you'll want answers to are:

- What product or service benefits do your competitors feature most often, and what points do their salespeople emphasize to customers?
- What media do they use and how frequently?
- What is their total (estimated) marketing budget, with separate estimates for advertising, promotion, and direct response?
- Do they have a well-known slogan or theme that serves as a common thread running throughout their marketing communications?
- To what degree do they target specific groups, or are they still using mass marketing?
- How does their pricing compare with yours? Do they have a discount policy?
- What weaknesses do your top three competitors have?

Where to Find Information about the Competition

An excellent source of information about the competition exists within your own organization. Staffers hear things from friends, family, and customers. Involve employees by discussing with them the kinds of information you're seeking. Requesting their input will also build enthusiasm and encourage participation.

And an even better way to get inside your competitors' heads—or at least find out what they're up to—is to talk to the people who work for them. Trade publications in your field might have articles about your competitors. And finally, the Small Business Administration might have information you can use.

DATABASES FOR EVERY KIND OF DATA

Let's say you've gathered the information you require, and you now have a clear, focused image of your present and future new consumers. How do you reach these people? George Arnold, CEO and president of Evans-Group, an advertising and marketing agency with offices across the country, tucks his tongue in his cheek and tells us how productive databases can be: "If you want a list of left-handed Irishmen with handlebar mustaches who live west of the Mississippi in manufactured housing, and you know where to call, the reply will be 'I can get you that list.' " Of course, first you have to know that you're looking for left-handed Irishmen with all those other characteristics.

You can—and probably should—develop your own database. That is hugely time-consuming, and usually you must seek out database lists to add to your basic groups such as 800-number callers and past and present customers. The consumer database industry is booming, the kinds of data available multiply rapidly. Computer software can help you produce a customized database. Visit any large computer store and you'll find programs for creating networked applications and client/server applications. And there are programs that will help you access the information superhighway and start using e-mail.

There is even software that examines the new technologies that are pulling televisions, computers, and telephone lines into a vast interactive network. Computer hardware is always getting less expensive and faster, and personal computers have almost no limit to what they can do. ·

D&B Marketplace

Dun & Bradstreet MarketPlace (part of D&B Information Services) is the creator of a business-to-business data warehouse that can pinpoint just about any desired group. Compuserve calls it "the single most powerful tool a small business has to increase profits." Its cost-effectiveness comes from your ability to choose—and buy—only the names that fit your requirements. So this is truly a customized list. Your choices are delivered as a mailing list in label form.

D&B MarketPlace can deliver three different kinds of reports. For each company, the full "Prospect Report" includes name, address, county, phone, top executive's name and title, SIC codes, annual sales, number of employees, whether ownership is private or public, type(s) of sites, and year started. The "Prospect Report—Short" lists company name, address, phone, chief executive's name and title, type of ownership and sites, business characteristics, and SIC codes. The "Prospect Report—Condensed" lists only company name, telephone number, location, executive's name and title, and primary SIC code.

Not only can new customers be located this way, but there is no minimum list size requirement, so you can create lists according to your own size specifications. You can test a large list by using small random samples, create small candidate lists for surveys or focus groups, or test new target markets by creating small lists with different criteria.

D&B MarketPlace can also be used to build a list of companies that meet a variety of criteria. It can also perform market analysis, merge and purge multiple lists, print labels and lists, or export lists to other applications.

Whether you wish to purchase database lists to fit your needs or develop your own lists, you will find helpful information in Mark Bacon's book *Do-It-Yourself Direct Marketing* (Wiley).

3

Case Studies:
Develop the Skill
of Copycatting

Marketing pros and a businessman offer examples of how they used MMMC to reach specific goals.

There are "wannabees," and there are "wannasees." This is the first of five chapters spread throughout the book for wannabees who wannasee how marketing pros do it. This chapter presents a broad summary and review of each of nine highly successful MMMC case histories. Specifics about these individual MMMC campaigns will be spelled out in other, appropriate "copycat" chapters. Copycatting can be your ticket to finding professional, lucrative ways to use MMMC for your own marketing purposes.

The information presented here is important—you won't want to miss it. But if you're looking for immediate help with a marketing communications problem that MMMC can help decode or unravel, skip on ahead to the section and chapter that deals with the specifics. Don't forget to come back later to these case studies so you can gain from their knowledge, their tips and techniques, and their examples of strategies that have been hugely successful and profitable.

JUMPING OFF THE ICE BLOCK

A story from *The Dallas Morning News* about filmmaker Mario Van Peebles is relevant here.

Talk is one thing—doing is another," says Peebles. "Me? I'm like a penguin. You know how they gather around the ice block to see if there's a shark down there? Suddenly, one jumps in—me—and the rest wait.

The marketers whose examples we detail here are like Peebles. They've jumped in and checked for sharks, so now you can safely follow.

In this chapter you'll meet four marketing professionals and a successful businessperson. The pros understand value, and practice using MMMC. The businessperson learned as much as he could about MMMC and then put it to work for his company—with phenomenal success.

These five will show you how they made MMMC work in nine specific situations. Each will walk you through the media mix he or she used, explaining the goals that were set and the approaches taken to reach those goals.

To make it easy to follow these case histories through this chapter (which presents an overview of each) and Parts II through V of the book, each case has been assigned a number.

CASE 1: FASTSIGNS

Gary Salomon is a businessman, not a professional in any of the various marketing disciplines. He's a do-it-yourselfer who built his business from a single test store in 1985 to a rapidly growing, international franchise network of more than 250 stores. FastSigns is the leader in the one-day signage industry.

FastSigns, headquartered in Dallas, consistently appears on *Inc.* magazine's list of the 500 fastest-growing private companies in the United States. *Entrepreneur* magazine has named FastSigns the number one sign franchise every year since 1992. Here's Gary Salomon's story—in his own words.

It isn't unusual for a beginning entrepreneur to handle his early marketing efforts on his own. What's unusual in the case of FastSigns is that, after building a worldwide franchise network with a ten-year track record of phenomenal success, we're *still* doing it ourselves.

Obviously, we're now at a point in our evolution when we could afford to hire an agency to develop materials and programs through which to market our stores and promote the continuing expansion of our network through the sale of FastSigns franchises.

Why haven't we? One reason is that no agency can ever know our business the way we do. We're in constant communication with our franchisees around the world. We know what their customers want from them and how we can help them provide it. We know where our industry's technology is going and how it will change our business in years to come. And we know where our own vision for the future is leading us.

So we've kept virtually all our marketing activities in-house, in the hands of people whose considerable talents are augmented by their intimate, day-to-day knowledge of our company.

For us, in-house marketing makes sense from a purely practical and realistic angle, too. In our single company, we have several different agendas:

- Our corporate headquarters works to expand the network through franchise sales;
- Our franchisee-governed advertising council works to increase store sales and market share;
- Our international stores work to overcome language and cultural barriers to efficiently develop marketing materials for their countries;
- And the final reason—because I like it that way.

I have strong tastes in marketing and advertising, so I like to keep a loosely guiding hand on these areas. My marketing staff often agrees with my judgment, but when they don't they say so loud and clear.

From such debate comes better marketing.

Effective marketing can be as whimsical as a dancing gas pump or as weighty as a photo of a family killed by a drunk driver. My point is that different kinds of companies require very different approaches. With as many different kinds of companies—all within the same industry—as there are among franchisees, FastSigns produces marketing across the MMMC spectrum. You'll see how we do it as you read through the copycatting chapters about advertising, direct marketing, promotion, and publicity.

CASE 2: MICROHELP

F. Richard Wemmers Jr. is president of Wemmers Communications, Inc., in Atlanta, Georgia, a company that offers marketing, advertising, PR, and promotions services to a variety of clients from computer and fountain pen retailers to hospitals and hotels. Wemmers' credentials include more than 25 years of marketing experience. Early in his career, he worked with the largest ad agency in the world and became one of their youngest vice presidents. He started his own full-service agency in 1978.

Here's the story of one of Wemmers' clients, MicroHelp, Inc., whose products include a general line of computer visual programming tools and special utility tools.

Location: Atlanta
Product: UnInstaller
Company started: 1985
Sales: Prior to 1993, $3 million. After UnInstaller, $20 million.

Until 1993, MicroHelp was a small and growing company, providing a line of visual programming tools to programmers around the country. Sales had virtually all been by direct mail and to a relatively small universe of programmers. The company's reputation was good, and its products and support services were perceived as being very good.

In early 1993, MicroHelp found and introduced a new utility program that made certain that, when an application was removed from a Windows-environment PC, it was completely uninstalled.

Without this tool, someone who installed and uninstalled numerous applications would accumulate a buildup of bytes and bits in his or her system or computer. Over time, this buildup would slow down the computer's operation and reduce space on the hard drive.

MicroHelp's goal, then, was to focus computer users' attention on the possibility that there were strange happenings inside their computers that affected the computers' performance. These gremlins couldn't be seen or heard, but over time they could reduce performance. Computer users couldn't correct the problem with traditional uninstalling procedures or products. Only UnInstaller could do a complete job, and if computer users wanted maximum performance, they needed to buy UnInstaller.

"We felt if we could build enough fear of the unknown, then people would buy UnInstaller. The purchase price of less than a hundred dollars made this an impulse rather than a planned purchase, thus helping the selling proposition," says Wemmers. No other software on the market was making any claims about totally removing unwanted applications.

A combination of three of the four MMMC tools was used to introduce this innovative product and build sales. The combination proved to be a winning one.

- Publicity gave the new product credibility and sales support from experts in places where customers sought news and advice on purchases. (In Part V, the section on publicity, you'll see how *The New York Times* picked up the story, expanded it, and put it on its syndicated news service so that it was picked up and run in newspapers across the country.)
- Advertising gave great awareness to the customer universe, alerting them to the benefits of the product as well as educating them about their need for it.

- Merchandising (promotion) made the product readily available and helped UnInstaller compete for shoppers' dollars.

We'll join Rick Wemmers, Wemmers Communications, and Micro-Help, Inc., again in Chapters 8, 12, 16, and 21, where we'll get a look at the way advertising, direct marketing promotion, and publicity were used.

CASE 3: TU ELECTRIC

EvansGroup is a $200 million agency with offices in Denver, Seattle, Phoenix, Portland, San Francisco, Los Angeles, Salt Lake City, and Dallas. It developed an MMMC program for TU Electric.

George Arnold, EvansGroup's president and CEO, says, "Clients aren't looking for advertising or PR or direct marketing. What they're looking for are solutions to problems, and they don't care [which marketing disciplines] deliver them." TU Electric's problem was an all-time-low customer favorability rating of 63 percent at the end of 1993. The objective was to achieve a customer favorability rating of at least 70 percent by the end of 1994.

Focus group sessions provided two strong insights into TU Electric's customers' opinions.

1. Customers felt helpless when it came to their electric bills: They couldn't choose their service provider, and their bills kept increasing.
2. Customers were not aware of many services and programs that TU Electric provided.

Monthly customer tracing studies indicated immediate results from the *Responsiveness* campaign. George Arnold says:

> We began the campaign in April with a 68 percent favorability rating. Following our initial airing, the rating grew to a peak of 77 percent in June.
> The increase in September is the first time in the company's history that favorability has not decreased in September. In fact, September was up to 70 percent, with an increase to 73 percent in October.
> We ended the year with a 77 percent rating—seven points higher than our original objective of 70 percent.
> EvansGroup used three MMMC routes to achieve this success:

- Advertising
- Direct marketing
- Promotion

We'll examine EvansGroup's techniques in Chapters 8, 12, and 16 when we learn how they achieved such success using only three of the four MMMC avenues.

HAVE YOU NOTICED . . . ?

By this point you've undoubtedly noticed that each of the three campaigns outlined so far has taken a somewhat different route, yet all have achieved phenomenal success. FastSigns used all the marketing roads, but UnInstaller and TU Electric used only three of the four.

Now it's time to meet a professional who will show how different avenues provided the right approach to the same end—success—for four decidedly different clients:

1. One used advertising and promotion.
2. A second used direct marketing exclusively.
3. The third used advertising and direct marketing.
4. A fourth used publicity and advertising.

Liz McKinney-Johnson is a founding partner and creative director of her Portland, Oregon, agency. The McKinney Johnson Amato agency (McK*J*A) serves clients from Seattle to Miami, and it uses MMMC to serve them. The following four case studies (Cases 4, 5, 6, and 7) demonstrate some of the agency's various approaches.

CASE 4: KPDX

The marketing problem at KPDX was one of awareness. After five years in the marketplace, KPDX was suffering from low public recognition, says McKinney-Johnson. The station wanted viewers to know that it was one of the five television stations in Portland, but it also wanted to position itself as unique from the pack.

The campaign goal became: "Make sure they remember us." "And our first research task was to find out who 'they' were," says Johnson. Monitoring KPDX and other stations in the metro area showed the target audience should be the television generation, adults 18 to 45.

Positioning

If you put together *what you want to do* and *who you want to do it to,* you get *campaign criteria.* By examining the station's audience traits and its goals, the agency put together a set of criteria that the campaign had to meet in order to be effective:

- It had to be attention-grabbing.
- It had to dare to be different.
- It had to position the station as separate but equal.
- It must not take itself too seriously.

What Set KPDX Apart?

To set the television station apart from its competition, the obvious approach would have been to examine what KPDX had that the competition didn't have. However, what turned out to be more effective was the exact opposite. What was it that KPDX *didn't* have that everybody else *had?* The answer was *news.*

How did other stations position themselves in the marketplace? *News* again. This was an opportunity waiting to be taken, says Johnson, and it provided the perfect identifier. It allowed KPDX to follow the same route as everyone else in the marketplace, but with a twist—NO NEWS.

The theme was then refined to *NO NEWS at 5:00, 10:00 or 11:00.* The balance the agency was able to achieve with this theme allowed KPDX to position its lack of news without leaving the impression that it thought news wasn't important. This allowed the station to applaud the wonderful job the other four stations were doing with the news, and then suggest that these stations stick with what they do best—news. That way, KPDX could stick with what it did best—great entertainment 24 hours a day.

The MMMC Message

Along with this main campaign theme was the overall positioning statement: *KPDX—Portland's Other TV Station.* This identifier was important as a continuity statement, to be used during the NO NEWS campaign and long after.

The final element of the creative strategy, says Johnson, answered the question: "Well, if you don't have news, what DO you have?" The answer? *Just a Lotta Fun.*

The MMMC campaign for KDPX used only two of the MMMC elements:

- Advertising
- Promotion

How McK*J*A put those two elements to productive use is described in Chapters 8 and 16.

CASE 5: SEWING CENTER SUPPLY/OMNISTITCH

Direct marketing and advertising were the two routes the McK*J*A agency took to accomplish the following two goals of Sewing Center Supply (SCS):

1. To create demand among home sewers for a new kind of machine they'd never heard of
2. To help SCS manage and fully utilize the resulting fusillade of retail customer inquiries (a different type of customer than they were used to)

Until this project, SCS had sold machines and notions on a strictly wholesale basis. The OmniStitch, a revolutionary embellishing machine, would be their first product marketed directly to consumers. The Omni-Stitch is a machine that a sewer would buy in addition to a traditional sewing machine. It had sold for up to $900 in sewing stores, but retail sales had been very slow, so SCS made the decision to go "factory direct" for $395.

Research

The agency's first question was: What do prospective home sewers like (or dislike) about OmniStitch? The first research done was with focus group sessions made up of sewers with various skill levels and interests. Next, a survey and prize drawing was conducted as part of an OmniStitch demonstration at a local sewing fair. This effort generated 1,500 responses.

Input from OmniStitch product demonstrators was also important. They had taken the OmniStitch to various sewing shows and could report from firsthand observation which features would help sell the machine.

Finally, the agency looked at the most popular patterns and projects that had been created for retail on the industrial version of the Omni-Stitch. The research showed that sewers loved the way the machine could embellish simple sewing projects. It gave their plain work a professional finish. Sewers also liked the machine's ability to work with a diverse array of embellishing materials, from fine thread to round cording, from sequins to wide strips of fabric.

Sewers saw the OmniStitch as a remedy for one of their biggest frustrations—projects that ended up looking homemade because they lacked the extra details of professional garments and home-decorating products.

Positioning

Because this was SCS's first direct-marketing effort, the agency knew that SCS would have to be positioned as a reliable company to buy from and viewed as a place where sewers would want to spend several hundred dollars. Even though SCS had been very successful in the wholesale market, most potential retail buyers would be hearing about the company for the first time.

The MMMC campaign for SCS used two of the marketing communications components:

- Advertising
- Direct marketing

How McK*J*A used these components is described in Chapters 8 and 12.

CASE 6: PROTECTION ONE

The Protection One campaign crafted an image from the ground up, according to Liz Johnson. It used print and television advertising and direct marketing to achieve its goals.

McK*J*A started work with Protection One right when Protection One began business, so the first goal was to build name awareness and educate the public about home security.

Research

Several research stages were required to track down the necessary information. First, branch managers were interviewed to get a feeling for what was happening in each of the three markets (Portland, Seattle, and Los Angeles). Then a series of focus groups was commissioned to tap into consumers' awareness and their reasoning behind selecting (or not selecting) an alarm company.

The focus group sessions confirmed that people were looking for more information about:

- Who the company was
- What the real benefits of the system were
- When the system would be up and running
- Where the monitoring was done
- How the system worked

These *who, what, when, where,* and *how* questions were the sales barriers
that had to be broken down, and the only way to do that was to answer
them.

Creative Strategy

The new strategy was named the "Know Campaign." Each of the MMMC
components addressed something the consumer wanted to know. The
closing theme summed up the desired effect of all this new wisdom: *The
More You Know . . . The More You'll Want Protection One.*

Outcome

After just 12 months of exposure, Protection One was consistently recognized as one of the top four security companies in the three areas, and
monthly leads increased in each market from 15 percent to 35 percent.

　　To accomplish these returns, McK∗J∗A used only two of the MMMC
routes:

- Advertising
- Direct marketing

The how-tos are spelled out in Chapters 8 and 12.

CASE 7: OREGON BURGLAR

At the heart of this campaign was the Portland police department's decision to stop responding to monitored alarms, citing high false alarm statistics, according to Liz Johnson. The challenge was to find out exactly
why the police felt the way they did and how their decision to stop responding was being tied to the recently passed property tax limitation
measure—Measure 5.

Research

Research included re-evaluating the actual circumstances behind the police
department's statistics, which were being widely quoted. Next, to solidify
their position, various companies comprising the Oregon Burglar and Fire
Alarm Response (OBFAR) membership were polled and asked to give their
customers' points of view. Finally, the agency researched other communi-

ties' solutions to similar situations and drew upon the established body of research on the crime-fighting effectiveness of monitored alarms.

Positioning

Convinced that the police had overstated their alarm burden, McK*J*A chose to position the issue as an example of local government wanting to save money at the expense of basic public safety—an action of great disservice to both the business and residential communities. Direct citizen response was needed to bring pressure on city hall.

Execution

The MMMC roads this campaign took were:

- Publicity
- Newspaper advertising

We'll follow the execution of these techniques in Chapters 8 and 21.

WISCONSIN'S WOMAN ENTREPRENEUR OF THE YEAR

Marsha Lindsay is founder, president, and CEO of Lindsay, Stone & Briggs Advertising, Inc., (LS&B) in Madison, Wisconsin. Her agency specializes in creative brand-building advertising for national and regional clients headquartered in the Midwest. The agency's name says "advertising," but LS&B practices the broad band of MMMC techniques and strategies.

With case 8 and case 9, we see a vertically integrated communications campaign for Caradco Windows and an anti-racism campaign that targeted teens. Case 8 is valuable as a commercial copycat resource. Case 9 provides insight into how to get messages accepted by teens at a time when teens are a highly profitable target audience for many businesses and service companies.

CASE 8: CARADCO WINDOWS

Marsha Lindsay introduces her review of an MMMC campaign her agency conducted, stating the remarkable results it produced:

Awareness of Caradco wood windows and patio doors increased from 47 percent to 55 percent in a ten-month period despite a share-of-voice [only] one-fifth that of the leading competitor: Andersen.

According to the independent national firm that conducted the research: "This is a highly unusual increase in awareness. We typically see this only after a two-year period."

The MMMC choices for the Caradco campaign included:

- Advertising
- Promotion

We'll see the methods used in Chapters 8 and 16.

CASE 9: MADISON ADVERTISING FEDERATION

This is a case history that breaks ranks with the others in this chapter. It is presented here because it offers several opportunities, the most important of which is an opportunity to study techniques for getting messages through to (and accepted by) teenagers. This is perhaps one of the most difficult jobs marketers face.

For companies with no foreseeable teen market, this case also demonstrates how professionals define a problem and conduct their marketing to diminish or surmount it. It also gives insight into conducting focus group sessions and the kinds of results that can come from focus group research.

Marsha Lindsay explains how the challenge came to her agency:

The Madison Advertising Federation thought our community would benefit from a diversity campaign, and the assignment was given to our agency, Lindsay, Stone & Briggs. We felt that we needed to choose one aspect of diversity and focus our attention there. Racism has been an issue in our community of Madison, Wisconsin, despite the city's liberal reputation and the influences of a Big Ten university and state government. At the time of the campaign's inception, there were racial incidents in restaurants and in employment opportunities.

Attitudes toward race differ in structure from those toward other groups, such as physical handicaps or mental illness. We decided these attitudes needed to be addressed through a campaign devoted to diversity education.

Research

We sought the assistance of the NAACP, and they endorsed our effort. With their help, we conducted focus group sessions with people of many ages and racial backgrounds to help determine which segment of the population held the most potential for positive change. Sample focus group questions included the following:

- Who are your role models? What do you admire in them?
- What makes you dislike someone? Is it something they say or do?
- Have you ever been made fun of because of your skin color or the way you talk?
- Has anyone been racist toward you?
- What is the best thing/worst thing about being of a particular race?
- Is society racist or just the people within it?
- Will racism ever be eliminated?
- How do you think someone becomes racist? Born, taught, or influenced?

From this research came some answers to the overriding question, *What is racism?*

Teens Were the Target

We listened for broad, generational attitudes instead of quantitative answers that confirmed our belief that the most attentive and accepting target audience for our campaign would be teenagers.

The decision was to target our messages to middle- and high-school age children, roughly 11 to 18 years old. Our reason? Teens want to make a difference. And our attitude was: Why not invest in the future? Teens are young enough to be influenced but old enough to get involved.

Lindsay, Stone & Briggs used three of the four MMMC routes to effectively reach this audience:

- Advertising
- Promotion
- Publicity

We'll meet Marsha Lindsay again in Chapters 8, 16, and 21 and learn how the routes were traveled.

FOCUS GROUP RESEARCH

Have you noticed how often marketing professionals rely on focus sessions to find what George Arnold says clients seek—solutions to problems? It may pay you to use this form of research, too. You can find more detailed how-to information in *The Handbook for Focus Groups Research* by Thomas L. Greenbaum (Lexington Books).

SEMIFINAL WORD

Don't settle for other people's dreams. Make your own. Oh, you can copy-cat another's dream, but always adapt it to your vision, your dream. Make a copycat version your own.

PART II

ADVERTISING: THE UNDERPINNING OF MARKETING

4

Why Advertise?

Advertising is the most popular marketing tool—but new tech is changing the way it's used. It's only part of the MMMC plan. The kinds of advertising and their virtues. New tech to transmit ads and commercials. Advertising on the Net and using cyberbucks.

Advertising may be the first road you think of when you want to carry a message to your target group. For many businesspeople, however, advertising is the only road they think of. Advertising is the most visible and the best-understood format in marketing. It is also one of the two most used formats—particularly by small and mid-sized businesses (and, of course, by advertising agencies). For users of advertising, everything centers on developing the most creative, attention-getting way of conveying their message. Often little thought is given to identifying the target audience or predicting how the message will play with that audience.

That is how things were during the long years that mass marketing was healthy and energetic and productive. But that's not the way things are today. Mass marketing can't pay the rent anymore and has had to move out. *Selective* marketing—aimed at specific, carefully selected groups—has moved in. Today it is absolutely essential that the needs, wants, thoughts, and interests of a specific group are foremost in every message.

A WHOLE NEW BALLGAME

At the 1995 annual meeting of the American Association of Advertising Agencies (AAAA), William T. Esrey, chairman and CEO of Sprint Corporation said:

Commercial communication does not mean reaching customers a billion at a time. Commercial communication [as typified by digital interactive media] gives us the opportunity to speak intimately to each and every customer—and to actually have them talk back to us.

Esrey also predicted that "in the future we'll know our customer by name, or else settle for having no customers at all."

The more you know about your customers, the better you can sell to them, and the more effective your advertising will be. It's a lot easier to fill a person's existing need or desire than it is to establish a new need or desire.

WHERE MMMC FITS IN

Advertising is sometimes thought of as the entire marketing plan. In reality it is only a part of a marketing plan and only part of MMMC, and sometimes it has no place in either. Agencies around the country are beginning to change their thinking—and change their names to reflect their new thinking. Foote, Cone/Chicago has made significant changes in its operations, even to renaming the company True North Communications, which its chairman and CEO, Bruce Mason, says "reflects its evolution to a communications company from an advertising company." All this, according to Mason, is because of the "rapidly changing communications environment," along with its clients' changing communications needs.

It's pretty obvious that this new marketing strategy calls for a completely new kind of marketer—someone who is comfortable with and understands all the mixed media communications avenues: advertising, direct marketing, promotion, and publicity. The changeover can be difficult for those whose reaction to all forms of marketing is automatically *advertising*.

IT ALL ADS UP

Let's assume that your previous research indicates, and your MMMC plan calls for, advertising as the best avenue—or at least one of the best— to effectively reach your target prospects. It seems appropriate at this point to take a look at a few things people sometimes hold against advertising. In recent years, advertising, like used-car salespeople, has tended to be thought of by the public as deceptive and perhaps even dishonest and manipulative.

It's very important to note here that *perception is reality*. When a perception is incorrect or negative, it is that perception that must be targeted in messages, not reality. For example, in the used-car business, some companies are making a concerted effort to reverse a negative image with a consolidated mixed media message that refers to their products as *pre-owned* cars.

True, there is advertising that is misleading and even false. But overall, advertising is a trustworthy marketing tool, an important part of the process that moves business forward.

HITTING THE TARGET

The Wall Street Journal works hard to give credibility to print media in ads that state, "Hard-to-reach audiences require exacting aim. And no medium gives you as much control and precision as print." *The Journal* goes on to state that, "although some marketing targets are as elusive as they are attractive—working women, young adults, and the affluent—it's still possible to reach each of these groups effectively and efficiently in print." These statements come as something of a surprise at a time when the impression—the *perception*—is that man, woman, and child across the board only watch television. The reason, according to *The Journal,* is that "readers lavish more time and enthusiasm on print advertising because they find the medium to be far more responsive to their needs and interests than television."

Some people claim that advertising is simply not cost-effective or appropriate for smaller businesses. But no matter the size of the business, try turning off the advertising spigot and see what happens. If you're still a little doubtful about advertising, take a look at the portrait on the other side of the coin.

ADVERTISING'S VIRTUES

Don't underestimate the power of advertising as a major element of marketing. There are 26 mountains in Colorado that are higher than Pike's Peak, but who has ever heard of them?

Advertising informs, it sells, and it enables businesses of all sizes to move forward and upward. It has unique strengths that work in good times and bad, and it plays a solid role in building markets and helping to drive prices down. One of this country's foremost economists says that the function of advertising is to stimulate demand, develop and shape consumer behavior, and provide the seller of a product (or service or image) with a measure of certainty regarding sales, an assurance whose absence could be financially disastrous. Economist John Kenneth Galbraith lists some other advantages of advertising: it shapes consumer behavior; it often induces a consumer response that otherwise would not occur; it creates wants and it often separates a particular product (or service or company) from its competitors and gives it a distinctive personality. Additionally it satisfies the need in all market transactions—to inform.

Galbraith makes another point: "Were informing the consumer the only purpose of advertising, the industry would be confined to the classified ads." This thinking predates two important developments: (1) technology that lets advertisers talk one-to-one to a potential customer, and (2) even more advanced technology that makes it possible for that potential customer to *talk back.*

Sprint Corporation's William T. Esrey, however, cautioned his AAAA audience that they must avoid the trap of falling "too much in love with our technological exploits. Our customers by and large don't buy technology; they buy solutions to problems. They buy satiation of needs." They accept the technology when it lets them ask the questions that provide the solutions to their problems.

Scott Nosenko, a copywriter at Miller Brooks, may have explained it best in a letter printed in *Adweek:* "Puh-leez!" Nosenko wrote. "Being PC nowadays is very PC. Advertising isn't brain surgery or a mental mind game. Its sole purpose is to sell a product or a service by speaking to the market. Period."

THE (R)EVOLUTION(S)

Customers don't buy technology, but technology can make your job a whole lot easier. Right now, today, you can have a videoconference with an advertising rep about the ad you intend to run in his or her medium, an electronic meeting using desktop or portable computers and regular phone lines. Both of you are able to view the same layout or video on your screens, and either of you can make changes that are immediately visible to the other. With some setups, you can actually see one another on a portion of the screen.

BBDO Worldwide, Los Angeles, is understandably one of the more sophisticated users of personal computers—they are the agency for the Apple Computer account. All their print ads leave the agency on SyQuest cartridges, each of which holds about 40 times as much information as a disc, and go directly to engravers. Computers also are pervasive at Foote, Cone & Belding/San Francisco, where elegant brochures and TV commercials are edited off-line and transmitted electronically to media.

Off-line editing with a software system saves hundreds of post-production dollars because it allows the creator to assemble the rough cut before it gets to the online editing stage. That's what's happening at ad agencies. It won't be long before it can happen for you. Actually, it won't be long before it *must* happen to you, because consumers' knowledge and use of these technologies is jumping out ahead of many businesspeople's. Consumers can now search interactively for electronic ads on demand, so *your* advertising should be available to them. It must be more informative, and you must be more available to answer consumers' questions than is possible with traditional ads. It's a world where old-line businesses must convert to front-line digital players.

THE KINDS OF ADVERTISING

This is the time when the strategy for using MMMC should rear its handsome head. Advertising is *not* a waste of money if it is on the right path to reach the right people, and when it gets there the information is what they want or need.

In his book *Magnet Marketing* (Wiley), John P. Graham says there are four major reasons that advertising fails:

1. It is used in the wrong media.
2. It is used to accomplish the wrong goal(s).
3. It sends the wrong message.
4. Its users have the wrong expectations.

Research International (RI), has been "building a body of knowledge about all aspects of market research," and some of what they've found appeared in an advertisement in *Advertising Age* in April 1995.

First, RI answers the question, Is advertising likability the best predictor of sales? RI refutes a major study by saying:

It ain't necessarily so. Many consumers who told us they "loved the advertising" didn't buy the product.

Rules of thumb: for standard package goods items, consumers have to like the advertising—as well as the product . . . and its packaging and price. On the other hand, for "big ticket" items, advertising that rubs people the wrong way might cause them to think more seriously about buying. . . . It can pay to stir people up.

Second, RI states that

Some advertising "communicates" so much to prospects, it leaves their heads spinning. . . . It's been gospel that the more benefits you jam into a commercial, the more persuasive it will be. We disagree.

Some of the commercials that do well in "communications" testing turn out to be least effective in the marketplace. Where do you want to be most effective?

Third, RI says that, unless you have a remarkable news story to tell, target your advertising toward users, not non-users:

> There's a growing body of evidence that the best advertising doesn't persuade a consumer to buy something she's not buying; instead, it helps to solidify her good opinion of a product or service she already uses.

(To persuade *potential* consumers, perhaps other MMMC routes may be more effective—promotion and publicity.)

And finally, RI presents the most convincing reason for jumping on the new-tech bus shuttling back and forth between advertiser and consumer.

> When the viewer talks back to the commercial, you might have made a friend. It's not all bad when a prospect argues with you, for you've got her actively thinking about you. Our research shows that even though people might play back the main copy points of your message, you won't make the sale until you've got 'em debating what you said. It's this kind of "processing" that can turn an enemy into an ally.

Constructing the right message is so important that an entire chapter is given to this information (Chapter 6). Equally important is choosing the right media, so that too has a chapter devoted to it (Chapter 5).

NEW TECH FOR TRANSMITTING ADS

Historically the Associated Press (AP) has been known for its ability to gather and disseminate news. Now it has dipped its foot into advertising, but only by offering another high-tech vehicle by which to digitally transport art and copy to newspapers. *Editor & Publisher* states that, as a general rule, digital delivery offers the highest-quality representation, partly because digital transmission reduces the number of production and handling steps, lessening opportunities for error that may accompany transitional delivery systems.

AP points out that the vast majority of ads still arrive at newspapers physically, by way of Federal Express, United Parcel Service, and the United States mail. After arriving, an ad is shot on a camera that converts the image to film. "At a fully paginated newspaper, the transmission comes off the AP satellite dish, and the bits go into the pagination system and are printed so that nothing is lost and there are fewer production steps," says the AP. And this system is as easy to inaugurate at newspapers as installing a high-end personal computer and some special software, which means that increasing numbers of papers will be jumping aboard, thus making things easier for you, the advertiser.

NEW TECH TO TRANSMIT COMMERCIALS, TOO

A Sony double truck ad carries a headline across two pages that tells what is possible for television commercials: "Distribute your commercial on Sony D-2 digital, and the copies will look as good as the original." The ad explains that a digital copy isn't just a dub. It's a clone. It's an exact replication of your original commercial. Which is precisely why, the ad says, there's no better way to distribute your commercials than on Sony D-2 digital video. Every digital copy you send out will have the same true color, sharp resolution, and crisp, clear sound as your original.

AD-VENTURE ON THE NET

By 1996, advertising may be spelled I-N-T-E-R-N-E-T. The Net may become the most readily available, most easily accessible place for you to make your advertising available to talk-back or talk-with customers. Which is not to say that traditional media won't be a healthy, vital, and viable means for carrying advertising messages to the public. However, it does mean that marketers must recognize the growing importance of the Internet, keep a close eye on almost-daily new developments, and be aware of the Internet's importance to their target audiences.

Although there are some feelings of animosity toward advertising on the Internet, advertisers who are using it by way of *HotWired* (an online offering by *HotWired* magazine) include such biggies as IBM, AT&T, Volvo, Sprint, MCI, Zima, and Club Med, among others. *HotWired* is available free to anyone with an Internet connection and a World Wide Web browser. The system requires users to click to call up an ad, and to overcome some of the anti-ads feelings, the advertisers have come up with some clever gimmicks to make scanners want to click.

What Is It? And Who Should Use It?

"What is this Internet thing?" asks—and answers—Walt Zwirko, a special computer reporter at the ABC television affiliate in Dallas. "Simply defined," says Zwirko, "[it's] the world's biggest network of computer networks." It links groups of computers" from local city to local city all the way around the globe from "Tokyo to Moscow and just about every place in between." And to assure understanding, Zwirko also points out what the Internet is *not*. "It is not a traditional pay-to-use online service like America Online, CompuServe, or Prodigy."

When the Internet was started in 1969, it was meant for military use only, to help control possible nuclear attacks. Now the government is withdrawing from Internet management, thus ending an estimated $12 million in annual subsidies, which raises the question of who will subsidize Internet operation in the future. Undoubtedly, a good portion of its upkeep costs will come from advertisers and marketers.

The New York Times says that no one disputes that the increasing commercialization of the Internet will accelerate its transformation into an international system for the flow of data, text, graphics, sound, and video among businesses, their customers, and their suppliers. "I see the commercial users of the Internet to be the big winners here," says Jordan Becker, an executive with an Internet subcontractor that is hunting down commercial users for the main network being vacated by the government.

Even classified ads are available over the Internet. And even *The New York Times*, previously considered slow to jump aboard new technology, makes its help-wanted ads available over the Internet. *The Times* also expects to expand its online service to include display advertising.

Cyberbucks

You recognize that more and more people are shopping in cyberspace, but you may have wondered how they pay for what they buy. That too is becoming easy. An electronic cash system has been developed that allows buyers and sellers to conduct their commercial transactions "entirely within the part of cyberspace known as the World Wide Web."

It works this way. A customer transfers a specific amount of e-cash (the term for space dough) to his or her computer, using a credit card or other conventional means of currency. Then when he or she shops the Internet and finds something to buy, a simple click on a designated area of the screen transfers e-cash to the seller. Software from Digicash Inc. automatically contacts the buyer's bank to confirm that the e-cash is truly available, all the while automatically protecting the buyer's privacy in the same manner as when cash transactions are handled by a bank.

Digicash has strong support from influential Internet users, but other ideas have been proposed and may be available soon for the electronic transfer of money over computer networks.

5

Choosing Media

So many to choose from. A company creates its own media. Traditional media's advantages and disadvantages. The right questions to ask. CPM is the way to compare media. Discounts and added value equal dollars. Co-op grows ad dollars beyond all other means.

Selecting appropriate media may very well be the most important decision you make in your entire marketing program. The greatest mixed media marketing message in the world won't do a thing to sell your image, product, or service if it doesn't reach the people who might need or want to hear it.

The intimidating part about choosing communications media is the variety of choices available. You have magazines, newspapers, Yellow Pages, billboards, broadcast TV, and cable to choose from—and those are just the traditional routes. Now that your research has given you an accurate picture of the individuals who make up your targeted audience, it's time to use that profile to choose a single communications medium or the combination of media that will carry your message to them. Be aware that some of the best salespeople on the planet are those who sell media, and some of them are more than simply convincing and forceful—they have histories that would make used-car salespeople appear saintly. In other words, you must check their sales pitches to establish that what is offered is in *your* best interests. Therefore, it's important (particularly if you have a limited budget) that you learn how to handle these sales reps by mastering the chore of obtaining honest data about the medium (or media) being considered, and then knowing how to negotiate to get the best rate—with perhaps some added values thrown in.

MEDIA **HAS DIFFERENT MEANINGS**

Before television, the word media didn't exist in the sense in which it is now used. We called it *the press.* Then, as advertising grew into marketing, publicity into public relations, and direct mail into direct marketing, like so much new terminology, they took on a multitude of meanings under the umbrella word *media.*

Sometimes companies even create their own media. It used to be that when someone said "media," traditional forms jumped to mind— newspapers, magazines, television, and radio. (These are the forms we will be examining in this chapter). The reality is that there are many, many things that qualify as media these days, hence the relatively new term *multimedia.* Very often a company or an agency representing a company creates its own media.

Such was the case for Clicks, a group of billiard parlors represented by RJC International Advertising and Marketing. Clicks has a total of 25 stores in the Dallas–Fort Worth area, Phoenix, and Orlando. They don't have a critical mass of stores in any one area that would justify the use of mass media such as network television, national magazines, or even metropolitan newspapers.

The situation called for research by RJC International to determine the nature of the stores, their exact locations, the degrees of concentration, and a sense of the product or service being offered—which was billiards with fast food and drinks as side offerings. The research showed that advertising was not what was needed. Not only was its too costly, but a tremendous amount of circulation would have been wasted because there was no critical mass.

The best, most effective way to market these stores, according to Ray Champney, president of RJC International, turned out to be through the invention of its own media. They used two invented media: (1) monthly calendars of activities primarily circulated on a store-by-store basis and handled by the general manager of each store; and (2) quarterly newsletters.

The monthly calendars can be likened to a monthly magazine—a very vertical-type magazine—that goes to a precisely targeted audience derived from a highly selective database. The database can be compared to the circulation of the magazine. Clicks' database of identified product users was built through a sweepstakes promotion. The agency sent a mailing to all residents within two to three miles of each of the Clicks' stores, announcing sweepstakes trips to Mexico. To register, one had only to stop in and play a free game and—not incidentally—fill in a questionnaire.

All of Clicks' existing customers took advantage of the offer, and new customers, some first-time billiards players, also came in to fill out questionnaires and enter the contest. Over months, Clicks' database grew to

60,000. The questionnaires, beyond providing a mailing list, also told managers at each location exactly what they had to offer in order to draw in traffic, keep people coming back, and build the business. Clicks' MMMC program consisted of conducting the sweepstakes, sending monthly calendars of activities and a quarterly newsletter, and conducting special promotions to take place throughout the year—all to keep interest levels high, keep people coming back, and keep traffic moving.

In actuality, there is no *media*, in the strictest sense of the word, involved in any part of the program. Clicks created its own media and used specific segments of MMMC—direct-response marketing and direct promotion.

What began when the owner of a chain of billiard parlors called RJC International because the owner initially believed an advertising campaign was needed, turned into a marketing communications program that concentrates on a tightly targeted, geographically selected, highly successful program.

With this sidetrip completed, and with a better understanding of media in terms of its use as part of an MMMC plan, let's now get back on the road and back to the question of choosing media.

TRADITIONAL MEDIA'S ADVANTAGES AND DISADVANTAGES

Each medium has its own drawbacks, and most have very strong advantages.

Newspapers

Newspapers, the first choice for most small businesses, reach a local audience. In the case of community papers or weeklies, that can be a very geographically limited local audience, one that may very precisely match a business's geographic area. Ads can be prepared quickly and changed easily. Space—no matter how large or small—is readily available. And space selectivity is fairly easy to attain: sports devotees can be reached through the sports section, businesspeople through the business section, and teachers and parents through the education or family sections.

One of the biggest pluses of newspapers is that they often are the first choice of manufacturers and vendors who underwrite co-op advertising, which is a great way for small businesses to double their ad dollars.

On the down side, newspapers often reach a mass audience and a geographic area far broader than a particular business needs.

Magazines

Magazines are similar to newspapers, but they're also like radio and cable. Although general-interest magazines—like newspapers—reach across the spectrum of people's interests, most of today's magazines are published for special-interest groups with niche titles. There are magazines for aviation enthusiasts and for people in the plastics business. There are magazines for women golfers, executive golfers, and golfers in Illinois, Michigan, or North Texas. No matter the subject, there's probably a magazine that zeros in on it. (To locate magazines in your prospects' niche area, consult a copy of *Bacon's Publicity Checker/Magazines*.)

There are weekly, monthly, and bimonthly magazines, but if time is a factor—if you need to get a message out quickly or change it at the last minute—keep in mind that magazines have longer lead times than other media, often from three to six months. And, although subject areas may be highly specialized, the geographic area in which each magazine is circulated can be quite broad. On the other hand, magazines can expand or decrease their length, something broadcast media can't do, so space usually is readily available.

Other advantages include high reproduction quality (magazines are printed on high-quality paper), a long life span, and a certain amount of space selectivity.

Magazines, which were initially wary of interactive media, are now cautiously boarding the interactive bus. In October 1994, Time Inc. announced a test offer to Internet users of an interactive version of some of its magazines. Although Hearst, Ziff-Davis, *U.S. News & World Report*, Conde Nast, *Playboy*, Times Mirror and a few other magazine publishers are dipping their toes in the water, according to a New York Times News Service story, the Time Inc. interactive version is a breakthrough.

What this means is that the large magazines are beginning to experiment. The smaller, very vertical magazines in which you decide to place your message will most likely not have this capacity at this time.

Radio

Like newspapers, radio usually has local audiences, and messages can be changed easily and quickly. Also, radio programming on many stations is highly selective. Stations offer so-called menu programming that speaks to groups of people with identical interests. And radio plays to people's imaginations. A well-written commercial can tap into what marketing professional George Arnold calls the "little theater of the mind," so that a well-constructed message can create pictures in people's heads and build feelings of taste, color, and motion. However, the number of time slots available to accommodate commercials is limited, and the times of your choice—those that are most likely to reach your targeted audience (drive-time, for example)—are not always readily available. Commercial time is also relatively expensive. But perhaps the biggest drawbacks to successful radio advertising are the brevity of the messages and the fact that listeners tend to use radio as background. They are not actively listening unless a message runs during a news or talk show.

Offsetting some of the minuses is the fact that, unlike television or cable TV viewers, radio listeners have loyalties to specific radio *stations* with their range of targeted programming (rather than to individual programs), so they stay tuned to the same station for longer periods of time.

Television and Cable

Both television and cable TV have numerous pluses and drawbacks. The combination of sight, sound, motion, and color makes a television or cable commercial the closest you can get to personal selling. They are both in-trusive mediums that take your message right into a person's living room, kitchen, or bedroom. Television and cable are so much a part of most people's lives that they're called an addiction.

But most television, unlike cable, reaches a mass audience, so it's very difficult to sort out target groups to fit your customer profile. And unlike radio listeners, television viewers are loyal not to particular stations but rather to individual programs. Therefore, messages presented between programs may not reach a specific group of people because they've already zapped to another program on another channel. But the biggest deterrent to television for low-budget advertisers is the sky-high cost of both the production of the commercial and the broadcast time in which to present it.

Cable, however, (like radio and many magazines) programs itself for very narrow-interest audiences. So narrow are most channel's interests that viewers can find channels that feature information only about books, health, the weather, news, movies, sports, comedy, travel, sci-fi, cartoons, home shopping, public affairs, finances, or education/learning—and even to exact types of learning such as that for nurses, caregivers, or doctors.

If home repair, cooking, or beauty how-tos are a primary interest of your target consumer, there are channels with this type of specialized pro-gramming. If your audience loves music, there are channels that offer only the kinds of music they prefer—country, rock, western, pop, rap, or whatever. There are even channels that cater to people who hate commer-cials, but those viewers must pay a price in the form of a subscription rate. The term *narrowcasting* was born when cable television came on the scene.

The biggest advantage cable offers is its similarity to television—a preference of most marketing professionals, but cable has lower commercial rates. There also are far fewer content restrictions for cable commercials than for television commercials. Commercial length is much more flexible on cable—from 15 seconds to 30 minutes, even up to an hour or longer for sales programs—and the availability of time slots is much greater.

YELLOW PAGES AND OUTDOOR

Yellow Pages are thought of by many as directories, not media, but they may very well be your most important advertising medium. They may not, however, fit well into the MMMC message plan because they must usually carry more than a single high-impact message, which is the intent of MMMC.

Your display ad's location in Yellow Pages directories pose problems. Some directories place display ads alphabetically, others according to the length of time advertisers have contracted for space. And in no other medium is your advertising totally surrounded by that of your competition, with your biggest competitor perhaps receiving much better placement because that company's name happens to begin with an *A* while yours begins with an *S*, or because the competitor has contracted directory space longer than you have. Therefore, your ad's graphics and message must stand up to all the enticements offered by your competition, which calls for greater copywriting, layout, and graphics skills.

There is one giant advantage to advertising in Yellow Page directories: this is where people look when they are ready to buy, whereas the job of other media advertising is to convince readers or viewers that they should buy. Research also shows that Yellow Pages advertising reaches customers who are not reached by other media and that Yellow Pages are an important producer of new customers.

Outdoor billboards are seldom used by small businesses except as a means to direct customers to their location. Brevity is the major disadvantage of billboards.

NIBBLE THE BAIT WITHOUT GETTING HOOKED

It's not easy to choose the right, the best, the most productive media to achieve your goals. It's difficult even for pros, although they have the advantage of having all the facts at their computer databases' fingertips. You must do some questioning and comparing, but if you know the right questions to ask, you can get the answers that make comparisons easier.

You'll be lessening your workload and putting the burden of digging out details and of proving their validity directly in the laps of the media reps you call in. Leave it to the reps to come up with the data you need. They probably already have it in their data files, and it's part of their sales job.

A major warning here: It is essential that you consciously maintain your objectivity. You must not choose media on the basis of what *you* like, the radio programs *you* listen to, or to the kinds of information *you* look for in publications or on broadcast media. You want only facts, not opinions—theirs or yours. A good example is an ad for and in *Modern Maturity* magazine. If you were a fast-food provider, you might assume that your best market is among teens or families with young children. If you continued to hold that opinion, however, you might be overlooking a tremendous market—older, often retired people. The head on the ad reads: "The readers of one magazine go for fast food more than teenagers." And the body copy provides convincing evidence:

> Over 226,947,000 times a month the readers of *Modern Maturity* head for a fast-food restaurant. They have a taste for a burger with everything on it. And a magazine with everything in it, *Modern Maturity.*

Bet you didn't know these stats, nor that a magazine would have these kinds of figures in its data file. But when a magazine's sales rep quotes you statistics, demand proof—the source of the data.

THE CONSUMER PROFILE FACT SHEET AND MEDIA REPS

From your consumer's portrait (which ought to be sitting on your desk right next to the pictures of your family members), you probably have a pretty good idea which medium will carry your message to him or her. Your research may have eliminated magazines and television, but you're still trying to figure whether newspapers are better than radio, or whether the entire budget should go into cable TV.

It's time to call in certain media sales reps. Common sense indicates that rock stations are out if you're looking for retired people who travel. But hang on to your objectivity, because that same common sense may be telling you that magazines for older people are out of the question if you're seeking hamburger lovers. Don't let common sense absolutely dictate who you should or should not talk to. Keep an open mind. It's pure good sense, though, if selling travel is your business, to call in representatives from cable travel channels, travel magazines, and travel newsletters.

Call in the reps one at a time and give them a copy of that picture profile of your targeted customer. Putting your profile in writing in the form of a Fact Sheet can prevent pleas of misunderstanding down the road. Doing so will also curtail attempts by reps to give you only the information or data they want you to have, rather than the facts you're requesting.

At this point, ask the following two questions:

1. Why should I use your medium (let's say, radio) to reach my particular prospect?
2. How does your entire medium (radio) compare in cost to other media (in this case, newspapers and cable)?

Remember, those are the only two questions you should ask at this time—and the only answers you should permit. This is not the time to allow a rep to make a sales pitch. That will come later, *if* his or her vehicle gets to a second-stage consideration. But first you must compare all the data from all of the media reps you've called in and reduce the media under consideration to only those that meet your specifications.

A Second Meeting

Your comparisons have now given you a notion as to which particular medium (or media) will give you the most direct route or routes to reach your prospects and your MMMC goal. You don't know yet whether you can afford the most appropriate media, but that question can be answered after you get other, more specific information.

Now it's time to call back, one at a time, the sales reps whose media are most likely to produce results for you. This is when you can get down to specifics. Ask the following questions:

- How many listeners or readers can the station or publication legitimately claim (verified by a recognized rating company such as Arbitron, Nielsen, or Audit Bureau of Circulations)?
- Where, geographically, are listeners or readers who match your profile located?
- What demographic data about readers or listeners does the publication or station have (e.g., age, gender, income, education)?
- How current are their stats and information?
- What psychographic data do they have that applies to your specific prospects?

When you talk to print salespeople, verify whether their stats are circulation figures or readership figures. Circulation numbers are smaller but more reliable than readership numbers. And check whether circulation is paid or free to readers. Also request information about editorial content and how it lines up with the interests of your prospects.

All of these are questions that media reps are asked by knowledgeable space or time buyers, so you can be sure the answers are readily available. If there is reluctance to provide specifics, you can be sure that it is because the salesperson doesn't want you to realize that his or her medium isn't right for you.

This call-back meeting is the time you can—and should—permit individuals to make their sales pitches. Listen to *all* of them before you make any decision or commitment. And remember that good sales people always concentrate on the best points about their product. Their job is to make it appear that their particular medium is the best in its field and the best for your purposes.

Cost per Thousand

Now that the reps have abided by your controls and you have solid data to work with, it's time to compare facts. But how can you compare radio, cable TV, or television data, which are measured in seconds and minutes, with newspaper or magazine data, which are computed in lines and column inches? It's impossible to compare time with space, but there is a formula that will give you a measure of the cost-effectiveness for each medium.

Richard Weiner's *Webster's New World Dictionary of Media and Communications* (Simon & Schuster) defines CPM (cost per thousand impressions) as "the cost of advertising for each 1,000 homes reached by radio or TV, for each 1,000 copies circulated of a publication, or for each 1,000 potential viewers of an outdoor advertisement." From the figures from the various media, you merely multiply the cost times one thousand and divide it by the total audience on a particular day of the week for a newspaper or by a certain time segment on a specific day for a broadcast medium. Any advertising sales rep will help you apply this formula to his or her space or time rates.

Go Figure

For most media, rate cards aren't much help in determining rates. They merely list asking prices. But rate cards are valuable for their listings of specifications that advertisers must abide by. So don't put much stock in the rate listings, but hang onto rate cards for other reasons.

Rate cards come in all shapes and sizes, from booklets to simple page listings to advertising rates listed on cards. In addition to standard rates, rate cards may also show discounts for volume purchases and added charges for such things as special positioning. Some rate cards give mechanical specifications for graphics, photos, and column inches and width sizes.

Look at the published rates, but count on negotiating if you want to get the best possible deal. Whereas most media have been willing to negotiate in recent years, newspapers and magazines stood firm until the recession of the 1990s. Today, negotiation of rates is a fact of life with all media. The publisher of a major news magazine admits, "Every piece of business is negotiated. I don't believe we will ever return to the industry we were ten years ago."

Be very skeptical about the rates on rate cards. Professional media buyers know that, with increasing frequency, the rates on rate cards are inflated in anticipation of negotiations. Among newspapers, the unwritten maxim is: The smaller the paper, the more flexible its rates. This probably is true of other media as well, so keep this in mind when you start negotiating rates.

Value-Added Negotiating

Negotiating doesn't always mean merely paying fewer dollars. The news magazine's publisher says, "We are putting together added-value programs to get away from discounts." Price might be negotiable, but it's more likely that a small business with a limited budget will be better off negotiating for a bigger ad, more repetition, delivery to segmented subscribers, a creative package, use of a publisher's lists for some form of database marketing, or better ad positioning.

No publication, station, or channel will break rate for a single insertion, but almost all will consider creative use or placement when there's a contract. Negotiation might include a special ad position—say, alongside the "Dining Out" column on the restaurant page if you're in the restaurant business. Or a paper might be willing to negotiate for what newspaper people call a "spadea"—a single sheet inserted in a special section and then folded over the front of that section. Or broadcast media might be willing to negotiate a better time period.

Or, thanks to new technology, you may be able to negotiate for something similar (although perhaps on a smaller scale) to what *Modern Maturity* did in a two-page Buick ad. The ad covered the inside front cover and extended across page one. The lefthand page read: "Special offer to you from Buick: Now save an additional $300 on any new Buick." Eight models were pictured, along with directions for the reader to "come in to your Buick dealer now, make your best deal, and then apply the cash toward your purchase."

But the pictures and text were not what grabbed the reader's eye. Rather, it was the *reader's own name* jumping out from the righthand page that did it. Set against the ad's black background was a half-page coupon. The reader's name, in large, all-caps type, was centered in a 2½-by-6-inch stark white block within the gray coupon. There's space elsewhere on the coupon for "Customer Name," address, and other pertinent (to Buick) information. It would be impossible for the magazine's subscriber to miss his or her name boldly shouted from the first page you see as you open the magazine.

Of course, this ad was for a major advertiser whose advertising budget is probably more than most smaller companies are worth. But this idea could certainly be adapted. There's no harm in trying to negotiate for an added-value feature that could stretch your advertising dollar.

Contracts, Standbys, and Mistakes

Contracts are another way to get more ads for less money. One-time rates are much higher (and translate into more commission for the salesperson), so they are usually the rates quoted. Also be sure to look for *special* contract rates that apply only for segmented business groups such as book dealers, travel companies, restaurants, mail-order advertisers, or purveyors of entertainment. Read rate cards carefully. There may be discounts or volume discounts for another category that you'd never hear about if you didn't locate the information for yourself.

A contract will also assure you that your rate will remain stable for the contract period, or that increases will be assessed last on contract holders.

Another, almost-unknown kind of rate-breaker among newspapers is called a "standby." This calls for putting an ad on standby with the newspaper, to be run when and where leftover space becomes available. You can request a specific day, but that can't be guaranteed. The benefit of a standby ad is a rate as much as a 50 percent below regular rates. The disadvantage is that you can't request a specific section or page.

It pays to remember that media make mistakes, and that can mean more space or added time slots if you keep track of your ads and insist upon credit for mistakes. For instance, a foul-up in technology at a radio or TV station might cut your spot so short that the entire message isn't heard. Or your print ad might appear on the wrong day or in the wrong section. A misspelled word in a headline could shatter a perception you're attempting to create that the work your business does is accurate, meticulous, and reliable. Demand a rerun.

More Added Value

Negotiating to use information in a publisher's database can amount to locating data you'd never be able to access otherwise. For example, a magazine can dip into its database to help market your product or service. There are no figures to show the degree of use by all magazines, but an estimate from *Time* magazine indicates that from 10 to 15 percent of all Time Inc. advertisers now use the publisher's lists for some form of database marketing.

For years, newspapers have had the reputation of being the least willing to deal, but they too are coming around and have undergone a dramatic attitudinal change in terms of negotiating both rates and value-added features.

Grow Your Ad Dollars with Co-op

Co-op is short for cooperative advertising. It can stretch advertising dollars up to double the amount budgeted. Take a moment to read the explanation Mark N. Clemente gives the term in *The Marketing Glossary*, because understanding co-op is essential if you're looking for budget-builders.

> [Co-op is] an arrangement in which two or more companies jointly produce or finance advertising. Co-op advertising takes one of two basic forms.
>
> *Vertical* co-op advertising involves shared promotional activities between a manufacturer and a local retailer. The advertising is paid for fully or in part by the manufacturer, and the retailer handles placement of the insertions. The manufacturer may reimburse the retailer for the ad costs or may grant an allowance on the cost of the advertised goods.
>
> *Vertical* co-op advertising lets national advertisers promote their brands in specific markets at local rates, which are typically lower than national ad rates.
>
> In *Horizontal* co-op advertising, independent sellers in the same or similar category combine to produce the advertising. A co-op mailing is one form of horizontal cooperative advertising.

In the most common co-op arrangement, a manufacturer or vendor shares advertising costs on a 50/50 basis, although the division can range from 25 to 100 percent.

Pay particular note to the words in the *Marketing Glossary* definition that spell out one of the chief reasons manufacturers and vendors are so interested in funding advertising for a local business's product. The key word here is *local*. Co-op arrangements allow national advertisers to buy space or time at local rates. The Newspaper Rate Differentials Study conducted bi-annually by AAAA shows that national advertisers pay an average of 74.6 percent more than local advertisers. They may be underwriting a major portion of the cost of your ads, but you can get them a 75 percent discount! For you, co-op means not only funding, wholly or in part, for your advertising, but the extra advertising that co-op permits may entitle you to volume discounts, which stretch your ad dollars even further.

There's another potential benefit for you, particularly if you'd like to use television advertising but can't afford the production costs for a spot that will stand up against the slickest, most enticing spots on the tube. Many national companies have co-op television spots that present their message but leave space and time to include your company's name as the local distributor.

National companies usually have other specially prepared materials for your use, such as logos, graphics, scripts, recordings, and professional layouts. Any such assistance can mean big-time savings in production costs. Your media rep probably has information about corporations in your field that offer co-op.

If your newspaper doesn't have a rep who can explain the pricing structure for co-op ads, ask a research librarian to help you locate current directories, or at least the addresses of organizations such as Co-op News, NCN, National Cable Television Cooperative Inc., National Cable Television Association Inc., and Television Bureau of Advertising.

As long ago as 1986 some $8 billion dollars—that's *billion* with a *b*—was available for cooperative advertising. It's estimated that much, much more is available today, but the bulk of what is available each year goes unused.

THE SWEET BUY AND BUY

The business of choosing media isn't exactly a walk in the park. Not only must you know how to handle over-zealous, sometimes-unscrupulous salespeople, but there are new concepts, new trends, and a dominant new inclination to decrease ad spending on traditional media to consider.

Heed a Pro's Words

The Wall Street Journal calls him Ludwig von Adhoven. He's Bill Ludwig, executive vice president, creative director, and member of the board of directors of Lintas Campbell-Ewald, one of America's premiere advertising agencies. In an ad for *The Wall Street Journal*, he said:

I think there's too much made of expanding media choices: the brave new world of 500 video channels; the thousands of emerging print options; vast libraries on CD-ROM. Technology may change, but the real issue continues to be the strength of the idea. And the important hurdle remains that of capturing someone's attention; involving the reader; communicating persuasively and memorably.

The new challenge—created in part by technology—is that of making a message warm and human.

That's advice from an advertising pro to advertising pros. And he has more worthwhile comments in the same two-page ad in *Advertising Age*.

Video is intrusive, the medium for creating brand awareness. Print isn't intrusive. It's invited into the home or the office by the reader—and any page can be rejected without a zapper.

But print moves the consumer from brand awareness, to brand preference, to product purchase. You can gain awareness with television, but you can gain customers with print. That's an important distinction. And print permits precise targeting so you can tailor your message for greater impact. At a time when efficiency is so essential, print has major advantages.

LOOKING FOR CONSUMERS' LOVE IN ALL THE RIGHT PLACES

You may now know more about media than you did earlier, but odds are you still aren't completely sure which media to buy space or time in or which media alternatives are best for your purposes. Well, you're in good company. The Survey on Marketing Effectiveness & Media Value showed that the perceptions advertising executives have about the effectiveness of different media don't always reflect where they put their dollars. Of 500 ad executives surveyed, 58 percent rated cable TV as "very/extremely" valuable, followed by special-interest magazines, 53 percent; radio, 39 percent; newspapers, 29 percent; and general-interest magazines, 23 percent.

Yet actual advertising placement according to Myers Marketing & Research, was: broadcast network TV, 72 percent; cable TV, 58 percent; direct mail/marketing communications, 55 percent; special-interest magazines, 53 percent; and general-interest magazines, 23 percent.

These two surveys make one thing clear: You should listen to the pros but make your own decisions, based on your own findings of what is best for your very special audience.

6

The Message: A Bill of Writes and Wrongs

The think-through process. Seven steps to creating successful MMMC messages. Using humor. Copywriting tips. The importance of the close. Layout is important, too. Test it.

Okay, put aside whichever hat you've been wearing, and put on your CD hat. Now you're Creative Director of your marketing program. This is where the communications aspect of MMMC kicks in. This is where you make decisions about the single, most consequential message—the communication—you wish to integrate throughout your MMMC program.

In Texas there's a saying: "If you're gonna run with the big dogs, you've gotta step off the porch." Since your message will be appearing alongside the big dogs' messages and you will be running alongside the big dogs in creating that message, just sit there on the porch a while longer and think through the basic communication that you will carry in whatever mixed media framework you choose.

This chapter is about message content and the basics of putting a message together, no matter which communications vehicle you use to get that message to your consumers and prospects. Once you know the how, it's easy to run with the big dogs.

THE THINK-THROUGH PROCESS

The think-through process can take place anywhere—alone in your office using a doodle pad and pen, or with staffers as you munch lunch, jotting notes on a napkin (or in one of the new-tech restaurants with tabletop hookups for your laptop). Napkin, doodle pad, or laptop. Office, porch, or restaurant. The important thing is to begin thinking and doodling.

STEPS TO CREATING SUCCESSFUL MMMC MESSAGES

No matter where you place your message—in a newspaper, on cable, on a package, in your targeted audience's mailboxes (or all of the above)—it should be basically the same message, should send the same communication. And it should accomplish the same seven goals.

1. Attract the right audience.
2. Pique their interest.
3. Knock on their doors and get their attention.
4. Create desire.
5. Abide by the WIIFM ("What's in it for me?") maxim.
6. Establish confidence.
7. Make it easy—to believe, to respond, to want, to buy—whatever is called for.

Stavros (Steve) Cosmopulos (considered a living legend in New England advertising) has advice worth setting in concrete. He indicates that the advice pertains only to advertising, but it applies across the MMMC spectrum. In a *Wall Street Journal* ad in *Advertising Age,* he says, "Make ads as if no one wants to read them—because no one does. People put a protective shield between themselves and advertising. To break through," he says, "focus on one point and express it in words as strong, forceful, sharp and penetrating as possible." Then he uses an example that should help you remember the point every time you consider communicating with your consumers and prospects:

> The fakirs of India can fall asleep on a bed of nails with many points. Load up an ad [or any MMMC message] with many points and none will penetrate. Make one point—and watch it penetrate.

Step 1: Attract the Right Audience

The research you did in Chapter 2 pinned down exactly who your selective audience is. But within each target group, there can be different bull's-eyes. For example, if you know that Hispanics are a substantial portion of your audience, you should think about tapping into and capturing a piece of their estimated $215 billion in purchasing power. Hispanics are the fastest-growing ethnic group in the United States and currently make up at least 10 percent of the population.

If your aim, then, were to reach Hispanics, it would be important for you to recognize that there are a variety of cultures, even a variety of nations, that contribute to the Hispanic population in the United States. In California and the Southwest, for example, the word *Hispanic* is usually used to describe people of Mexican descent. On the East Coast, however, the same term is used to describe people of Puerto Rican descent. People whose ethnic origins are in Guatemala, El Salvador, Cuba, and South America are also described as Hispanic.

Some of these potential customers speak both English and Spanish; some speak only Spanish. And the same words might have different meanings in different Spanish cultures. Not to mention different Spanish accents. One Hispanic teacher says he has no trouble communicating with his Spanish-speaking students or their parents, but some students say he speaks a different kind of Spanish. "They say I sound like people in the *novelas*," he says, referring to South American–produced TV soap operas. The difference might be likened to the difference between English as it is spoken in Texas and English as it is spoken in England.

Those with Chilean ancestry point out that their country is very different from some other Latin American countries. There is, they say, more of a connection to Europe than to North or Central America. They feel closer to Paris than to New York.

So the challenge is to not only choose a single message to convey and appropriate media in which to place it (in this case, a Spanish-language newspaper or radio station might be called for) but also to offer the message in a way that the recipient can and will relate to.

Step 2: Pique Their Interest

One proven means of catching the eye and arousing the interest of your targeted individuals is to cite a benefit you *know* they want. You may need to change your thinking somewhat to focus on selling a benefit rather than a product or service. In reality, the only thing that really matters is what the product or service can do for the consumer or prospect—how it benefits him or her.

If you believe that if one benefit is good, ten would be ten times better, forget it. Set down all ten benefits (or as many as you can come up with) on your doodle pad, but choose only one to focus on. (Save your notes, though; this list will save time and work when you change your message or decide to go after another target group.

Keep in mind that certain words are guaranteed to pique interest. One word that catches every eye is *free*. If you have something you can offer for free, by all means accentuate the word, but make sure to use it along with the benefit. Free alone isn't enough.

To demonstrate how two words that appear to have the same meaning can have completely different effects on people, a list of word substitutes follows. This list is from a booklet called "Write It & Reap: A Comprehensive Guide to Real Estate Ad Writing." It states that certain words and phrases stimulate interest and instill confidence. "Some words even have a negative connotation, while another word with the same meaning seems more appealing." It also warns, "Never misrepresent a home by using words that don't actually describe it."

"UGH" WORDS: "DYNAMIC" SUBSTITUTES

Commission: marketing fee
Contract sale: seller financing
Development: area of new homes
Down payment: initial investment
Good area: established neighborhood
House: home
Huge: oversized
Land: property
Lot: homesite
Mortgage: financing
Older: well preserved
Owner: seller
Price: value
Priced low: affordable
Sales contract: purchase agreement
Sign: authorize

Many of these words can be applied to other kinds of businesses, but since words are highly important in any marketing message, you may wish to consult a book that could help you choose the most effective words. One such book is *Words That Sell: The Thesaurus to Help You Promote Your Products, Services, and Ideas* by Richard Bayan (Contemporary Books).

Step 3: Knock on Their Doors

You've piqued their interest. When you drove up, they looked out the window and saw the words on the side of your delivery truck. That piqued their interest; now it's time to knock on the door, talk your way inside, and keep a strong grasp on that interest.

Lively writing, an easily recognized logo or package, an identifying slogan—anything that carries over from an ad, a promotion, a package, or a direct-marketing piece—anything that creates friendly recognition—is what you're striving for when you knock on the door. If you're writing an ad, your headline (and possibly a stunning graphic) is what catches the reader's eye. Your knock on the door is your headline. That's where you ask prospects to let you inside so you can answer their unasked questions and tell them how that benefit in the headline will benefit *them*.

Your lead paragraph is crucial. It should continue the thought from the headline and never let go. This can be accomplished with a quote from an authority, a testimonial, or a challenge to the reader. Or you can do what the most popular current television commercials do—tell a story. People love stories. Sometimes it's a challenge to keep the opening graf concise and sparkling, but if you can get your point across in the form of a snappy, interesting anecdote, you'll not only get inside the door, but the reader will invite you to sit down and tell her or him more. If your message begins with a story, you can keep the entire ad in the form of a story, or you can complete the story in the first graf and then switch to a more straightforward form for the rest of the ad.

Step 4: Create Desire

John Caples wrote in his book *Making Ads Pay* (Dover):

> The headline of your ad, if it contains a believable promise to the right audience, will cause your prospect to drop his guard for a fraction of a second. You can then deliver, not just one sales argument, not just two sales arguments, but a rapid fire of sales arguments.

Two highly respected figures in marketing, Theodore Levitt and George Arnold, assert that people don't buy things—they buy solutions to problems. Which means that your best MMMC strategy is to determine what problems people have that your product or service can help them solve. You've already done that; it's time to apply it.

Don't lighten up now. You may know what goes in the pot, but you still have to light the fire under it. That fire is words. Use words that sell, words that spark desire. (There is more about writing messages later in this chapter.)

Step 5: Abide by the WIIFM Maxim

"What's In It For Me?" WIIFM. It's the aphorism by which most Americans live. This should tell you that the words *I, we,* and *our* are taboo. *You* and *your* are the only acceptable pronouns in addressing your targeted audience.

Step 6: Establish Confidence

Trust is becoming as rare as high-fat donuts at a health resort, particularly when it comes to advertising. The public's credibility has been tested to its limits. Desire alone is seldom strong enough to convince prospects to buy your product or service if they don't trust it and the company selling it. It boils down to this: When the public can't trust advertising, it has to be able to trust the advertiser. Therefore, it is essential to build that trust with every word you put out—in advertising, direct marketing, promotion, and public relations.

Perhaps you've noticed that you're seeing more and more advertising that is pure image. Image advertising is often used to build trust and confidence. The truth is that every ad, every message your company delivers, transmits an image. A Dillard's department store ad featuring a piece of furniture is an example of an excellent image ad that did a lot toward establishing confidence at the same time that its layout indicated the store is not a discount store and the ad as a whole was selling the product. The ad consisted of a drawing of a single piece of furniture and its price alongside four statements that were set off from the rest of the ad by heavy lines.

1. **HONEST PRICING POLICY:** We strive to bring every customer the best value for their dollar every day.
2. **SELECTION:** Choose from over $12 million of stocked merchandise, or take advantage of our complete Customer Order Program in living room, bedroom, or dining room furniture. Our custom orders are at a substantial savings off the manufacturer's suggested retail price.
3. **A NAME YOU KNOW AND TRUST:** Dillard's is proud to offer you the finest products from such discriminating manufacturers as Henredon, Century, Lexington, Lane, Sealy, Simmons, and more.
4. **DILLARD'S SALES ASSOCIATES:** Whether you're looking for that one special piece or furnishing your entire home, you can be sure that our sales associates are continuously trained to offer you the newest, most fashionable trends in furniture.

You Can Violate the Inviolate

While we're discussing image, another once-inviolate rule that's now being broken is: "Thou shalt not attach a price to products sold on image." So says *Advertising Age*. Now even the toniest ads have prices slipped into them. There's a tactic behind the artifice, according to *Ad Age:* "Advertisers don't want consumers to believe that, if they have to ask a product's price, they can't afford it." However, *Ad Age* points out, some advertisers soften the single price figure by showing an item that costs $385, but running a line that says "from $75 to $1,000."

Step 7: Make It Easy

The final step in creating a successful MMMC message encompasses a number of elements. Do everything you can to make it easy for prospects to believe, trust, respond, want, and buy—whatever is called for. To do this requires a creative layout, perhaps humor, a concise and simple message, and the manner in which the message is written or said.

Layout Matters

Good ideas shine through poor layouts but beautiful layouts can't help poor ideas. That's the cosmetic school of advertising: the use of makeup to create the illusion of beauty. But no matter how much pancake makeup you use, it can't disguise the lack of a real idea. Focus on the concept. Make your layouts rough; make your ideas fancy.

Stavros Cosmopulos

A strong headline that tells readers what's in it for them (and perhaps an attention-getting graphic or photo) is what draws readers to your ad. Holding their interest beyond the headline is the big problem.

Subheads really work. Use them to carry readers' eyes down through the text and to break up dull, grey blocks of type. Subheads make the layout more attractive, but most importantly, they make your points with those who read *only* the subheads.

Never use half-and-half layouts. Everyone prefers an unequal size arrangement— a two-thirds/one-third arrangement of graphics/headline and body text. If, for instance, an ad has a photograph and a small block of text, two-thirds of the space is given to the photo and head and one-third or less to the copy block. Get out your copycat file and notice eye-catching layout arrangements. Some things to consider while you're focusing on layout include:

- It's currently popular to use headlines without photos and to space heads two-thirds down the space.
- Round shapes are more pleasing to the eye than square shapes, and vertical lines are more pleasing than horizontal ones.
- Borders work well for a print ad that is smaller than an entire page. A border sets an ad apart from clutter and attracts readers'

eyes—particularly if the ad incorporates a large proportion of white space. Make the border heavy enough (six to ten points) to fulfill its beckoning assignment.

- Use a simple, easy-to-read typeface, in a size large enough to be easily read. Your ad rep at the publication has books of typefaces and styles and can help you choose style and size to fit your needs.

Entertain Them and They Will Come

Humor can bring a smile to recipients of your message, and as Victor Borge says, a smile is the shortest distance between people. A smile-creating message can also make a company seem friendly—or friendlier. Unfortunately, some people equate humor with jokes and punchlines. There *are* times when a punch line can also be a groan-up joke and exactly what your audience enjoys. "We have found the best way to get a serious message across is to approach it somewhat humorously," says Dick Dunsing, coauthor with Ken Matejka of *In Search of Humor*. "Having a little fun with something is one of the ways to get through to people without turning them off," says Dunsing's coauthor Ken Matejka. When something is too serious to take seriously, try humor. At least try to put a bit of a wink into it. Humor can be especially effective if you consult your prospect profile and use the particular kinds of humor that your very targeted audience enjoys.

Always keep in mind, however, that humor can be totally ineffective—even offensive—if it's not done well. Test every use of humor on everyone within your circle, and particularly those who fit your audience profile, as many times as possible before you go public with the message. You have to be absolutely sure that your humorous, witty words don't come off sounding smart-alecky or tasteless.

Keep the Message Concise and Simple

Simple is more important than concise. There are times when a message can be long but every word will still be read if the content has high value to readers. Roper Starch Worldwide examined the 15 print ads that were rated as 1993's most successful in capturing reader attention. They noted that simplicity and lack of clutter were the key factors, although color played a big part in attracting attention.

Being concise is important even when your message is meant to be long. Rambling, wordy sentences are an absolute taboo regardless of the length of the message. It is important to be concise *before* you write your message. Make sure that the very idea you wish to express is concise. Is it short enough to fit on a T-shirt or a billboard where drivers have less than seven seconds to get your message? (T-shirts are sometimes used as offbeat billboards. President Clinton is known for wearing T-shirts that offer his message for the day.)

MORE TIPS FROM THE PROS ABOUT COPYWRITING

Jack Hart is so good a writer that he dares to be the writing coach at the *Portland Oregonian* and writes a how-to-write column for *Editor & Publisher* magazine. His lessons are worth learning. He makes some points about writing news stories and features that bear remembering for MMMC messages. He says there are numbers of ways to begin, but . . .

> You probably won't pull many readers along unless you get moving.
> Step right out. Grab readers with a concrete noun and yank hard with
> a strong, transitive verb. Then hang on tight and keep pulling.

In his book *Ads: Design and Make Your Own* (Van Nostrand), Abraham Switkin says that clarity and force are characteristics of effective copy. And the [message] should bubble with enthusiasm, although that doesn't mean that exaggeration or meaningless superlatives should be used.

Brian Tracy, one of the country's busiest speakers on the subject of selling, stresses that a caring attitude is one of the most important attributes a salesperson should project. If the goal for your message is to sell, then as the salesperson carrying the message to buyers, you should transfer Tracy's thinking to your MMMC message.

Together, a caring attitude and enthusiasm may be just the combination needed to escort each reader through your message to the close, where he or she reaches out to buy your product (or whatever it is you're asking them to do).

THE CLOSE

Don't let your prospects get away! Don't mince words; don't dance around the subject. Come right out and tell them what to do. If your MMMC message appears as an ad, don't waste your bucks, or your time, by omitting a close, a request for action. After all, a salesperson *always* asks for an order.

This, too, is part of the think-through process—deciding what exactly it is you want your reader to do. If you're making an offer—of a sample, some literature, an 800-number to call for more information—or asking for an order, come right out and clearly and concisely say so, explaining exactly how to do it. Make sure you keep this information at the close, at the end of the message where it is expected, and don't make readers search back through your message to find a telephone number where an order can be placed, whether credit cards are accepted, or any other information a person might need to make a purchase (or do whatever else is being asked). Keep all of this information together in the closing graf(s), a boxed space, or on the mail-in coupon.

WRITING: CREATIVITY OR CRAFT?

It had better be both. For unless you can think creatively—by sensing what to say and how to say it—what you write won't grab many readers or listeners or viewers. Of course, other people's creative thinking can be copycatted. But once you get to the actual writing—now that's a craft. It requires skill that can be learned through practice. Part of the skill is speaking in a language those you speak to will understand. Otherwise, why bother?

TEST YOUR MESSAGE AGAINST THOSE IN YOUR COPYCAT FILE

With the completion of the first draft of your MMMC message, suddenly you're one of the card-carrying, legitimate MMMC big dogs. You're off the porch!

One suggestion: get out your own copycat file, the collection of print ads that attracted or repulsed you, and pick out the best ones, then candidly compare yours with theirs. The likelihood is that your message will be far stronger than any in the collection. Don't compare graphics or layout, only the message. Their deeper pockets may have purchased a fancier-*looking* message, but for now you're concerned only with comparing whether your *words* will get through to your audience.

THE WHETHER FORECAST

Pretest your ad. Call this step the "whether forecast." This is when you find out whether it will play in Peoria (or with whomever you're targeting) or whether it needs a little adjusting. Run your ad past every person you can personally contact who fits your niche target. If the budget permits, buy a small run in the publication you intend to use and do an actual test, realizing of course that the test does not allow for building recognition and that with repetition and recognition come acceptance and sales.

7

Seeing Is Believing on TV . . . But Radio Gives Great Pictures, Too

TV is for the masses; cable targets individuals. How to construct your commercial. About production companies and using semi-pros. Writing the script. Choosing spokespersons and getting them to act the part. Cable is priced right. Radio: "little theater of the mind." Using humor.

When you don't know exactly who your audience is—and *if* you have the big bucks required—then television is the way to go. Television advertising is like hunting with a scattergun, hoping you'll hit something. But when you know exactly who the quarry is—and you want the benefits of broadcast media, but not its mass audience—you head for cable TV or radio.

Radio has long been a communications medium widely used by small businesses not only because it reaches local people, but because there are stations that can zero in on just about any selected group.

Cable has the same vital links in distributing MMMC messages. Cable commercial time and production costs are plummetting, so this entire chapter is devoted to making the distinctive construction of television, cable TV, and radio commercials more understandable. Chapter 17 is devoted entirely to methods of constructing and transmitting *publicity* messages on television and radio.

THE EYES HAVE IT

Much of what applies to television applies to cable TV. The two primary differences are: (1) television is for mass audiences, whereas cable with its menu programming is for highly vertical audiences; and (2) time and production costs for television are mostly beyond the budgets of most small businesses.

Television in general has made addicts of people who wish to be passively informed and entertained, and the zapper has become the greatest threat to productive television and cable advertising.

A report in *Adweek* under the headline, "Thanks for the Show, Guess I'll Skip the Commercial," offers stats about zapping.

> How much do ratings tumble in TV's primetime when the program gives way to a commercial?
> For affiliates of the three big networks, the primetime rating for commercial minutes averaged 7.9 percent lower than for program minutes. For independents and Fox affiliates, the differential was wider, with commercial time getting ratings 12.8 percent lower than the programs.
> Cable networks showed an average drop-off of 14.3 percent from program to commercial time.

(Things that can be done to overcome these hazards will be described later in this chapter.)

Aside from actually sitting down with a prospect, television—and now cable—comes closest to providing everything a viewer wishes to know about a product except smell, taste, and touch. But words can go a long way toward simulating these senses for a viewer.

CONSTRUCTING YOUR COMMERCIAL

From your investigations in Chapters 2 and 5, you should know whether cable or radio (or both) is right for you, and which cable or radio stations best fit your audience profile. And from your doodling in Chapter 6, you should know the basics of the message you want to get to these viewers or listeners.

The two main questions at this point are: (1) Is this a project you can do yourself? and (2) if so, how do you do it? There are several answers to these questions, but the best recommendation is always to get as much professional help as you can afford. If you can afford experienced professionals who understand your business, who understand at least as well as you do integrating messages the MMMC way, and who can relate to the person you want to reach with that single message, then that's the way to go. But don't think of your company as being underprivileged or discriminated against if you can't afford an agency or can't find one that measures up to your needs. Don't panic. There is low-cost freelance, even no-cost semi-professional help available, and we'll discuss that later in this chapter.

You should know that, in almost all agencies, writers are the dominant creative force. They're the ones who almost always conceive and create the idea. You already have the message, which will more or less dictate the visuals and the sounds that accompany it. Your challenge is to squeeze that message into as few as 40 to 50 words and find pictures and sound that will strengthen and intensify it.

Production Companies

Advertising agencies do all manner of advertising in all kinds of media, but production companies specialize in doing video commercials, from scripting to producing the finished product. Most specialize either in live action or in animation. Some produce on videotape, others on film. Shooting with 35 mm film is the acme for high-grade production. There is also 16 mm film available at a lesser cost, but videotape is by far the least expensive (yet still quite adequate) means for recording almost any spot you might contemplate producing.

Some production houses have the latest high-tech equipment to handle special effects such as morphing (a computer technique for transforming one image into another), but at prices that very few small companies can afford.

What you really need is someone who knows and understands the technicalities of producing television commercials. If you can handle writing the script and conceiving the visuals, perhaps you can find a freelancer or a production company who will handle only the technical part of the job. Ask around.

Semi-Pros

If you have easy access to a college or university that has a marketing, advertising, or television production department, check whether competent students might be able to assist with the job. Instructors are often delighted when a local business gives students the opportunity to do real-world work. Sometimes the work is done for course credit under the supervision of the instructor; other times, qualified students can be hired for minimum rates upon the recommendation of a department head or an instructor. If you hire students, be absolutely sure you have as serious an agreement or contract as you would if you were contracting with a professional production company. To avoid misunderstandings, be sure the agreement includes a clause that allows you to turn down the finished product if it doesn't measure up in content or quality. Agree in advance to pay equipment rental charges, to purchase the needed videotape or film, and to cover any other charges.

Even if you don't use student talent, an instructor who teaches construction of television commercials can be an extraordinary source of information about where to locate script writers, locations for shoots, and freelance camera crews. Some television and cable stations will also assist in producing commercials.

WRITE A SCRIPT

Whether you're writing a television or radio spot, a script is called for. And each type of script has its own format. We will discuss television scripts first and cover radio scripts later in the chapter.

Cable is merely television aimed to a select, highly vertical audience, so much of what applies to television works for cable. Cable messages, however, can be simpler and less glitzy because they seldom have to compete against the super-sophisticated commercials that mega-corporations run on network TV, network affiliates, and even on local independent stations.

The most popular script form has VIDEO descriptions (what the viewer will see) and instructions in chronological order on the left half of the page. The right side is the sound or AUDIO portion of the script—the words to be spoken. The second script form is a reversal of this. Audio and video are separated, but audio is on the left and video on the right. In a third format, the first two formats are blended—sort of. The instructions are centered, usually in capitals or italics and set between lines of dialogue. It will be easier to write—and edit—your script using the half-and-half page format.

A sample script for you to use as a model is presented in Exhibit 7.1.

Make it Friendly and Conversational

Words on television and radio are spoken—and heard—not read as we read books or magazines. So the words must be written to be spoken. Most people speak informally, with contractions: they say "don't" in place of "do not," "doesn't" for "does not," and "I'll" in place of "I will." Be sure your words are written to be spoken, then speak them aloud yourself, and *listen* to them to be sure they sound conversational. If they sound friendly, they'll receive a far friendlier response.

Exhibit 7.1 Script for a 30-second commercial for TU Electric showing how video instructions and the audio portion are set up.

TU Electric
:30 TV
9/12/94
Mr. & Mrs. Hammerbacher
"Spud"

VIDEO	AUDIO	
WALK UP TO FRONT DOOR	MK:	We asked our customers to tell us how we could build a better electric company.
KNOCK ON DOOR		
CLOSE-UP OF MARILYN KOSANKE		
SPUD ANSWERS DOOR, LAUGHING	ANCR:	Do you remember this?
LETTER HANDED TO SPUD		
CLOSE-UP OF MARILYN	SPUD:	It's a letter I sent to TU Electric.
CLOSE-UP OF SPUD	MK:	I read 8,000 letters.
CLOSE-UP OF FAMILY PHOTO WITH NOTE WRITTEN TO TU	SPUD:	Please use more renewable energy sources.
CLOSE-UP OF MARILYN		
CLOSE-UP OF SPUD WITH BABY	MK:	We're going to use the ideas from customers to plan new programs. At Energy Park we're looking at wind power, solar power.
CUT TO SPUD RIDING BICYCLE		
CLOSE-UP OF SPUD		
CLOSE-UP OF WIFE	SPUD:	I've always considered myself a nerd.
CUT TO SPUD PLAYING WITH SOLAR TOY		
	MRS:	He had one good year. In third grade he had a girlfriend.
E-PROGRAMS LIGHT BULB VISUAL		
	ANCR:	E-Programs, made from customers' suggestions. Maybe one of them was yours.
FAMILY WAVING GOODBYE		
	ANCR:	Enjoy the hats! What did we pay for those anyway?
TU ELECTRIC LOGO WITH TAG		

Listen for double entendre, too—for words with a double, perhaps risque, meaning. For instance, the announcer in a reducing salon's commercial said, "It's in your jeans."

Whaaaat?

That's what the announcer said . . . except the spelling in the script was actually "genes," and a lot of listeners misunderstood.

Listen, too, to be sure listeners hear what you mean to say. For example, a car's price of $20,966 can be heard as "twenty-nine sixty six"—$2966. And don't count on just spelling out the price on-screen. Often television is merely background sound while people do other things.

Be sure to speak the words aloud in order to time them, to be certain they fit comfortably into 28 or 57 seconds for a 30- or 60-second time slot. Technology is so refined that if a commercial runs the barest fraction of a second overtime, it is cut. Allow a couple of seconds extra to accommodate an announcer who speaks a trifle slower.

SFX FOR VIEWERS WITH EARS

Have you ever watched a television commercial with no music or sound effects (SFX)? With the mute button on? Almost without exception, commercials have music, a dog barking, the background clatter of a manufacturing process, a baby crying, or some other sound effect. Sound effects accompany spoken words and are always used when only words or visuals are flashed across the screen.

Have you ever watched a commercial where the sound and picture weren't integrated? That kind of disharmony can create unconscious unpleasant reactions among viewers, so be aware of this possibility.

Sounds are chosen to grab the attention of viewers and to heighten the impact of the message. The letters SFX denote and describe the sound effects that are called for at specific places in the script.

Remember: sometimes less is more. If sound effects are difficult to locate, apply the keep-it-simple strategy and adapt whatever is handy. This is an excellent safeguard against the tendency to overuse sound effects in an attempt to attract attention. Such overuse sometimes works against you by automating listeners' mute buttons or zappers.

The Sounds of Silence

Occasionally, no sound is the best sound. Dead air can grab listeners' minds—particularly with radio—and make them wonder what's wrong at the station or with their equipment.

In describing SFX, we said that sounds are "always used when only words or visuals are flashed across the screen." An exception to that rule was an especially effective Bayer Aspirin commercial that ran completely without sound. None. The entire commercial was a woman speaking in sign language while a translation ran at the bottom of the screen. There can be times when a few seconds of dead air can be highly effective. Just make sure it's appropriate and matches the storyline, so the viewer or listener understands that it's intentional, not a glitch. And use the technique sparingly.

The Music of Advertising

"To many non-musicians in the creative end of the advertising business, music is as foreign as Sanskrit or Swahili," grouches Wayne Dykes in *Adweek* magazine. Dykes is cofounder of Acous Tech Sound Production, an Atlanta-based music design firm. He describes how to come up with music that is both unique and effective and says that those designing the music "need to cultivate the art of listening. Music for advertising should have one ultimate goal—to help communicate a concept. If it doesn't, the ad is as good as dead."

Ask yourself these questions:

- Will the piece be used to set a mood?
- Is the music's role to establish a connection with a certain demographic group?
- Should the music accentuate the point of the ad by building and releasing tension?

Television stations have libraries of music and sound effects they will let you use if you run your commercial on their stations. Cable stations, because they're smaller and operate on more limited budgets, often can't offer you this assistance, which means you'll have to locate your sound effects or music somewhere else and pay for using them.

Music, unless it's in public domain (meaning the copyrights have expired) calls for paying royalties to those who recorded it and possibly to the person who wrote it if the composer's copyright is still in effect. Some stations have special CDs that were recorded especially for use as background for commercials. It just takes a little digging to locate them.

CHOOSING YOUR SPOKESPERSON

Well-Known Celebrities

The qualities Chevrolet looked for when it chose Janine Turner (best known as Maggie on "Northern Exposure") for their commercials were outlined by a Chevy spokesperson: "Of all the individuals we looked at we were very impressed with Janine because she did a good job in conveying the sincerity, honesty, and believability we want."

Candice Bergen ("Murphy Brown") was chosen for Sprint commercials for other reasons. "We tend to have a technologically sophisticated, somewhat younger audience with somewhat of a female skew," Sprint's vice president for corporate advertising told *The New York Times*. And it was felt that she "speaks to the baby boom generation, the economic base of the population," and to a Sprint kind of audience that is generally better educated and with higher incomes.

Real People

Those are undoubtedly the same qualities you'll want to test for among the real people (non-celebrities) you'll be auditioning. Here are some guidelines for getting your non-pro talent to act the parts they've been assigned. (We've adapted these rules from Bob Eric Hart, writing in *Adweek* magazine.)

1. You be you, and let them be them.
2. Encourage them to be creative. Give them a shot at doing it their way.
3. Remember that tape is cheap, but magic is priceless. As you give your talent emotional rein, relax. Do ten different takes on the key lines. Give your editor a lot to work with. There is no economy in low tape costs and a mediocre final product.
4. Know when and how to be firm. Constructively challenge people to stay on course without doubting their creativity.
5. Don't be negative. People draw energy from positive feedback but can get totally bummed out by negative comments—or even silent frowns.
6. Let your talent in on the big picture. Try: "Now Brit, this new amusement-park spot is aimed at kids, but we want their parents to think it's a good idea, too. It needs to be fun but not too silly."

SOME THINGS TO THINK ABOUT

The major challenge with every commercial you construct is to hold the interest of viewers throughout the entire message and to make the spot memorable. A special sound repeated in every commercial for your product or service or a certain melody that is always used as an introduction to the spot (or run as background music), can become almost as recognizable as a slogan that is always used with the name of your company. (More about slogans in Chapter 13.)

Three more things to remember about commercials are:

1. Surveys show that people respond more readily to commercials that tell a story or offer a real-person testimonial rather than merely present the message as a report.
2. Always include a call to action. Tell the listener what to do and how to do it.
3. And always, always allow five seconds at the end of the commercial to run your logo with your location and phone number.

CABLE—THE PRICE IS RIGHT

Costs for creating cable spots are extremely low when compared to costs of producing network television spots. Jay Conrad Levinson, in his book *Guerrilla Advertising* (Houghton Mifflin), gives a real-life example. Med 7, an urgent-care center in Sacramento, California, signed a contract to run one-minute TV spots on cable for one year.

"We produced two commercials," Levinson says, "for a total cost of $3,000—that's $1,500 per ad. The cost was low because of a tight script, use of Med 7 employees instead of professional actors, rights-free music, and a non-union announcer."

What results did Med 7 earn?

"After the commercials ran one month at the rate of five spots a day, five days a week, three weeks each month, Med 7 did a postcard mailing to the citizens of Carmichael. At the end of the second month, patient count rose to thirty each day. At the end of the third month, it went up to fifty each day—our goal for the *year.*"

Pay special notice to the relationship between using the MMMC strategy of integrating direct mail (the postcard mailing) with cable—and the ultimate results. Also note Levinson's tips about effective cost savings being achieved by means of "a tight script, using Med 7 employees instead of professional actors, rights-free music, and a non-union announcer."

MORE TIPS TO REMEMBER AS YOU CREATE A TV COMMERCIAL

TV (in this case, cable) is the nearest you can get to an in-person visit to a prospect. With television, you can demonstrate your product or service, and your words can almost make that prospect taste or smell it. Viewers aren't just looking at still pictures. TV moves, it *sounds.*

So don't water down TV's advantages by showing only mouths moving. Many novices place an attractive person in front of the camera and give him or her words to recite. "Talking heads" they're called. Show moving pictures, people doing things, action that captures both the eyes and the minds of viewers. And it isn't necessary to use exceptionally beautiful people. Real people, ordinary-looking people, people who look like neighbors or other people viewers might see every day—if they are doing things—can be many times more effective than the most attractive talking head in the country.

Creating and producing cable TV spots yourself has another advantage. You can forget simulating an agency-designed storyboard that locks the crew into doing only what is scripted. Let things happen spontaneously. When you're shooting, let the people act naturally and say your words in their own manner. Once they're comfortable with the camera, let them portray *themselves*. It will come across as honest.

Finally, check your open and close. Be sure the spot opens with a compelling two- or three-second visual or sound-grabber and then goes on to state the message in simple words or actions and ends with another compelling visual or sound call to do something—a close. Make sure the company's name is presented both visually and by voice so that if your audience isn't watching or the mute button is on, they'll know whose message they've just received.

RADIO

One of the greatest things about radio is that it follows people wherever they go, whether they are out jogging, in the car, in the shower, in bed, doing chores at home, sitting in an office, at the grocery store.

And most radio junkies (unlike television viewers) are loyal to a specific station rather than to certain programs on a variety of stations, which means your message won't get zapped if it's placed between programs, as so often happens to between-shows spots on TV. Each radio station directs its programming to a very narrow interest group—to people who want news, talk shows, country, rock, classical, or rap. The range of interests that radio offers is as broad as the range of people's interests, and each station's programming is as narrow as the single, narrow interest of its listeners.

The Little Theater of the Mind

If a commercial is done right, people get a better picture from their radio than they would from TV. But it's not the easiest job in the world to make radio listeners see with words alone. The best radio dramas and commercial spots play to listeners' imaginations, to their mental visions. People who remember radio in the days before television reflect on how much more they enjoyed dramas back then. There is general acceptance that people get a better picture when their imaginations do the picturing. Pros know this and play to the imagination factor.

Pulling Your Spot Out of the Background

Radio is often used as background while people are doing something—biking, working, studying—and radio commercials become background, too.

Drive time is usually a good time to reach an audience, because people tune into a specific station to listen to the programs that station offers. Listeners are locked in their cars with their radios—and your advertising messages.

Of course, that doesn't mean that individuals' minds don't occasionally tune out (particularly when the programming is music) as they think about what happened at work or other things going on in their lives. That's why an opening grabber—or dead air for a second or two—works so well to bring listeners back to the present and to your message.

Keep the following points in mind as you prepare your radio spot:

- With radio you have no double impact of sight and sound to implant your company name in a listener's memory. So try to work your organization's name in three times—in the beginning, the middle, and the end.
- People don't remember numbers well. Therefore, don't give phone numbers or street addresses. Tell them that your number is listed in the phone book or that you're located at the corner of two well-known streets, or across from or next to a well-known landmark or store. Try to implant a visual identification.
- Quality can vary widely if your script is read live by radio station personnel, so to control the quality level of your spot, tape it and distribute the dupes.

A Script Is a Script Is a Script

Go back to the section in this chapter about writing scripts for television and cable and check out the angles that apply to radio, remembering of course that words and sounds are even more important for radio than for television. Words and sounds are all you have, but with them you can create very vivid pictures in your listeners' minds.

In Chapter 3, we urged you to develop the skill of copycatting. There we presented an overview of the marketing routes EvansGroup chose on behalf of TU Electric (Case 3: Taking TU Electric Past Its Problems). One of the routes used was television and radio advertising. (The TV script is shown in Exhibit 7.1 on page 71.) For copycatting purposes, here is a radio script for that same campaign, not only to show you how a radio script is formatted, but also to give you a peek at how EvansGroup targeted two specific audiences—English- and Spanish-speaking people.

Exhibit 7.2   Script for a 60-second radio commercial that ran on both English- and Spanish-language stations. (This is the English version.)

"Gente Como Tu"
(People Like You)
English Version
:60 Radio

ANNR: People like you are helping TU Electric make some very important changes . . .
            Like Mr. Joe Guzman, who wants us to offer tips in Spanish on how to save energy:

MAN 1:   "It would be good to have information in Spanish for people who don't know English."

ANNR: Or like Mrs. Violeta, who suggested we design a bill that's easier to read:

WOMAN: "I would like for my bill to be less complicated."

ANNR: Mr. Zuniga would like to have different payment options:

MAN 2:   "I believe that if I could make my payments in another way, it would be better for me."

ANNR: These are only some of the many ideas that people like you have given us. But this is not all. In your bill you will find a brochure where you can give us your ideas—ideas to serve you better . . .
            TU Electric.
            Building a Better Company.

Humor

People who listen to radio for anything other than background while they're doing something love humor. Television commentator John Leonard observes, "This is the comic-book '90s," so humor is almost expected. A tiny taste of humor, with a tinier whiff of mild offensiveness, adds up to a smile on behalf of the huge discount store, Incredible Universe. Their opening line was: "We've gone to Dell and back to bring you incredible deals on Dell Computers."

Try it. You have nothing to lose. If you can get prospects to laugh, you can get them to buy. *But how?* you ask. Be of good cheer. Bob Hope's joke writer, Gene Perret, said that "everyone can learn to use humor effectively."

Your local library has how-to books and articles on the subject of humor. Study a few of them and learn the skill. Not only might it make extra dollars for you, but it seems to be something that is demanded in today's advertising world.

Radio Is Glancing at Interactive

Radio spends most of its own marketing time concentrating on establishing an online presence, on both the Internet and commercial online services. However, out of the corner of its eye, radio has been watching what's been happening elsewhere in interactive media. Ron Rodrigues, managing editor of *Radio & Records,* tells *Advertising Age* readers that radio "has more finitely targeted audiences. But a lot [of stations] don't know what to do with it other than soliciting feedback from listeners." As late as 1995, almost all radio stations were hunting for ways to gain revenues from online offerings. A very limited number are dipping their toes in the water.

KMPS-AM/FM in Seattle is fishing for advertisers from its own Internet location. They offer a monthly magazine—in both print and online versions—that provides information, music reviews, and station promotions, with an average of 6,000 responses per month. The station was also experimenting with a technology that merges radio with personal computers. Another station, KKSF-FM in San Francisco, offers a weekly online newsletter, which it says receives 13,000 inquiries a month. For radio stations that don't individually have the budget to go online, there's CompuServe with its version of talk radio.

The bottom line to all this is that by far the biggest number of radio stations are still testing the waters, while a few are diving in, knowing everyone's watching them jump the waves and try to swim.

8

Case Studies: How the Pros Used Advertising

Advertising was the foundation for all of the experts' campaigns. How each used it: Case 1—FastSigns; Case 2—The UnInstaller; Case 3—TU Electric's *Responsiveness* campaign; Case 4—KPDX *No News* image builder; Case 5—OmniStich; Case 6—Protection One's *Know* campaign; Case 7—Oregon BFA's "Call to Action"; Case 8—Caradco Windows' campaign to reach two targets; Case 9—It Takes All Kinds

Advertising was the foundation of each of the MMMC programs described in Chapter 3, although advertising was secondary to direct marketing in one case and to publicity in another. In this chapter, the businessman and the pros you met in Chapter 3 explain how they used advertising in their MMMC campaigns.

CASE 1: FASTSIGNS DOES ADVERTISING

When Gary Salomon sat down and began thinking through how advertising would accomplish his goal (to reach potential entrepreneurs with the right kind of message), he recognized something in others' ads that he did *not* want to duplicate in FastSigns' ads. He explains it in his own words:

> Even the best business magazines usually carry at least a few ads that promise would-be entrepreneurs $5,000 a week for stuffing envelopes. No matter how blatantly exploitive these ads are, they continue to draw response—but anyone with good business sense instantly recognizes that kind of ad for what it is.

So our first goal in advertising was to take the high road—*never* to look like an envelope-stuffing scheme. And when you're working with limited funds, that can be difficult.

We tried to do it not so much by what we put into our ads, but by what we left out. In a publication filled with screamer headlines (such as "Fire Your Boss!" and "Make Big Money Fast!" and the ever-popular "$$$$$$$!!"), an ad that shows some restraint will have a unique appeal. It will speak to the more experienced, more realistic businessperson who's looking for straight talk, not pie-in-the-sky.

And that's exactly who we were trying to reach.

Getting the Picture

As our company grew and we were able to place larger ads, we encountered the photography problem: good photos are usually expensive, and bad photos can make you look . . . well, *bad*. But there are ways to get better photos without spending a lot of money.

The first step is to decide exactly what you want to communicate through the photograph. For example, we devised one particular photo that allowed us to make several fundamental statements about our business without saying a word.

- The prominence of the computer in the photo says that we're a clean, high-tech business—not a warehouse-based paint shop.
- Readers can see that the design on the pad is being reproduced on the computer screen, which demonstrates that we can do custom artwork.
- In the background, you see a customer being assisted at the front counter, which clearly implies that this is a retail-style, service-oriented business. Employees and the customer are dressed neatly and professionally. The message their appearance sends is subliminal, but effective.
- On the wall beyond, "menu boards" display some of the materials, typestyles, and colors available, and suggest that FastSigns has a wide range of graphic capabilities.
- We even managed to work in our name, frosted on the glass between the computer room and the counter area.

Use a Photo That Tells Your Story

With that single photo, we managed to paint a fairly detailed picture of what a FastSigns store looks like and how it operates. That picture is worth much more than a thousand words—because it allows the prospective franchisee to *literally* envision himself in our business.

And what did that photo cost? At first, almost zero. An untrained person with a good eye and a mid-range 35 mm camera set the shot up and snapped it in ten minutes. Later when we were ready to invest in the services of a professional photographer, we had the same set-up reshot. The pro's photo, shot with a large-format camera, is indeed better—it has sharper focus throughout the depth of field, consistent lighting, and models who were better prepared for the session. The professional photograph was well worth the two or three hundred dollars it cost. But that first photo, which cost only the price of film and developing, was good enough to do the job until we were ready to invest in a more expensive photo shoot.

When we made the investment in professional photography, we planned and prepared for every shot in detail before engaging the photographer on a day-rate basis. In order to make efficient use of the pro's time, we handled as many logistical issues as possible beforehand, then stood by to assist as needed.

Sending the Message

Traditional wisdom says that people won't take the time to read a lot of copy in an ad. In fact, statistics indicate that the vast majority will read only your headline and, possibly, the captions under your photos.

After much thought and a few trial runs, we decided to defy traditional wisdom. We reasoned that we didn't need 100 percent readership. We only needed that small percentage of people who were actually qualified prospects for our franchise, people with

- Business acumen
- Entrepreneurial spirit
- Solid financial resources

And those people, we believed, would appreciate an ad that contained some real information, rather than the usual puff piece. We decided to give them an ad worth spending some time with.

The FastSigns Ad That Targets the Target

We designed the ad to resemble an editorial piece, albeit with the word ADVERTISEMENT displayed at the top.

Headline
We gave the ad a provocative headline to engage the reader's curiosity. We included a growth chart as a strong visual expression of our company's progress. And, because photo captions are more likely to be read than body text, we made sure our captions emphasized the most compelling facts about our concept and our company.

Writing Style

Another departure from tradition was the style of our writing. We wanted to strike a professional tone, but not to bore the reader with the dry, soulless prose of most business-to-business advertising. We developed a style that reflected the personality of our company and the profound sense of commitment we felt toward our franchisees.

Results

It worked. Our "advertorial-style" ad, placed in only one major magazine, drew roughly 300 inquiries per month for a period of nearly two years. During this period, our network growth peaked at the astonishing rate of one new FastSigns store every week for a full year.

Testing

The system we used to test and refine our ads was simple: We asked each new franchisee to critique the ad he or she had responded to. We paid careful attention to their comments and adjusted our message to provide the information they felt was most important.

Other Factors

We also took into consideration the mood of the country and shifted the focus of our ads to address concerns that appeared to be relevant. For example, during a particularly unstable period in the economy, we devoted some of the space in our ad to the fact that we had started our business during one of the worst economies Texas has ever seen, and it has prospered nonetheless. We backed up that statement with some details on how the type of business-to-business service we provide helps make FastSigns inflation-resistant.

Cost Containment

Because color separations (the actual artwork from which the magazine prints the ad) are costly, all this adjusting and updating would have been prohibitively expensive if we hadn't planned for it. To keep the cost down, we designed some of our ads so that each new version could be produced by changing only *one* of the four pieces of film that made up the color separation.

We did that using only black ink for all the elements we might want to change, such as the headline and the body copy. The color photos, the red-and-blue logo, and other color elements remained the same from one ad to the next—so when we wanted a new ad, we only had to produce new film for the black plate.

Staying Current

Our black-plate-only revision system had one obvious drawback: The ads all looked basically the same. Over time, regular readers of the magazine became overly familiar with our ads, and response began to dwindle. It was time to recapture their attention with a new look. We invested in some better photography and used the results to create a new series of ads that relied mostly on the visual to draw the reader's attention.

CASE 2: WEMMERS COMMUNICATIONS FACED A CHALLENGE

In order to break through the high level of noise from other software advertisers, an unusual ad campaign had to be designed for the UnInstaller, a new product to be sold by MicroHelp. The campaign was, to say the least, a bit controversial.

Advertising was the major route used to raise sales for UnInstaller in the initial launch stages. It was the way MicroHelp told the world about the product and the benefits it offered to a specific segment of the computer audience. "We also knew we had to reach potential consumers where they read—in computer user magazines," says Rick Wemmers. "But we faced a fact that the four magazines chosen for the campaign had more than 100 different software and Windows products advertised, per average issue."

The challenge Rick Wemmers faced for his client, MicroHelp, was getting magazine readers to stop and read the UnInstaller ads, an especially difficult challenge because the problem UnInstaller was designed to solve was not widely recognized.

Ads Were Designed to Break Others' Noise Levels

Wemmers designed ads that would break through the noise level of other software advertisers. One of the somewhat controversial ads carried a headline:

> Like it or not, a bunch of trash
> has moved into your computer.

Below the head was a photo that was sure to attract everyone's attention, a photo of three men and a woman who fit the 'trashy' look. The copy read:

> It's shocking to look through your Windows and suddenly see that the electronic equivalents of the Clampetts have put down roots in your system. These are the homeless remnants of every program you ever thought you had replaced.
> UnInstaller chases out these useless, no-count data, restoring disk space and operating speed in seconds. For a suggested price of

only $69.95, UnInstaller takes out the trash, leaving your Windows as valuable as the day you bought it.
Only UnInstaller Cleans Windows.

Below the body text was the logo for UnInstaller Version 2.0 and information about where it was available, plus an 800 number for ordering.

The Ad Scored Big

That ad was one of three designed for the 1994 campaign. It scored the highest response rate of all advertising in the January 1995 issue of *PC Computing* magazine. It was the second-most-remembered ad in the same issue. (The photo in the ad was also used in other promotional materials at the time the ad debuted.)

CASE 3: EVANSGROUP'S CAMPAIGN FOR TU ELECTRIC

TU Electric's objective was to stabilize residential customer favorability and achieve a rating of at least 70 percent. To achieve these goals, Evans-Group chose several advertising avenues, but the primary media selected were spot television and spot radio. Secondary support was local newspaper advertising and outdoor advertising. Their thinking was:

- Spot television provided the high reach and mass appeal needed to maintain positive top-of-mind awareness. (See Exhibit 7.1 for TU Electric's TV commercial script.)
- Spot radio allowed the agency to build frequency among a variety of loyal listeners. (See Exhibit 7.2 for the script of one of TU's radio spots.)
- Newspapers, both community- and market-wide, were used to reinforce TU's message.
- Outdoor boards served as a continuity medium throughout the entire campaign.

The Initial Campaign Appealed to "Folks Like You"

TU Electric began the initial "Folks Like You" *Responsiveness* campaign with television, radio, and newspaper ads that asked customers to send in their suggestions via the form in their bill insert. There were 8,000 responses, all of which TU Electric personally answered.

The Secondary Approach Focused on Specific Programs

Subsequent radio, newspaper, and magazine advertising messages (as well as a direct-marketing bill insert) were focused on specific available customer-service programs, says George Arnold, president and CEO of EvansGroup.

It was tabbed the *Responsiveness* campaign, which was a follow-up and extension to "Folks Like You." Three television spots highlighted actual customers who had written to the company and TU's response to their suggestions.

CASE 4: THE KPDX *NO NEWS* IMAGE CAMPAIGN

This campaign was run by the McKinney Johnson Amato agency for one of the five Portland, Oregon, television stations. Liz Johnson describes their media-buying strategy:

> In deciding where to place our message, we once again reviewed our audience and our goals, then added in the initial budget and creative information.
>
> The overall budget showed us what type of media we could afford. The creative strategy gave us direction as to each medium's effectiveness to carry our simple message.
>
> A strong outdoor and transit advertising schedule was suggested along with print, radio, and on-air support. Collateral materials were also planned.

Re-evaluating the Budget

> During this phase of preparation, we shifted dollars to accommodate media selections, target particular media vehicles, and earmark appropriate production amounts.
>
> For example, we had set aside cable TV advertising dollars in our original budget, but then saw that those dollars would have more impact if they were shifted to augment outdoor boards. At the same time, television production dollars were moved to the outdoor production allocation for maximum effectiveness.

Execution

Everything was mapped out, and the challenge was to meet all the deadlines.

The advertising campaign elements included: three print ads, two radio spots—one 30-second on-air spot and more than twenty 10-second teaser spots—plus outdoor paints and posters, and transit. (Paints, also called "painted bulletins," are outdoor billboards that are painted directly onto the boards. Posters, also known as "printed posters," are prepared in a plant and are "posted" on panels on outdoor boards.)

During phase two, graffiti-like additions were made to all transit and outdoor boards, which proclaimed: "Just A Lotta Fun."

CASE 5: ADVERTISING IN A SECONDARY ROLE FOR SEWING CENTER SUPPLY

Even though direct marketing was the primary avenue for marketing the OmniStitch machine by Sewing Center Supply, a magazine ad kicked off the campaign. Later in the campaign, ads would continue to run in selected magazines. McKinney Johnson Amato Marketing's Liz Johnson describes where advertising fit into their overall marketing plan:

> We decided the initial full-page ad should be colorful and full of visual information, showing a variety of OmniStitch projects in-progress and finished.
>
> We chose "The Difference Is In The Details" as our headline—with the question "Are your garments and crafts stunning?" as a subhead.
>
> The purpose of the ad was to get sewers to call the 800 number featured at the bottom of the ad for a free video and printed information.

Research Led to a Media-Buying Strategy

> After the introductory ad, we re-evaluated the necessity of additional magazine advertising. Because the OmniStitch was a new kind of product, it remained to be seen exactly which magazines the best prospects would favor. We heavily researched the magazines that reach home sewers nationally. We found magazines for home business sewers, home sewers who use fashion patterns, decorating craft sewers, apparel craft sewers, holiday craft sewers, and more. Also helpful was a portion of our sewing show survey that asked which sewing magazines the entrants read.

After looking at all of the available information, we chose the four magazines that would give us the fairest possible test of the major home sewing segments. It soon became obvious that the magazines aimed at non-business home sewers and craft sewers were pulling the best. The next flight of ads was adjusted accordingly.

Ads They Could Respond To

Knowing that OmniStitch users liked lots of color and detail, we created the magazine ads with a colorful, bright border and enough information to make home sewers want to call the 800 number and request the free video. Response was overwhelming. We could tell immediately when each publication the ad was in arrived at subscribers' homes, because a wave of calls would flood the 800 number, as many as 186 a day. Another wave would hit when that same publication reached newsstands, and calls have continued at an average of 65 a day.

CASE 6: PROTECTION ONE'S "KNOW CAMPAIGN"

Research conducted earlier by the McKinney Johnson Amato marketing agency for Protection One's home security system was reviewed, questioned, and reviewed again in order to come up with a summary of the common reactions and concerns of the target audience, according to Liz Johnson:

This summary gave us the building blocks for our campaign. It showed that much of our job was explanatory and educational—to increase name awareness and educate the public about home security. We also saw that a number of unnecessary facts could be weeded out to simplify the marketing message.

Creative Strategy Set the Course

The quest for knowledge was a recurring theme in all of the research. Therefore, each of the ads or spots within the campaign was designed to address something the consumer wanted to know. The closing theme summed it all up: "The More You Know . . . The More You'll Want Protection One." This concept not only spoke to consumer concerns, but it gave Protection One a stronger position in the marketplace because it looked and felt so different from the competition's advertising.

The creative strategy dictated where media buys would be made. A combination of print, radio, and television would give the message the strongest impact. And because media plans were outlined for a year, we were able to initiate some contracts for more desirable rates and additional promotions such as contests and sports sponsorships.

Real People with Real Stories

The focal point of the creative was a series of six television spots that used real people to tell real stories about Protection One. (The only exception was an actor who portrayed the burglar.) A homeowner, Protection One employees, and a policeman rounded out the cast.

Interview segments were broken up within each spot to emphasize the underlying messages:

- Theme
- Company logo and slogan
- Price
- Phone number

The radio spot reproduced the feeling of the television spot. Print ads featured pictures of the same spokespeople and their theme lines.

CASE 7: OREGON BURGLAR AND FIRE ALARM RESPONSE ISSUE

This campaign, alerting the public to a decision by the Portland Police Department to stop responding to monitored alarms, was based almost exclusively on publicity. (For a better understanding of this entire campaign, refer to Chapter 21.)

Advertising was used, however, as a climax to the campaign, with placement of call-to-action ads in the *Oregonian* newspaper.

Advertising Paid Off

The ads, according to Liz Johnson, founder of the McKinney Johnson Amato marketing agency, made the phones ring at City Hall, generating the most public response of any Measure 5 issue.

CASE 8: CARADCO WINDOWS

This is what Lindsay, Stone & Briggs calls a "vertically integrated communications campaign." It targeted both builders and retail consumers and produced a highly unusual increase in awareness.

Advertising Across Trade and Consumer Media

The trade advertising campaign incorporated two-page spreads and was based on repositioning the brand with a more benefit-oriented message that would raise builders' expectations of what a window supplier can do and deliver. These two-page ads in trade magazines went right to the heart of builders' expectations. One headline declared:

> Caradco Windows.
> The Only Limit Is Your Imagination

The first two sentences of the text read:

> Imagine more glass, more features, more profit. You can get more than you ever imagined by combining standard Caradco windows and patio doors.

Success Called for Including Consumers

The positioning and integrated execution across all ads and promotion materials was so successful that the campaign was extended to consumer print ads and television. Ads placed in consumer publications went to the heart of consumers' concerns. One headline read:

> Look Closely.
> (You'll Be
> Living With
> Them For
> Decades.)

The headline tugged at a concern all homeowners have. The picture caught the eye and returned it to the head and then on to the copy. The picture was a morphed photo of a man crouched on a stool, peering through a drawing of a telescope that is aimed at the sky, which is showing through the uniquely designed windows. The copy presents information in a conversational, friendly manner:

> Let's face it, windows are not something you think about, much less buy every day. So when you do, you should look closely. When you look closely at Caradco, you'll find. . . .

The rest of the copy concisely spells out benefits homeowners look for.

The headline in another ad establishes integrity, dependability, and reliability. It states:

A Study In Craftsmanship
For Over 128 Years.

And the first lines of copy go on to further build Caradco's attributes:

> Caradco has been making wood windows and patio doors longer
> than anyone else in America. And with that experience comes the
> knowledge of how to build windows and patio doors that last.

The text then offers details.

The company's logo carries the words "Since 1866" and "Wood Windows & Patio Doors." Part of each logo signature is the company's slogan: "Raising Your Expectations."

Consumer Television Co-op

Lindsay, Stone & Briggs also created an attractive co-op television spot that was consistent with the look and tone of Caradco's print ads and sales materials. Through a national Weather Channel package, distributors could, at very low cost, put their names on the spots appearing locally, if they ordered 25 sets of Caradco French Manor patio doors. Caradco distributors signed up for the program in record numbers, far exceeding the company's goal to break even on the TV spot production and media placement. Sign-up was so great that Caradco actually made money on the program itself.

CASE 9: IT TAKES ALL KINDS

Remember, this case history is unlike the others in that it involves what is basically a social issue (diversity awareness) rather than a commercial campaign to build sales. The campaign was conducted by a professional marketing agency—Lindsay, Stone & Briggs—and that professionalism is what sets this campaign apart from similar campaigns that are often developed by dedicated but inexperienced politicians and businesspeople. There is a good reason for including this campaign as a part of what otherwise is a book purely about business marketing: This campaign successfully targeted teens and demonstrates how to talk to and get through to kids—something even pros usually have difficulty doing.

And kids are worth talking to. They represent a $10 billion market, up from $5 billion in 1987. And that's just from their allowances. Their purchasing power totals $165 billion dollars, and they influence $400 billion in purchasing decisions, according to a research company called Packaged Facts.

The Objective

There was no commercial motive here. The objective was simply to create a better understanding and appreciation for individuals of different races among teenagers (the age when prejudices are solidified). The targeted group was roughly 11 to 18 years old. Marsha Lindsay explains that Lindsay, Stone & Briggs' objective was to reach the target audience through both traditional and nontraditional media during periods of high media consumption.

The Thinking Behind the Strategy

We initially thought that schools and teachers would be excellent avenues for our message. But instead our research showed these to be exactly what teens tune out. The authoritative tone is seen as negative and goes in one ear and out the other. Teens are so desensitized to messages in this tone that we decided to put our message into a positive context—a context within which this issue had never been presented to them.

The source and tone of a message are just as important as the message itself. The creative allows teens to accept an issue into their own world and make it a topic of conversation. We attempted to quell worries of peer acceptance and self-consciousness so teens would feel comfortable talking about racism and then hopefully do something about it.

With the adoption of different-colored smiley faces as its logo and a tagline of "It takes all kinds," this campaign made it cool to be against racism.

The Message Was Carried across the Media

Whether it was a billboard, an interior bus sign, or any of the other advertising media, the message was the same. Just said in different ways. One set went like this:

Opposite the tagline on the right, which is:

It Takes All Kinds

was one of the following messages:

If ZITS can
ignore skin color,
why can't we?

or

> All belly buttons are
> created *equal,*
> some just hold MORE
> LINT.

or

> We are
> ALL
> COLORED
> People.

Some of the wordings did not use "It takes all kinds." One, for example, was a half-and-half board, one side black, the other side yellow, with type overprinted on each side. On the yellow half, in black type, was printed:

> "Funny, you don't
> look stupid"

And on the black half, in white type:

> "FUNNY, YOU DON'T SOUND BLACK"

Media Choices

Marsha Lindsay also explains that all of the media time and space was donated, so, although advertising on bus signs and billboards was in traditional formats, television spots were in the form of public service announcements (PSAs), because government regulations permit the government-regulated PSA format when the message is for nonprofit reasons.

Which Media to Use Was a Question

"We knew," says Marsha Lindsay, "that print would be a challenge because readership is low among our target audience. And television presented a problem because our creative would have to cut through the clutter." But when you view the PSAs, you can understand how and why the message got through to the teens. It becomes obvious what Lindsay means when she says, "We presented the target audience with images of their own generation in their own voice to break through their defenses." The messages are neither preachy nor a lecture.

Positive—and Negative—Feedback

Teens responded well, and there has been positive feedback from area organizations about Lindsay, Stone & Briggs' communication strategy for reaching teens. But there has also been negative feedback from parents and grandparents who think the campaign is off-base and promotes rudeness.

"Actually, we view this as positive feedback because these adults are complaining because they don't get it," says Marsha Lindsay. "And they are not supposed to get it. Our strategy was to give teens a message tailored to them, and let them feel they 'own' it. When adults don't quite 'get it,' that gives teens even more ownership."

PART III

DIRECT-RESPONSE MARKETING: IT'S DIRECT MAIL AND MUCH MORE

9

Direct Mail, Direct Marketing, and Direct-Response Marketing—What Are the Differences?

Person-to-person marketing. The differences between direct marketing and direct-response marketing. The influence of hi-tech. V-mail—direct mail people pay attention to. Electronic coupons—new form of direct marketing—and fax-on-demand—one form of direct-response marketing. Inserts as direct marketing. Keep old customers—it's five times cheaper. 800 numbers as a marketing tool.

Marketing. Direct marketing. Direct-response marketing. And what about direct mail? Where does it fit in? These questions will be answered, but first it is important that you recognize three things:

1. All the members of the direct marketing family are the person-to-person branch of marketing.
2. The MMMC concept of taking a single high-impact message with you wherever you venture in marketing is all-important—whether it's to visit direct marketing or advertising or promotion or publicity.
3. All these different names are merely separate branches of an enormous family called marketing.

DEFINITIONS 101

Everyone who has a mailbox knows what direct mail is. But when it comes to the difference between direct marketing and direct-response marketing, things become a little confusing. Even marketing professionals are somewhat baffled. If you look in marketing dictionaries and glossaries, you'll find a laundry list of explanations with similarities and differences that only add to the confusion. The terms *direct marketing* and *direct mail* are often used synonymously, but they are not really synonyms. The biggest difference between the two is that direct marketing is not limited to the mail, although mail is its most popular use. Direct marketing is marketing that delivers a message directly to present and potential consumers, and direct mail is but one form of direct marketing. *Direct-response marketing* is when the consumer can respond to an ad or a commercial by returning a coupon, making a phone call, sending a fax, or by some other high-tech electronic means.

UNLESS YOU WANT TECHNO TRAUMA, APPLY MMMC

A cartoon in *Editor & Publisher* shows the high-tech circus that publishers have to deal with these days. A lion tamer with a whip and chair is trying to keep four lions on their pedestals. The lions, roaring and growling, are named CD-ROM, Fax-on-Demand, Interactive TV, and Database Marketing.

Some people call the job of trying to keep all these high-tech advances in line "techno trauma." Others, such as Allen Rosenshine, the chairman and CEO of BBDO Worldwide, one of the nation's largest ad agencies, said in an interview with *Advertising Age:*

> It was hard enough in the old days when technology—interactive media, 500 channels, computerized agencies—wasn't all over us with its ever-changing perspectives. The massive changes people are talking about are in response to new opportunities from changing technology. And little of technology is created with a clear understanding of who wants it, who needs it, and who will pay for it.

Rosenshine reported that his agency talked with one of its largest clients about the consequences of having so many sources of marketing communication. The end result, according to Rosenshine, is that "their message becomes very fractionated," and "they need to integrate under one entire strategic approach." He told *Ad Age* that it all goes back to the simplistic example of *integrated marketing communications*, which is just another way of saying MMMC.

V-MAIL

Everything old is new again, and everything new is newer. V-mail is new technology that is real. It's not techno trauma, nor does it fit Mr. Rosenshine's depiction. It's here now, it's working, and it takes the word *junk* out of direct mail.

When Nintendo of America Inc. wanted to introduce a new product, they sent 13-minute videocassettes of a mock documentary about their new game's development to nearly two million specially targeted customers. The effort was backed by a $17 million marketing budget, but don't let the size of the numbers turn you away. Individual grocery stores, furniture stores, and other small, independent businesses are also using direct-mail videos to market their services to neighborhoods. This is one use of technology that can be adapted to the smallest budget, and it can be highly effective if your mailing list precisely targets your specific audience.

Video marketing began in the 1980s, but only for top-of-the-line products. Videos that used to cost $6 a tape 10 years ago now cost as little as $1.50 to $2 a tape. Technicolor Video Services (TVS), introduced in November 1995, promises that "your video message can be duplicated, packaged, and delivered for less than $1.50 per tape, *including postage!*" When you compare that with the usual cost of about $2.50 each for printed mailing pieces, videotapes can be winners.

One professional told *The Dallas Morning News* that "there is something exciting about getting a videotape in the mail. Compared to typical junk mail, a person is much more likely to pick it up, stick it in the VCR, and watch it. It breaks through the clutter."

From your standpoint, as Technicolor Video Services explains, video lets you demonstrate your products and services in a way that no brochure or 60-second commercial can. Most impressive is that surveys show that 89 percent of people will watch V-mail the same day they receive it, according to TVS. And people don't toss out videos the way they toss out junk mail, especially when a video contains news—when it's informational, educational, or entertaining.

Most businesses invite recipients to recycle the video—either pass it along, share it with others, or return it to the business (to be reused) and get something *free* (there's that magic word again), such as "a FREE sampler of freshly roasted gourmet coffee."

And speaking of junk mail, did you see the "Close to Home" cartoon by John McPherson? The man of the house is stoking the stove as he tells his friend, "So far we've been able to heat the entire house using nothing but junk mail." Don't let anyone tell you junk mail isn't valuable—for something!

OTHER NEW DIRECT MARKETING

Vending machines have been around for the length of most people's lives, but now there's a new twist—vending machines that accept electronic coupons. It's not direct mail, but it is direct marketing. The machines must be specially equipped with software that reads electronic coding that's printed on one side of the coupons. The other side of the coupon contains a marketer's ad.

Fax machines have been around for awhile, too, but now direct-response marketers can use fax-on-demand to distribute messages. According to *Editor & Publisher,* fax-on-demand is a synthesis of computer-controlled voice response and personal computer fax technologies. The faxed messages include numbers (fax, phone, or 800 number) to which the fax recipient can reply and request more information.

> While the interest of the reader is high, information is delivered to the reader. Delivery of product information by fax-on-demand is a supplement to printed product information, not a substitute, and is viewed as an additional service to prospects and customers.

Hewlett Packard began using this fax system successfully after it recognized the need by prospects and customers to receive product literature immediately—before their interest cooled—rather than waiting days or weeks for the information to be sent by mail, according to *E&P* magazine.

Predictions by Hewlett Packard and others are that this new use of fax technology will create a shift from delivery of product literature by mail to delivery by fax-on-demand. As a result, service bureaus for small-business vendors are being established, and it is looked on as an opportunity for newspapers and magazines to offer a document delivery service to their advertisers. It's even been proposed that such a service could be offered as an added value to advertising in publications.

FAXES GO BOTH WAYS

Because fax machines are everywhere, invite people to use them—to their benefit as well as yours. On a coupon or a survey—any form that requires filling in information—add a couple of lines:

> Call Toll Free 1-800 (your number)
> or fax this card to (your fax number)

Advertising Age is particularly adept in this regard. On one card enlisting subscriptions, they use a headline to shout:

Fill it out. Fax it in. Save $41.

On another card, a line in boldface type runs across the bottom of the self-mailer:

In a hurry? Fax this card to . . . Or call 1-800 . . .

NEWSPAPER AND MAGAZINE INSERTS

Did you see the Bill Rechin and Don Wilder comic panel where two "Crock" characters are atop a very tall structure, and one asks the other, "New magazine came today, huh?" The other character is shaking the magazine, from which is falling what could be hundreds of inserts.

There are times when your morning newspaper reminds you of the "Crock" message. But a Dan Piraro "Bizzaro" cartoon also offers a smile about what's happening in this regard. A newspaper the size of the entire front yard lies in front of a home. The inset box says, "Scientists estimate that by the year 2015, the Sunday edition of *The New York Times* will be roughly the size of a humpback whale."

One Sunday, a full-size Kraft grocery bag was inserted into the *Wenatchee* (Washington) *World*, giving the newspaper's readers 25 percent off for all the groceries they could get into the bag. In many communities, hardly a week goes by that the plastic bag that shields the newspaper from rain or snow doesn't contain at least one product sample—a packet of Malt-O-Meal, boxes of Wheaties and Sun Cruncher, a packet of Coffee-mate nondairy creamer, or a bar of Irish Spring soap. Or the plastic bag is printed with a message such as one that said, *"The New York Times* and 100% Columbian Coffee: The perfect combination to start your day."

INSERTS

Neither the bagged samples nor messages on the newspaper's wrapper can technically be classified as inserts. They are, however, a form of direct marketing. Inserts—many people call them stuffers—can be part of any direct-marketing effort. Inserts that accompany statements are also popular. Such inserts are an excellent means to put a punch-out Rolodex-type card into the hands of people you want to keep your phone and fax numbers handy.

One such insert announced the opening of a copy center. Included along with the punch-out telephone card was a description of services offered, pricing information, and a map showing where the business was located. TU Electric often inserts a tiny newsletter called *TU E Answers* into its bills. The headline says, "We've been reading more than meters" and tells readers that it provides the answers "to our customers' frequently asked questions." A stuffer with a bank statement breaks into three credit-card-sized cards for Hertz. One is a member discount card, one a discount on a weekly rental, and the third an offer of a free upgrade.

HITTING THE REPLAY BUTTON

Lane Kirkland said it this way: "Go where the customer is and don't expect him to come to you. The only way to convert a heathen is to travel into the jungle."

The point is that it pays to put customers first—whatever form of marketing you use—and speak directly to those customers. It's even better when they can talk back.

Joe Griffith tells a story that emphasizes the importance of knowing who your message is going to and understanding the person who is buying your product or service.

> A fisherman went into a sporting supply store. The salesman offered him a fantastic lure for bass: pointed eyes, half a dozen hooks, imitation bugs—a whole junkyard.
>
> Finally, the fisherman asked the salesman, "Do fish like this thing?"
>
> The salesman said, "I don't sell to fish."

Back in 1989, *Fortune* magazine accentuated the importance of placing customers first—ahead of employees, shareholders, and the community. The magazine's cover story quoted Du Pont Chairman Richard E. Heckert:

> Knowing what's on the customer's mind is the most important thing we can do. . . . Giant General Motors, tiny Techsonic, and countless other smart companies are keeping customers loyal by listening to them.

But then *Fortune* advises: "Think of yourself as the customer."

There's only one thing wrong with *Fortune*'s advice. Thinking of yourself as the customer can lead you to think you already know the customer, which can be an excuse for bypassing ongoing research that keeps you updated on what customers really are thinking. That means you end up knowing what *you* think and nothing more.

THE COST OF A NEW CUSTOMER

As you're shaping your direct-marketing plans, keep in mind this information from *Fortune* magazine:

> The biggest payoff to knowing what prospects want is in building loyal repeat buyers. *"Holding on to them costs one-fifth as much as acquiring new ones."*

Yes, every business must hunt new consumers, if only to replace those that relocate in today's highly mobile society. But too many marketers tend to forget all about the customers back in the barn. You recognize how expensive this memory loss is when you remember that it costs you five times as much to capture new ones.

800 NUMBERS

Toll-free numbers are almost as prevalent as fax machines, because marketers know that 800 numbers are probably the best way to stay close to customers. They are the equal of good old-fashioned complaint departments, but they are also the embodiment of direct-response marketing.

Toll-free numbers work two ways. Customers can grouse and grumble about perceived inadequacies or problems, or they can place orders. But equally important, an 800 number can be a direct line into consumer thinking. No focus group session or survey is any better at finding out what customers or targeted individuals want, need, or perceive.

In their book, *The Wall Street Journal on Marketing,* Ronald Alsop and Bill Abrams quote John Goodman, president of Technical Assistance Research Programs Inc.: "Only about 4 percent of dissatisfied customers complain to a manufacturer. Instead they usually stop buying the product and also bad-mouth it to 9 or 10 people."

"In contrast," Goodman says, "complaints that are resolved quickly lead to repeat purchases in 95 percent of the cases involving inexpensive items and 82 percent of those involving products that cost at least $100."

10

Snail Mail
(and E-mail, Too)

Direct mail's popularity is awesome as a vital tool that's
cost-effective. Target lists are essential. Envelope shapes,
sizes, and messages that compel opening. Eight steps to
writing direct mail messages. Seven steps to good letters,
the most prevalent DM form. Best mailing times. E-mail,
the Internet, and E-tech.

According to *Advertising Age*, direct mail's share of ad dollars in 1991
jumped to 19.3 percent from 17.4 percent in 1987. And one-fourth of all
U.S. mail—$12.7 billion a year—is third-class advertising mail. Ad spend-
ing estimates for 1995 are predicted to total $159 billion, and direct mail's
portion is also expected to increase, which would put direct mail's share
well above $31 billion. That's mighty impressive when direct mail has ac-
quired such a scornful moniker as junk mail.

OTHERWISE KNOWN AS JUNK MAIL

Q: What's the difference between a direct mail piece and an onion?

A: Nobody cries when you chop up the mail piece, because it's probably just junk mail anyway.

Letters, card decks, postcards, catalogs, fliers, brochures, reprints,
circulars, newsletters, audio- and videocassettes, and self-mailers (which
can be folders, brochures, or reply cards)—all of these can be direct mail.
Some are strictly direct mail and some serve double duty.

Then there are direct-mail *packages*. These can be big enough to include just about anything you want to put directly into a person's hands,

or they can contain a very detailed description of your product or service when that is necessary. These packages, Richard Weiner tells us in *Webster's New World Dictionary of Media and Communications,* are most effective when the sales message is too long or complex to be explained in a print ad or a broadcast commercial.

In this chapter, we'll look at only those items that are thought of strictly as direct mail. Envelopes are a logical place to start, because they hold the key to whether recipients will ever open the correspondence. Then we'll look at postcards, card decks, and finally letters, because they're the cornerstone for all direct mail, and their content is the expanded version of your message, from which even the most concise wording will be extracted and integrated throughout all your direct marketing messages.

A POPULAR CHOICE

If direct mail is frowned upon by so many people, then why do so many marketers use it so often? A 1991 USPS Household Diary Study offers some pretty impressive statistics:

- A full 43 percent of all third-class mail and 58 percent of all first-class mail is opened and read.
- Only 8 percent of third-class mail and 5 percent of first-class mail is set aside to be read at a later time.
- A total of 30 percent of Americans looked at but did not read the third-class mail they received, and 23 percent looked at but did not read their first-class advertising mail.
- Only 19 percent discarded their third-class mail before reading it, and 14 percent discarded their first-class mail before reading it.

See Table 10-1 for more information about the effects of how the envelope is addressed and how familiar the recipient is with the sending organization.

A VITAL TOOL THAT'S COST-EFFECTIVE

In a special section in *Ad Age,* the United States Postal Service notes that direct mail is a vital tool because of its popularity due to changing consumers and the needs of a new marketplace.

Table 10-1   Direct Mail Reading Rates

	Opened and Read (%)	Set Aside (%)	Looked at but Not Read (%)	Discarded and Not Read (%)
Personalized address	50	9	27	14
Addressed to "occupant"	40	7	32	20
Sent to customer by known organization	61	11	22	6
Sent to noncustomer by familiar organization	33	7	37	23
Unknown sending organization	26	8	35	31

> Consumers have changed and advertisers are changing as they realize the old advertising and communications paradigms led by mass marketing techniques are no longer effective.
>
> Instead, the new emphasis is on selectivity, efficiency and effectiveness.

The Postal Service survey makes yet another point—that direct mail is cost-effective: "You control your advertising costs through testing. Once you know what works, you can spend advertising dollars more wisely."

The Postal Service's arguments make sense when you take time to listen to them. They say that "Americans are starved for time," yet magazines are proliferating. And where once there were three television networks, there now are four (and five hundred cable channels are not far off). So many new choices will make competition for consumer time and attention still more difficult. The Postal Service also points out that 32 million Americans regard English as a second language, which means that specialized approaches and materials are required to reach this huge submarket. Direct mail can reach them when other avenues are either limited or nonexistent.

Julia Adamsen, director of print marketing for Pizza Hut, told the Postal Service that they use direct mail marketing because it "allows us to be more relevant to the consumer because we understand the details." Then she says something that should be remembered by everyone considering any kind of a marketing program: When you send a message by newspaper, magazine, television, cable, billboards, or just about any other medium, what you say is open for scrutiny by everyone. Send it by mail, and only you and the prospect know of your offer. It's an advantage that few people—even professionals—think about, a "mystery factor" that can give immense strategic advantages. It is possible to mount major programs without your competitors' knowledge, because direct mail is a secret medium, literally unmeasurable by ordinary tracking services.

Other advantages of direct mail include:

- *Selectivity.* You can sort customers from noncustomers, diversities within ethnic groups, and any other classification you wish to separate out.
- *Flexibility.* You control size, shape, layout, and format.
- *Control over printing.* You have a choice of printing processes, paper stocks, and colors.
- *Timing.* You choose the time(s) to relay your message.

In a nutshell, direct mail is targetable, confidential, flexible, measurable, and effective.

COST: THE MOST APPARENT DISADVANTAGE

Headlines that shouted "Postal rates may climb 20%" kept direct-mail marketers on the edge of their seats for a couple of years. *Advertising Age* predicted that "a double-digit rate hike would cause many [direct-mail users] to more narrowly target prospects so they could send out fewer mailings." But precise targeting has been known and used for years by knowledgeable, aware marketers as a means of lowering costs by sending out fewer mailings. These savvy marketers won't be able to consolidate more effectively; they can't save a single dollar.

1995 Rate Hikes

When the most recent postal rate hikes were authorized at the end of 1994, the Postal Service didn't wait a minute to put them into effect. First-class jumped from 29 cents to 32 cents, effective on January 1, 1995. Mailers who use third-class, which already had an excess of delivery problems that most marketers don't need, had been hoping for rate relief instead of an increase. After all, their rates had jumped 41 percent in 1991. But the new bulk rates increased even more than first-class—by an average of 14 percent.

All of this makes tight targeting crucial.

TARGET LISTS: THE MOST CRITICAL ELEMENT

The best way to make direct mail as cost-effective as possible, regardless of postal rates, is to direct it only to individuals who have been identified as prospects in your own or a rented database.

A special section offered in *Entrepreneur* magazine, entitled "Mail Order Gurus: Their Secrets of Success," contains suggestions for locating good mailing lists. One is New York City–based Hugo Dunhill Mailing Lists Inc., which offers a free mailing list catalog. Another is Standard Rate & Data Service (SRDS) that publishes the "Direct Marketing List Source," a resource of more than 12,000 consumer and business mailing lists. Your local reference librarian undoubtedly can offer other suggestions.

DATABASES: THE SECRET TO SUCCESS

Although the use of direct mail to attract consumer attention has been commonplace for more than a century, the newer world of databases now provides marketers with information about customers' behavior that was never available earlier. Databases are discussed in Chapter 2. If you skipped that section, take the time now to study it. It could be the difference for your company between a success and a dud.

TASTE TESTING

No matter how good the mailing list, testing is essential to find out if you have the right mix. Does your message need a little more spice or a little less flash? Is it "tastefully appropriate"? Big dollars can be saved when small tests are run in advance of any direct mailing.

One of the most critical (literally) names and addresses on your mailing list should be your own. The trick to accurate tests can be a very simple process—coding your name on the mailings. For example, if you're sending more than one test mailing, add your own name to each test list, but add different middle initials for each different test mailing. Make a note, of course, of which initial you used to signify which test mailing.

Adding your name to each mailing list also gives you a way to track how long it took from mailing to receiving, particularly if a piece is sent third class. You can also assess the condition in which a piece arrives. The interval between mailing and receiving a piece can also give you much-needed objectivity so you'll be able to see the piece more as prospects view it.

YOUR ENVELOPE IS YOUR BILLBOARD

If a shortage of time is a critical factor among your audience, perhaps your best guide is to think of the problem as similar to constructing a billboard message. In high-traffic areas, you have only three to five seconds to catch a traveler's eye. The most time you have on the lowest-traffic roads is seven seconds. Think of the envelope or the outside of a self-mailer as your billboard. You must use those few seconds to not only grab the eye but to pique a strong enough interest that your recipient will open the piece or at least set it aside to read later.

The Envelope, Please

Envelopes come in every size imaginable—from small social sizes that give the impression of a note from a personal friend all the way up to 9 × 12 inches. Some envelope sizes are standard and can be purchased in small numbers, whereas others must be specially ordered in large quantities and are therefore considerably more expensive.

What you need is an envelope that is distinctive enough to separate it from the mound of mail that every person receives daily. Size can certainly be a distinguishing feature, but color may also be the characteristic that sets your piece apart.

Three things almost everyone looks for in that first hurried run-through of the day's mail are personal letters, checks, and important business documents. You might conspire to place your piece among those precious few by choosing a social size envelope with a return address on the flap that appears to be handwritten (no company name) and the recipient's name and address actually handwritten.

Or you might select the envelope most commonly used for business correspondence (a No. 10), again eliminate the company name, and print only the return address in a dignified, business-like typeface (in the upper left corner or on the back flap) in such a way that the recipient might believe the envelope contains information important to him or her. Credit cards and confidential documents regarding PIN numbers are transmitted in this manner. Perhaps the best tactic is to use a window envelope and make what can be seen through it so intriguing, so *real*-looking that a recipient can't resist opening it. If none of these tactics fits your needs, then give serious consideration to putting a grabber-type message on the *outside* of your direct mail piece.

Provocative Prose

The words on an envelope that are forged to compel the recipient to read what's inside constitute provocative prose. And perhaps the best brand of provocative prose is a teaser, something that elevates curiosity to action.

One technique that's almost guaranteed to work uses a No. 10 window envelope. The company's name or logo and return address are in the traditional corner, but through the window the recipient's name and address are visible on what appears to be a check. The words "The sum of" (and perhaps even a dollar sign and some numbers) are also clearly visible through the window.

Evans Pontiac/GMC Truck Clearance Center used this tactic, although the company's name was not included on the envelope. Inside, there was a dated check (on check paper, as authentic-looking as any check you've ever seen) with "The sum of Twelve Hundred Fifty and 00/100**" printed on it. It was a tear-off check, part of a regular business-size sheet of paper that addressed the recipient by name and told her she was "invited to attend a TWO-DAY AUTOFLEET SALE ... [for] only a select group of local customers who may be ready to purchase a new vehicle in an entirely different way."

Not until you'd gotten the gist of the message would you check out the check again and discover that it was unsigned. If you bothered to read the tiny print beneath the line where the authorized signature should have been, you'd see:

Redeemable at Dealer Within
One voucher per customer
Valid Only on Above Dates
Non Negotiable This is Not a Check

But the company had done its homework, and the mailing had only gone to people with older cars who definitely needed a new car or truck. These people undoubtedly read the entire message.

Another example of provocative prose is a boxed message alongside an envelope's window that says:

IMPORTANT INFORMATION
on your legal documents enclosed.

A similar tactic is the message CONFIDENTIAL DOCUMENTS over- and underlined in red ink, with "Preferred Customer Account summary statement enclosed. Open at once!" is printed next to it in a handwritten-script typeface. What makes this piece even more unique is that it's enclosed in an envelope that looks like a regulation-size file folder. On the tab, in white type on a black background, is the recipient's full name. Inside are sweepstakes entry forms and information about ordering the company's product.

If you're enclosing a gift or a token in a direct-mail package, say so on the outside. For example:

YOUR
PERSONALIZED
ADDRESS LABELS
ENCLOSED

Of course there are the WIN! WIN! WIN! messages. But savvy marketers realize this tactic isn't enough, so one adds a white sticker on the manila-color No. 10 envelope. It says, "Use these stickers to enter!" and includes a red "Winner-Take-All $1,000,000.00" sticker (take note how spaces for cents amounts are included to make the dollar amount seem even larger) plus a green "Chevy Blazer Early Bird Prize" sticker.

Some direct mailers use every square inch of space on an envelope, both front and back, to shout things they believe will catch and hold a recipient's attention. That tactic almost guarantees a slam-dunk into the nearest wastebasket. Unless, of course, you do what Parsons Technology did. They used a soft-yellow No. 10 envelope, but it was covered front and back with attractive blocks of other pastel colors. Each colored block contained a message that included the recipients name:

Jeanette Smith, now you can
create your own cards,
posters, banners and more!

It's time to celebrate, JEANETTE!
Introducing Announcements 2.0 for Windows!

Party at
Jeanette's!

Jeanette, send a message that
could only have come from you!

Inside a circle was printed, "30 Day Money-Back Guarantee," and inside another circle was printed "Just $19" in reverse type.

Inside the envelope was a four-page folder with information about the product and a business reply envelope with the recipient's name printed in the return address position on the back flap. There was also a tear-off that showed "Jeanette's priority code is [special number]," plus a check-box that said, "YES, I want to create posters, cards and banners that could only have come from Jeanette Smith—for just $19!" .

If recipients don't read the contents to learn about the product or service and to order, they'll surely scan them just to see how many times the company has used their name throughout the message!

Other examples of words that act as letter openers are:

- PRIVILEGED CUSTOMER PORTFOLIO ENCLOSED
  - Confirmation of Payment Receipt
  - Lifetime Security Certificate
  - Confidential Record of Service
  - Private Sale

The Blair mail-order house effectively builds and maintains image by using envelopes with an address on the rear flap but no company name. On the front, left side of the envelope are five step-down blocks that read:

VALUE
  QUALITY
    COMFORT
      CONVENIENCE
        Yours with
        IMPROVED LIVING

If your location is difficult to find, you might print a small, simple map on the left front of the envelope. It's not exactly provocative prose, but it might really be appreciated. Why on the envelope, rather than inside? Because it's easier for an interested prospect to tuck a folded envelope into a purse or pocket than to carry the enclosed letter or brochure. It may convince a prospect who had always thought of getting to your place as a real chore that it isn't that hard to find after all.

Keep Building Your Copycat File

So it's not how much you say on an envelope but *what* you say that counts. Make a note of every piece of mail that catches your eye enough to open it, and decide if any of the tactics that worked on you will snare your target. Then attach your written reaction right when you receive the piece; a later reaction may not be as spontaneous or as realistic.

HOW TO WRITE DIRECT MAIL

The rule that contends that "the most critical element of a mail campaign will always be the list" is true *if* you merely wish to put your message into the hands of people on your target list. But if you want to catch the eyes and attention of the people on those very finely tuned lists, if you want them to read your message, to reach out and respond to your message, what you say is equally important.

If you don't already have a copy, you should take a minute right now to order an 88-page booklet produced by the U.S. Postal Service in late 1992 called *The Small Business Guide to Advertising with Direct Mail: Smart Solutions for Today's Entrepreneur.* If direct mail is any part of your marketing plan, this booklet should be a part of your marketing library. The booklet is free, but most impressive is that it was written by some of the country's foremost direct-mail experts. The toll-free number to order it is 1-800-THE-USPS, extension 804.

By calling the same number and extension, you can also arrange for a consultation with your local Postal Business Center about preparing your direct-mail advertising. The consultations and assistance, like the booklet, are complimentary.

In the booklet, the marketing pros list the following eight basic guidelines to consider when writing copy for a direct-mail package.

1. Keep Copy Simple and Easy to Understand

Simplicity was stressed and restressed in the chapter about writing a marketing message (Chapter 7). There is, however, no more important place to practice this dictum than in a direct-mail message, where readers will merely glance at the piece and—unless the message can be understood instantly—will toss it.

2. Make Effective Use of Headlines

Headlines beckon readers to follow. Of course, the copy that follows has to produce, or the most tempting, beguiling headline is for naught.

Headlines and subheads also serve as excellent ways to visually break up blocks of copy. And for people who are skimmers (if they were viewing TV, we'd call them "channel surfers"), a main headline is a way for you to summarize the point you want them to grasp instantly and entice them beyond the headline and into the copy. For channel surfers, subheads are like an outline of your main points, and perhaps they'll be the nudge that will get a prospect to actually read the copy. Offer a benefit, if possible. The most successful copy—in *any* type of selling message—follows the WIIFM strategy. Good copy answers the reader's first (and sometimes only) question: "What's In It For Me?" Be sure to answer that question as quickly as possible. And make sure to personalize your headlines. Let the reader know immediately that this message is directed to him or her personally.

Whenever possible, include your company or product name in your headline. Let everyone know who's talking. If they already have a friendly feeling toward your business's name, that alone may be reason enough to check out the rest of your message. For people who look at nothing but the headlines, including the company's name in the headline can at least build name recognition.

3. Tell Your Customer How to Respond

Good salespeople don't beat around the bush, and they don't mince words or mumble. You quickly get a very clear picture of what their message is, and exactly what you should do to complete the transaction. Be a good salesperson. Don't mumble!

4. Warn of Limited Supply or an Impending Price Increase

There's an old law governing supply and demand: if supply is low, demand usually skyrockets. It's a principle that can be used to great advantage. People naturally want something when there are only a few left or when it will soon become more expensive. Let your audience know if your present price is only a temporary reduction, if it will increase soon, or if supplies are limited. The strategy will undoubtedly increase sales.

5. Emphasize Guarantees and Establish Dependability

People want to know they can believe your message about the product or service—that it will perform as stated. Guarantees are an excellent way to establish dependability and accountability.

Another effective means of establishing dependability is to stress your years in business. When you can state something like, "Serving homeowners in [your town] since 1989," they know you're not just someone working out of a truck who will be on your way out of town before warranties run out on the work you do. If you can say that you've served the community for two or more *generations*, they know that both your work and your company are dependable and accountable.

Be certain, however, not to make claims that, if found to be false or enlarged beyond what is real, could become the "bad news, true lies" story of the day for your company. Remember that repairing image is vastly more difficult than building it.

6. Use Testimonials

Words of praise for your product or service are never as convincing as when someone *else* says them. When such words of approval come from local people (or from people who appear to be everyday, next-door-neighbor types), the testaments carry added substance and credibility.

7. Use Action Devices or Offer Bonuses for Action

According to the USPS booklet, "Using a premium with a time limit or a bonus if action is taken before a certain date encourages immediate action from people who may put off responding to a direct-mail solicitation." Just think about how successfully Disney has used this tactic in selling videocassettes of such movies as *Snow White, Dumbo,* and others.

8. Emphasize Special Prices

Whenever your goal is to sell something, be sure to mention price. All sorts of surveys and studies prove that when price is omitted, people automatically believe that the price isn't mentioned because it's very high. They believe it's *too* high, so they don't even ask, "How much?" Of course, if yours is a high-image business, that may be exactly the impression you wish to make. On the other hand, if a discount or low price amounts to a benefit for your particular targeted group, shout about it. Special financing plans also can amount to benefits that should be prominently displayed in your piece.

Use Humor—It's a Fun-Raiser

Humor, when used well, adds readability to just about anything except an obituary. If it's in good taste and it's applicable, use it. Surveys show that people are looking for a light touch, and they react favorably to anything that brings them a smile or a warm-hearted feeling. (The use of humor is covered in several areas in this book. Please refer to the index.)

LETTERS: THE MOST WIDELY USED FORMAT

Our direct-mail copywriting suggestions begin with direct-mail letters for two reasons:

1. Letters are the most prevalent form of direct mail mainly because they are acknowledged to have the most impact and because many times they are used in combination with other items.
2. Constructing letters will do wonders for your ability to write other types of direct-mail copy. Follow the basics suggested by the Postal Service, but write them the same way you'd write them in a letter to a friend—a good friend. Make your words friendly, conversational, and enthusiastic.

If you're an executive with a long history of writing business letters, you may pooh-pooh that second reason. Most executives feel that, given their extensive experience, they are able to write good business letters of all types. If you truly qualify, sit back and congratulate yourself, but be aware that writing good direct-mail or direct-response letters is probably the most demanding and most difficult copywriting assignment in marketing.

It is difficult for most businesspeople to write direct-mail letters because their style of writing is so—well—so business-like! Forget business letters as you know them. A direct-mail letter is to people you know well enough to think of as friends. You want to tell them in a friendly way about something you're enthusiastic about, something you believe in, something you're sure they want or need. If your recipients think of you, your company, and the message you're bearing as friendly, you're a long way down the road toward winning their business.

Common Sense in Letter Writing

William H. Butterfield wrote *Common Sense in Letter Writing,* on the cover of which is a statement that describes the book's merits:

> A unique letter writing system that shows you how to keep and increase the goodwill and confidence of your clients and open untouched sources of profit for your business.

Butterfield does this with seven questions and seven steps you can use to test your letters. First ask yourself if your letters are correct, clear, concise, courteous, constructive, conversational, and considerate. Butterfield calls these the "seven C's."

The seven steps to creating good letters are:

1. Get all the facts.
2. Say what you mean.
3. Don't take half a day to say it.
4. Keynote each letter with courtesy.
5. Focus your message on the reader.
6. Make it sound friendly and human.
7. Remember the *tact* in *contact*.

Tracking down Butterfield's book through interlibrary loan (it's out of print) is well worth the effort. Following is a summary of the seven steps.

Step 1: Get All the Facts
Getting the facts comes from knowing your product or service, knowing your competition, and knowing your customer or client.

Step 2: Say What You Mean
There's no doubt that "double meaning can be ludicrous," as Butterfield points out . . . *unless you mean it!*

Double entendre can be a real "fun-raiser," and a little humor, including double entendre, can be the very thing that bumps readers into paying attention, and it may firmly implant your message and company name in their brains.

One effective example of double entendre shows up in a midpage, page-wide, one-inch-high newspaper ad for the SPCA of Texas. It had four inch-high panels: The first panel shows four adorable, tiny pups looking directly at you, with the words "Lawn Sprinklers now in stock!" Second panel: a totally relaxed cat, also with direct eye contact, and the words "Overstuffed Recliners in patterns, stripes & solids." Third panel: Two dalmatians depicting the words "Imported Lickers stocked for the holidays." The fourth panel gave pertinent information about the organization and it's location.

Along these lines, Butterfield has some further advice worth remembering: Make your message clear, and be sure your reader understands it. "If he can't understand your message, it will probably irritate him," writes Butterfield. "If he actually misunderstands it, the results may be still worse."

Step 3: Don't Take Half a Day to Say It
Needless words make up 30 percent of an average business letter. That means that one-third of all business letter writers use ten words to do the work of seven, according to William Butterfield.

Another book you may want to track down, through interlibrary loan if your own library doesn't have a copy, is *Words That Sell: The Thesaurus to Help You Promote Your Products, Services, and Ideas,* by Richard Bayan, published by Contemporary Books. This book can help you say what you mean, not only by using necessary rather than needless words, but by using words that motivate and persuade the reader. Bayan cites eight writing rules:

1. Don't lose sight of your primary goal: to sell your product or service.
2. Don't fill your copy with empty overstatements.
3. Be accurate.
4. Be specific.
5. Be organized.
6. Write for easy reading.
7. Don't offend.
8. Revise and edit your work.

Step 4: Keynote Each Letter with Courtesy

Butterfield lists qualities that spell COURTESY:

Cooperative
Open-minded
Understanding
Reasonable
Thoughtful
Even-tempered
Sincere
You-minded

Step 5: Focus Your Message on the Reader

Businesspeople are often so concerned with their own reasons and purposes that consumers' concerns become secondary. Don't let that happen!

Step 6: Make it Sound Friendly and Human

Read the draft of your letter, and ask yourself two questions:

1. Does anyone actually talk this way?
2. Would I like to know the person who wrote this letter and the company he or she represents?

Step 7: Remember the *Tact* in *Contact*

Tact isn't usually called for in direct-mail letters unless there's a negative to be handled, such as righting a wrong the company has inadvertently done or overcoming and explaining some bad press. But tact is a virtue in any form of business communications, in writing or in person.

A WELL-DESIGNED LETTERHEAD

Entrepreneur Magazine Group's Small Business Development Catalog includes tips on designing a letterhead:

- Use a style that fits your market and customers. If they're conservative, your letterhead should be too.
- Avoid flamboyance. You can cut loose later on, when you're fully established.
- Choose a design that can be extended to your ads, brochures, and printed material. Projecting a consistent image will give your business credibility.
- Print your company's products or services on your letterhead, and it becomes an instant brochure!

Remember, your letterhead is many people's first impression of your company.

WHEN TO MAIL

Common sense again rears its head. If your mailings are to businesspeople, use your own experience as support for surveys that show it's best (obligatory, even) to avoid reaching businesspeople on Mondays or any day following a holiday, when large quantities of mail in need of prompt attention have accumulated. Friday or Saturday should also be avoided, because people tend to be tired or headed for a weekend of R&R.

Surveys show that Tuesday is the best day for businesspeople to receive direct mail, and Wednesday is the second-best day.

To a certain degree, the same applies for mail sent to homes. No overworked stay-at-home child- or elder-care provider (or anyone who has spent a long day at work) will take the time to read your message when there's a bigger-than-usual stack of other mail—including competing direct mail. And try at all costs to avoid mailings from Thanksgiving until after New Year's, when not only do the numbers of personal cards and letters surge, but so do the numbers of direct-mail pieces. With the postal service barely able to handle the flood, it's doubtful there will even be timely delivery, which could mean disaster for a dated event.

THAT WAS THEN . . . THIS IS E-MAIL

He is called Dr. Tomorrow, and he recently gave a warning to a group of editors that is equally appropriate for all businesspeople: "If you're not part of the bulldozer of change, you're going to be part of the road."

Marketers are heeding the warning. The bulldozer, in the form of electronic mail, is bearing down on this stretch of road. People have become so used to up-to-the-minute reports on television that they've come to expect everything to be immediate. The post office cannot provide same-day delivery, and even overnight delivery isn't fast enough. The feeling is growing nationwide that if it doesn't come by fax or electronic mail, it's not very important. And software allows e-mail to become voice mail and vice versa, so recipients receive a message in the form they prefer: they can see it or hear it.

Dr. Tomorrow, whose real name is Frank Ogden, also says, "You've got to look through new eyes, not through industrial-age eyes. Knowledge is doubling every eighteen months. Ninety percent of the products that will be used in ten years still don't exist."

"Students with a computer," he told *Editor & Publisher*, "already have access to more information in one evening than their parents had in a lifetime."

When Ogden was asked about information overload, he said, "It's a myth . . . the human brain will adapt to handle an increasingly digital world."

The Internet Gives Access to E-Tech

In September 1994, the Internet celebrated its silver anniversary. It's the world's biggest web of computer networks, with access to 12,200 computer networks around the world, and the number of individual users is growing between 12 and 15 percent *every month*.

Twenty-five years old! Yet how many people were aware of the Internet even five years ago? Cyberspace is uncharted ground for most of us. Some people are comparing the changes the Internet has caused to the social and personal revolutions that came following the advent of railroads, the telegraph, and television.

E-Mail Advertising

Full recognition of e-mail advertising seems to have come in April 1994 when Laurence A. Canter and Martha S. Siegel posted an advertisement offering their immigration legal services on thousands of Internet bulletin boards (called Usenet news groups), according to a story in *The New York Times.* Previously, businesses had been more discreet and had camouflaged their ulterior commercial motives. The couple's action, called "spamming" in Net jargon, created head-to-head confrontations about free speech versus commercialism. The spamming earned the married lawyers $100,000 in new legal business.

Did Canter and Siegel continue to perform legal services? No. Instead, they formed a consulting company to help businesses and individuals use the Internet to market their products and services. Their book, *How to Make a Fortune on the Information Superhighway,* was published at the end of 1994.

Get an Address

If you're planning to travel the Internet, you need an address. Anyone can register an address, but the single restriction for businesses is that their addresses must include the suffix *.com,* which is short for *commercial.* An administrative body called InterNIC does the registering. It's unclear, however, whether trademark protection extends to Internet addresses, according to Lynne Beresford, the trademark legal administrator at the U.S. Patent and Trademark Office. In mid-1994 there were 17,000 *.com* names registered, but it's expected that the number will grow to 50,000 a year.

11

Beyond Envelopes and Letters

Where and when will they receive your message? Inserts. Booklets and brochures. Newsletters. Coupons. Postcards. Card decks. Telemarketing.

Have you ever heard the sound of one hand clapping? In a way, direct mail, when it travels only one way—from your company to your customers and prospects—is one hand clapping. But there are many ways to turn one-way mail (one form of direct marketing) into direct-*response* communication, including using electronic means.

Remember, direct marketing delivers a message directly to a prospective consumer. Direct mail is one form of direct marketing, and all of the subjects covered in this chapter can be used as direct mail. Direct-*response* marketing is when the consumer can respond to an ad or a commercial by returning a coupon, making a phone call, or sending some sort of electronic message.

RANGE OF DIRECT-MARKETING OPTIONS

There is a lot more to direct marketing than direct mail and direct response. For instance, some junk "mail" doesn't even get mailed anymore. Every time you open the street-side door of your home, there are doorhangers.

And now there's T-mail—telemail. There's serious speculation among marketing professionals that *individually* targeted telemail messages might be another big change that's just ahead. Fiber optics available over phone lines are a key to whether this direct-marketing technology will merely coast or race on ahead. At the moment, audio and video messages processed in this fashion may not be affordable or realistic for many small businesses. It's important, however, for everyone with a direct-marketing program to be knowledgeable about this technology and prepared to use it should costs plunge once it has proven its strengths. (In the meantime, audio- and videocassette messages *can* be used relatively inexpensively, via direct mail, to target special groups.)

This variety of message carriers merely adds challenge to selecting the right ones. They offer opportunities to expand your MMMC strategy and new ways to deliver that individual message to your targeted audience. This chapter will explore the immense array of direct-marketing communication methods that are often used for direct mail but can also be used as handouts, inserts, or electronic messages, and it will offer some ideas about ways to use each of these methods effectively.

Judging by the deluge of coupons you receive, you almost expect every letter you open, even those from family and close friends, to include a coupon that entitles you to a free phone call or free gas if you'll call or visit. This chapter will also cover coupons. And there's one other direct-response vehicle that also merits consideration. Although unpopular with the public, it's so widely used—300,000 solicitors make 18 million calls daily, according to the Direct Marketing Association—that it's doubtful if there's anyone who doesn't know of it. It's called telemarketing.

THINGS TO CONSIDER

Before sorting through the direct-marketing options, there are some important things to consider. Whatever vehicles you choose, first think about *where* your customer will receive your message:

- Will she have just dashed in from work and be rushing to get chores done or to attend an evening meeting?
- Will he be standing in a crowded, busy store?
- Will she be handed your piece by a salesperson who keeps right on talking and doesn't give her a chance to read it, so it has the added challenge of restimulating her interest when she picks it up again later?
- Must he take time to use the VCR or a tape recorder to play your message?
- Is she retired, perhaps a little bored, with plenty of time to sit down and browse through the contents of your package?

In other words, how much time can you realistically expect your recipient to have to digest your very important message?

The answers to these questions hinge on deciding ahead of time how the piece is to be used and knowing your customer as well as you know your close friends. In today's world, retired people may not necessarily be looking for ways to occupy themselves, but rather are out doing volunteer work or working at part-time jobs, and their schedules may be as hectic as anyone else's.

WHAT'S INSIDE

Okay. Your envelope worked. It passed the first test. They didn't toss it; they opened it. Now it's time to get out the doodle pad and come up with ways to convince them they should really pay attention to what you have to say—and then act on it. The look of your envelope and the words on it, as demonstrated in Chapter 10, are crucial, but it's what's inside that counts from here on.

It's doubly crucial, because what's inside undoubtedly can be used in ways other than just as direct mail. Therefore, to make each direct-mail piece as cost-effective as possible, seriously consider other uses it might have. Can the piece double as a leave-behind for salespeople, as an on-site handout, or as an insert with billings or statements? To make a piece this versatile, you may have to omit time factors such as "Return the order form before [a certain date]." And you'll want to omit references to limited quantities.

No matter how prospects receive your piece, you still have to grab them with a headline or lead paragraph and then hold their interest until they've gotten the message and are convinced! It's not easy, but it's not all that hard if you know who your prospects are and what they want. Remember the WIIFM strategy: "What's in it for me?" And don't forget to conduct small advance tests before you send out *the* mailing.

Inserts

What you put inside your envelope can be just about anything that will fit. A letter (see Chapter 10) may be—and often is—the main communication piece, but there can be a variety of inserts, from brochures, booklets, and folders to reply cards, newsletters, and coupons.

Booklets and brochures seem to add a more elegant note than folders. An elite image created by a brochure or booklet can clinch a positive first impression. And a booklet or a brochure provides the space and a layout style necessary for extensive copy, yet the amount of text on each page isn't as overwhelming as it might be on a panel of a folder.

What is the difference between brochures and booklets? Actually, they're more or less the same. A booklet is a group of bound-together printed pages, whereas a brochure is more of a pamphlet that may or may not be stitched or stapled. (A word of caution about staples: Some people strongly resist anything with staples because they are likely to tear up nails and fingers.)

Because booklets and brochures are costly to produce, budgets usually don't permit using them very often. But well-worded and attractively constructed booklets and brochures can become a company's principle information pieces. Because they're planned for permanence, they live a much longer life than most other inserts or enclosures. Therefore, the information in them must remain current for the estimated use period of the piece.

Also keep in mind that a booklet or brochure should be used only when you're certain that the information in it is of sufficient interest to the targeted prospect that he or she will take the time to read it. Brochures and booklets can essentially guide prospects page-by-page through your marketing message, whereas there's no way to control the order in which a recipient sees and assimilates information contained in an envelope with several inserts.

Folders are a slightly different type of insert. They vary in size from an 8½ × 11-inch sheet folded to fit a No. 10 business envelope to an 11 × 17-inch sheet folded to 8½ × 11 or smaller. The paper for a folder should be heavier than the standard 20-pound business letter paper. If the piece will be used as a self-mailer, it should be printed on at least 70- or 80-pound stock.

Testimonials are another kind of insert that can ride along with just about any letter or other direct-mail piece. General Electric has one 8½ × 3¾-inch piece, printed on both sides, that says:

A Few Words
About Us
From Customers
Like You.

In much smaller print, immediately below the headline, the piece is justified with an explanation: "To us, quality service is personal as well as technical. Here's what our customers say about the people who serve them. They'll tell you that we're . . ." Then there are quotes with customers' initials and hometowns beneath a series of headlines saying *Dependable, Responsive, Knowledgeable,* and *Courteous.* Even a heads-only reading of the piece has impact because it capsulizes GE's message.

Business reply cards are probably the most frequent form of insert. They can be just that—a standard postcard-size reply form—or they can be eye-grabbers that serve dual purposes, such as one used by Sears Installed Home Improvements. The eye-grabber was an 8½ × 11-inch piece printed on heavy stock folded lengthwise that was an accurate reproduction in black and white of a $500 bill, complete with President McKinley's photo and Henry Morgenthau Jr.'s signature. Upon opening it, the recipient finds complete information about Sears Vinyl Siding along with a punch-out Free Estimate Request Card with check spaces to request information. The postage-paid, addressed side of the card is also printed over a duplicate of the currency reproduction so that no matter which side of the folder the recipient first glimpses, that $500 bill undoubtedly will make him or her wonder "What's this?"

The headline on an *Advertising Age* reply card uses another effective tactic. Above all the blank lines for requested data, it says:

FILL IT OUT.
FAX IT IN.
SAVE $38.
FAX NO. 313/000-0000

Another subhead says:

or call toll-free 1/800/000-0000

This card plays to something that is well known among marketers—that people like and want choices. Here they can choose to fax—a preference of many businesspeople—or phone or mail a reply.

NEWSLETTERS

Not everyone thinks of newsletters as direct mail. They're certainly seldom likened to junk mail. Therefore, newsletters can serve business purposes more subtly than perhaps any other medium, and they can establish a personal camaraderie with consumers that's not readily available through any other means. And with today's easy-to-use, affordable desktop publishing technologies, every business should consider using newsletters as a direct marketing tool.

Newsletters are proliferating rapidly, but they are still received much more willingly than mail that is straight advertising. If a newsletter contains information that is useful or of interest to its recipients, it can contain advertising messages throughout its pages.

Some advantages of newsletters are:

- They're personal.
- They can soften undesirable, even unpleasant, news by submerging it among cartoons, tips, techniques, and other tidbits of positive, worthwhile, desired information.

- They are a wonderful way to pat your company on the back, to disguise otherwise irritating bragging about service or dependability in feature articles or news stories.
- When published on a regular basis, newsletters keep your name before would-be customers and thereby become an ongoing reminder that when they need what you offer, they should do business with you.
- Like a hometown newspaper, over time newsletters become a familiar, welcome offering that is readily received. But unlike any newspaper, a newsletter carries the advertising of only one business—yours.
- They are a place where the publisher—you—can have a column in which to offer comments, anecdotes, recommendations, or suggestions—which gives readers a chance to get acquainted with you. People feel more comfortable doing business with a company when they feel they know the person who runs it.
- They can be a place for jokes. People enjoy humor and seldom remember jokes, so they're inclined to save issues that tickled their fancy. That means a longer life for your publication. Also, three-hole-punching newsletters before mailing them is an unwritten invitation to readers to save issues.
- They're a place for gentle pokes at your competitors' products, but only if it's done tastefully and subtly.

Newsletter Formats

Although newsletter size and style can vary widely, most are four pages—one large sheet folded in half. The most common size is a 17 × 22-inch sheet folded in half to form four standard letter-sized pages. Folded in half or in thirds, it can fit into an envelope or be used as a self-mailer.

It's important to design a masthead that is attractive and includes your company's name (or a play on the name) or your familiar, recognizable logo. If you have a slogan, include that, too. Once you've come up with an attractive, suitable masthead, don't change it. Maintain it to build recognition.

If you think a newsletter may fit your direct-marketing needs, collect samples, not only to use as copycat examples but to see what works for you and what doesn't. For example, pages of solid type turn people off. Break up story blocks with illustrations—of people, your product, drawings, cartoons, even charts and graphs when the information in them merits the space. And use headlines and subheads to break the gray look of solid type.

Purchased Newsletters

In certain businesses, there is an alternative to publishing your own newsletter. You can buy one that fits your needs from a service that specializes in producing such publications. That's what Realtor Becky Hensley in Plano, Texas, does. Hensley, who is affiliated with Henry S. Miller Realtors, sends only 200 newsletters a month, which she purchases for less than $75 and mails bulk rate for less than $50, and she believes they pay off handsomely for her. The name of the publication Hensley purchases is *Homeowner/Handi Hints,* and it's published by The Publishing Company in Kingwood, Texas. The newsletter contains things like steps for conserving water, travel ideas, hints for cooks, a gardening calendar, best buys of the month, and "Pricing Your Home: What to Forget." Few people would toss such a wealth of tips and news. Most would save something in it, and undoubtedly it's welcomed each month when it arrives.

Newsletter How-tos

If you don't purchase a ready-made newsletter, there are two ways to construct your own—the old-fashioned way or by using desktop publishing (DTP) technology. The latter is by far the easier. Visit your local computer software store, explain your needs, and you'll no doubt find everything you require, including graphics and art, in one software package. Or, if time and know-how are in short supply, get in touch with a graphics instructor at a community college or university and request the help (for an agreed-upon fee) of a student who has the necessary knowledge and access to software and computer equipment.

Whether you're using DTP or doing the job the old-fashioned way, you'll need what is called a dummy. Sketch each page, showing the position of print articles, illustrations, and graphics. The most popular and easiest-to-read format is two columns per page. Short lines of type are easier on the eye than long lines. And choose a friendly typeface and size so people won't need to strain their eyes in order to read your words.

If you are using the older, paste-up method and you don't have access to computer graphics, stock art—collections of ready-to-use drawings, cartoons, and graphics of all kinds—is available. Your local office-supply store or bookstore most likely will have booklets with clip art that is ready to cut and paste into place. If the stock art of your choice is too large or too small, it can be reduced or enlarged to fit a designated space.

COUPONS, COUPONS, COUPONS

"The best things in life are free. (With coupons, of course.)"

That's the head that tops a Dunkin' Donuts ad offering four coupons. Many companies add coupons to their advertising and marketing messages, but the coupons usually seem to be more or less an afterthought. Dunkin' Donuts uses coupons as the focus for the whole ad, boxed and centered in a photo of a mouth-watering assortment of their products.

Coupons work, and *The Dallas Morning News* has tracked down some interesting facts to prove it:

- A total of 7.7 billion coupons were redeemed in 1993 (the latest year for which figures are available) for a savings of $4.8 billion dollars.
- That same year, manufacturers distributed 323 *billion* coupons.
- The average face value of each coupon was 54 cents.
- The average coupon had an expiration date of 3.8 months after it was issued—one-half the average life span of a coupon issued five years earlier.

Coupon Writing Rules

There really aren't any rules for coupons, although there are some commonsense things you should do, such as providing adequate space when a coupon requests a name, address, or other information. It also makes sense to tell the consumer an expiration date or if there is no expiration date. And it certainly makes sense to spell out terms such as:

- One coupon per purchase
- May not be used in combination with any other coupon
- Good only on the product(s) indicated

POSTCARDS: TRAVELING BILLBOARDS

In her book *How to Get Big Results from a Small Advertising Budget*, Cynthia Smith says that, with postcards, there are "no envelopes to fight through. A postcard just hits the desk and spills its story straight out. It's an instant billboard that cannot be missed. It has to be seen and can be read even as it's being thrown away." That is the biggest advantage of using postcards.

Postcards can be just about any size, from standard on up to those that are almost literally "traveling billboards." When you're deciding on size, consider that a larger size seems to shout "advertising," which may result in a faster slam-dunk into the wastebasket than a postcard that compares in size with those you might receive from a friend on a trip.

One more thing to remember about postcards is that the message side—the grabber side that carries your artwork and main message—will be buried when the card is received. Mail carriers line up all names and addresses to make for easier mail delivery, so your recipient will see the address side first.

"Free Postcards Showcase Hip Advertising"

That headline above a story in *The Dallas Morning News* tells of a new marketing use for postcards. The article describes free postcards that feature hip ads aimed at young, upscale consumers. The cards are given away at shops and other sites in selected cities.

The idea—which comes from New York–based Gitter, Anapol & Glazer Communications—is simple. "Postcards showcasing a company's products or ads are placed in display racks, which in turn are placed in high-visibility locations where consumers can pick them up for free. The result is a targeted and low-cost marketing tool," says *The News.* "The beauty of it is that people think they are getting something of value with the postcards, and there is a positive ruboff with the advertisers," says Sylvie Anapol of Gitter, Anapol & Glazer. She says that studies show that 59 percent of patrons who take the postcards from the high-tech metal racks mail them off to friends and family, and 46 percent make some kind of purchase from the advertiser.

CARD DECKS

Traditional forms of direct mail can be thought of as solo direct mail. The opposite of that is card decks. Within their own industry, card decks (or card pacs) are referred to as a form of cooperative direct-response media because of their established performance records in supporting traditional media programs, especially solo direct mail. (Other cooperative direct-response media include package inserts, statement stuffers, and catalog ride-alongs, bind-ins, blow-ins, and take-ones. In cooperative direct-response programs, the marketer buys space in a direct-mail package targeted toward a specific audience.)

A number of companies sponsor card decks. The American Management Association offers them. *Entrepreneur* magazine has one it calls "Portfolio Direct Response Card Deck." Then there's New York–based Venture Communications, which has so many card deck offerings that it prints a

60-page catalog to list them. Venture, a company founded in 1983, claims that "there is no other organization on a par with our breadth of direct response media knowledge and services." According to Venture:

> A card pac is a package of business reply postcards mailed to a defined target audience. The cards are generally 3½" by 5½" or 5" by 7" business reply cards, each bearing a marketing message.
>
> The cards are stacked in deck form, poly-sealed, and mailed bulk rate to prospects. The recipient opens the pac, selects the cards of personal interest, and mails them back to the [advertisers/marketers]. Coupons, product samples, and other non-card inserts are often included.

Effective Cooperative Direct-Mail Inserts

Not even in the clutter of a newspaper page crowded with small ads is there greater competition than in a card deck. Because each card in the deck must grab—and hold—the recipient's attention all by itself, the copy and visuals must be kept to a minimum while producing maximum impact. Here is some valuable guidance in constructing these inserts from Venture Communications:

> Sometimes, as with card pacs, the challenge may be to generate a satisfactory response/cost ratio with a single postcard. At best, your copywriters and designers will have a small dimension, multi-panel insert with which to communicate your message.
>
> *Headlines Rule:* Any promotion with limited space is somewhat headline driven. You only have a chance to sell if you can stop the prospect at your insert. Make it big, bold, and obvious to grab the reader's attention. Headlines that promise a strong benefit generally work best. Don't forget to identify your key prospects in the headline copy.
>
> *Make Your Visuals Sing:* Strong visual treatments that harmonize with the headline will catch and hold the prospect's attention. Generally speaking, the bigger the better. If your product lends itself to color, you'll probably benefit from the extra investment. Even a simple line-illustration will help your insert attract reader attention.
>
> *Get Right to the Point:* Persuasive copy maintains the reader's interest and helps substantiate your product or service. You must remember to abbreviate features and benefits. Above all, keep your objectives in mind. Leave the prospect wanting more information if you're trying to generate an inquiry. On the other hand, offer as much detail as possible if you're trying to make a sale.
>
> *Don't Forget to Close:* Never assume that the prospect knows what action to take. Give precise instructions such as, 'Complete the postage paid reply card and mail today.'

These guidelines can also apply to postcards when used as direct-mail pieces. And no matter what the means for getting your message to your target group, never forget that there's a four-letter word that may be the biggest attention-getter in marketing: *FREE*.

TELEMARKETING

Telemarketing has been coming undone for years. It's broken, and most people think there's no way to fix it. If you think the words *junk mail* are derogatory, consider the public's displeasure and irritation with what goes on, seemingly ungoverned, in the telemarketing industry. The Better Business Bureau reports what appears to be a new low: Unscrupulous telemarketers who have bilked and cheated consumers are now calling their victims back, pretending to be official "recovery" agencies that will help them get their money back—for a fee!

The public's outrage is growing, and telemarketers must either police themselves or expect new regulations that will police them. In 1991, Congress passed the Telephone Consumer Protection Act (TCPA), which prohibits telemarketing to hospital rooms, cellular phones, or fax machines—any phone where costs are incurred merely by answering the calls. There's also a law that bans the use of taped sales messages with no live caller, although this law has been found unconstitutional by some courts and seems to be ignored in many areas of the country.

In spite of the TCPA, however, many unpleasant tactics still exist. For example, frequency is unlimited, which means there is no limit to the number of calls telemarketers can make to the same phone number—even in a single day. And there are no restrictions on calls made after 9 P.M. or during the dinner hour.

The many negatives associated with telemarketing don't seem to have diminished profitability for the industry. Americans buy $275 billion annually through telemarketing. There are 300,000 solicitors making 18 million calls daily, according to the Direct Marketing Association.

More Information

If your plan calls for this form of direct-response marketing, Jerome S. Gladysz offers advice on the subject in *The Advertising Kit: A Complete Guide for Small Businesses,* by Jeanette Smith. (Lexington Books/Macmillan). Gladysz is president of Market Relations, Inc., in Fort Worth, Texas, and represents business-to-business clients in a variety of industries.

12

Case Studies: How the Pros Used Direct Marketing

> Only five marketing campaigns called for direct marketing: FastSigns, the UnInstaller, Sewing Center Supply for OmniStitch, Protection One, and Caradco.

Case histories from the pros serve as models for imitation, but—more importantly—they give you a peek inside the minds of and insight into the decisions made by professionals when they start from ground zero to develop an MMMC plan. Only five of the nine cases involved direct marketing. Gary Salomon used it for FastSigns. Rick Wemmers used it for the UnInstaller, but only in the initial phase. Of the four cases designed and carried out by Liz Johnson's agency, Johnson believed that only Sewing Center Supply and Protection One would profit sufficiently from using a direct marketing approach. And when Marsha Lindsay's agency mapped out a plan for Caradco Windows, they incorporated direct marketing in only a limited way.

Why such limited use of direct marketing when advertising was used for *every* case? Perhaps they used advertising because it is the foundation, the underpinning, the infrastructure of marketing, whereas direct marketing is often considered junk mail by the targeted audience.

CASE 1: DIRECT MARKETING PRODUCES FOR FASTSIGNS

"My first job after college," says Gary Salomon, "was as a Val-Pak representative, selling coupon advertising to small-business owners and managers in San Antonio, Texas."

After five months, I worked out an arrangement that allowed me to buy my own territories over time. It was through a coupon sale in Austin a few years later that I met Bob Schanbaum, who became my partner in FastSigns. Handling Val-Pak led me to develop a full-service direct-mail agency through which I compiled and maintained mailing lists, brokered professional lists, and developed solo direct-mail pieces for my clients. Although I've long since sold my direct-mail businesses, that experience gave me a good general understanding of how to use the medium effectively. Here's what I learned:

Your mailing list is a crucial asset. You may compile it yourself from your list of customers and prospects, or you may rent or purchase it from a professional list company. Either way,

- It must be maintained regularly.
- Defunct or duplicate companies [or individuals] should be deleted.
- Addresses should be checked and updated.
- If your list includes contact names, those names must also be updated with every change in personnel.

Depending on your arrangement, a professional list company may do all this for you—but the marketplace is always changing, and even the most well-maintained list is likely to be only 90 percent deliverable at any given time.

Couponing is a double-edged sword. Sure, the right offer can motivate new people to come into your place of business, and once they've discovered you, they may become regular customers. But when used too often, coupons can train your customers to expect a discount every time. Some people actually wait until they get another coupon before they buy again. When that happens, you have devalued your product and, in effect, cut your prices. Some retailers try to avoid the problem by printing "New Customers Only" on their coupons, but that can alienate existing customers, who may feel that their loyalty isn't appreciated.

Keep your expectations realistic. If your product is an impulse buy, you can expect to see a little stronger response to your mailing than if you're selling a needs-based product or service, such as the signs we sell in our stores. For us, direct mail is a good way to build awareness, but we don't expect it to bring in a huge blast of business overnight.

Designing Direct Mail the FastSigns Way

In 1985, FastSigns was a brand-new business in need of print materials to introduce itself to the public. And, like most entrepreneurs building a new enterprise, my partner and I wanted to do everything ourselves. Luckily, that fit right into our budget!

We developed our own logo, took our own photos, wrote our own copy, and designed a small self-mailing brochure for our new company. The one area in which we didn't scrimp was color. We felt that color was the only way to communicate the graphic nature of our business, so we took the money we'd saved on design and put it straight into full-color printing.

A Mail Piece That Doubled as a Handout

The result was a self-mailer that, although amateurish in retrospect, was by far the best thing the Dallas sign industry had seen at the time. It showed examples of our product, offered a discount, and gave a brief explanation of the then-new process of computer-generated signmaking. It did the job admirably.

An Oversized Postcard

The next piece we developed was geared for flexibility: an oversized, full-color postcard left blank on the back, to be surprinted [superimposed] with whatever offer or announcement we chose, in whatever quantity we wanted.

Again the photos were only snapshots, and the design was weak (despite the involvement of a professional artist), but the piece served its purpose at the time.

Upgrading the Image

[Part of what follows is actually a part of the promotion process, but it's needed here to explain why FastSigns switched the look of its mailing pieces.]

Despite FastSigns' early success, we knew we were fighting an uphill battle against the longstanding image of the sign industry. Traditional signmakers worked with chemicals and heavy equipment in remote warehouses or garages. They were industrial artisans—painters, metalworkers, sandblasters—and though they might produce outstanding work, they were generally not very good at making their customers comfortable with the sign-buying process.

FastSigns, on the other hand, offered a clean, bright showroom in a convenient retail location, staffed by professional sign consultants with special training in customer service. Our streamlined manufacturing process involved only a humming computer, a wall display of colorful vinyls, and several neatly attired signmakers working at sparkling white tables beyond a glass wall.

Exhibit 12.1   A black-and-white reproduction of FastSigns' first self-mailer—
an 11 × 17-inch three-fold that offered photo examples, with explanations,
of the variety of services performed by FastSigns.

FASTSIGNS

The One Day Sign & Lettering Experts!

- *Real Estate Signs*
- *Site Signs*
- *Truck & Vehicle Lettering*
- *Window Lettering*
- *Parking & Traffic Control*
- *Ready-To-Apply Lettering*
- *Trade Shows*
- *Vinyl Graphics*

- *Banners*
- *Magnetic Signs*
- *Interior Graphics*
- *Informational Signs*
- *Building Graphics*
- *Logos & Symbols*
- *Directional Signs*
- *Fleet Markings*

*FASTSIGNS uses cutting edge computer technology
to provide custom signs within 24 hours of placing an order.
FASTSIGNS Centers offer a large selection of typestyles in a
rainbow of colors. Ensure highly visible, attractive signage,
quickly and economically with FASTSIGNS.*

Exhibit 12.2   A black-and-white reproduction of FastSigns' giant—
8½ × 14 inches—postcard. The card, on heavy-duty card stock, folded
to two 5-inch panels, on one of which was a single 4-inch tear-off return card.
Part of the 8-inch width on the return card was a tear-off Rolodex-style card
that listed all the services offered on one side and a "Satisfaction Guaranteed"
list of benefits for customers on the reverse side.

For the business professionals who were our primary customers, buying from FastSigns was a very different, and a much more
comfortable, experience.

But as FastSigns evolved, we recognized that, in order to communicate those differences, we needed to develop a more polished
style [in the direct mail pieces]. We worked with better designers to
create a crisper, more corporate look in our mailing pieces. We used
larger photos, less text, and more white space to project a more refined image.

Black Is White Space

"White space," of course, is a figurative term. Sometimes the space is
black, as on our second oversized postcard, which used a glossy black
background to make a few selected sign photos stand out like jewels
on velvet.

This postcard was very different in appearance from the usual
"junk mail" at the time. It got noticed, and it got response.

The "big black postcard" was so successful as a marketing tool
for our stores that we decided to try it in franchise sales as well. A few

Exhibit 12.3   The "big black postcard" that served several
purposes as a mailing piece.

weeks prior to exhibiting at an International Franchise Association
show in Los Angeles, we surprinted the new black postcards with an
invitation to visit our booth at the show and mailed them to individuals in southern California who had inquired about FastSigns and also
to a major business magazine's list of Los Angeles–area subscribers.

CASE 2: WEMMERS COMMUNICATIONS
FOR MICROHELP, INC.

Rick Wemmers explains his agency's thinking about the limited use of direct marketing on behalf of UnInstaller—in introducing this new, innovative product and in building sales. Direct marketing was used, but not ag-
gressively, during the launch stage of UnInstaller. Direct sales were
gained through insertion of an UnInstaller listing with several major computer software catalogers. These catalogs were—and still are—sent to
hundreds of thousands of computer buyers and owners. They offer a
wide variety of software products. But UnInstaller was only one of many
software products in these catalogs. It was the addition of general media
advertising that began to pump up sales for UnInstaller.

Proposals by the agency for targeted mailing to heavy users were considered but not implemented during 1994. Mailing to current owners of UnInstaller was delayed until 1995.

The Right Decision

In the case of UnInstaller, limited direct marketing, with greater emphasis on the integrated use of other marketing communications tools, was the right choice. Remember the profit figures for MicroHelp, Inc.? Before 1993, profits were $3 million. After UnInstaller was introduced according to Wemmers' marketing plan, profits were $20 million and rising.

CASE 5: SEWING CENTER SUPPLY

Direct marketing *was* a major component in McKinney Johnson Amato's plan for the introduction of OmniStitch, the revolutionary embellishing machine that was parent company Sewing Center Supply's first product marketed directly to consumers. Advance research had shown that home sewers saw OmniStitch as a remedy for one of their biggest frustrations— projects that ended up looking homemade because they lacked the extra details that professional garments had. But, even though advance research indicated that sewers embraced the idea, this was SCS's first direct marketing effort, so the company had to be positioned as reliable to buy from.

Ad Reprints Recycled as Direct Mail

The ads that had run in selected magazines were reprinted and, along with a letter, mailed to each of the 1,600 entrants in the earlier sewing-show drawing. The ads had been created knowing that users liked lots of color and details. They featured a colorful, bright border and enough information to make home sewers want to call the 800 number to order a free instructional video. A major effort was made to ensure that each printed piece would look professional and polished.

Overwhelming Response

Although there is no breakout of response figures between ads and direct-mail pieces, because both included the 800 number, a sizable portion can be attributed to the direct-marketing efforts. Sewing Center Supply went from zero to more than 7,000 inquiries in 120 days. "They received more than 24,000 inquiries through 1994," says Liz Johnson. Perhaps most gratifying was finding that the total cost per lead—including production of all materials, reprints, and media—was under $20. "Ten percent of all leads have been converted into sales," says Johnson.

CASE 6: PROTECTION ONE

Another of the four McKinney Johnson Amato marketing campaigns relied on direct marketing. This campaign was on behalf of Protection One, a home security company in Portland, Oregon, and it focused primarily on advertising with direct marketing playing a backup purpose. The goals of the "Know Campaign" were to establish name awareness and to educate the public about home security. The focal point of the campaign was a series of a radio spot and six television spots, but print ads were also used. Throughout the campaign, real people told real stories. All collateral materials, including a direct-mail piece and a series of doorhangers, incorporated the burglar and three other spokespeople from the ads as continuity elements.

The Right Choices

According to Liz Johnson, after the "Know Campaign" began, monthly leads steadily increased in each of the three markets (Portland, Seattle, and Los Angeles) from 15 percent to as high as 35 percent. An awareness survey in the southern California market showed that, after just 12 months of exposure, Protection One was consistently recognized as one of the top four security companies in the area.

CASE 8: CARADCO WOOD WINDOWS AND PATIO DOORS

Lindsay, Stone & Briggs' campaign to develop awareness for Caradco's products focused mainly on advertising and promotion, but a mailed catalog was also used. The catalog, however, doesn't fit the usual description. It was a 112-page, 8½ × 11-inch publication printed on coated magazine-type paper. Considering the breadth of its contents, the catalog could almost double as a magazine.

The first two pages of the catalog (the inside cover on the left and page one on the right) include a small but easy-to-read table of contents,

Exhibit 12.4 A black-and-white reproduction of the Caradco catalog cover art. As with all art in the catalog, the cover blends a drawing with a photo.

but the major portion of these two pages is devoted to two boxed articles. One article carries the headline, "America's Most Experienced Window Makers" and tells readers about the company. Underlines have been added to the following passage to highlight kinds of information your copy should include.

America's Most Experienced Window Makers

Back in 1866, the first Carr and Austin Window was installed in a home in <u>Dubuque, Iowa</u>. Since then, across the United States and around the world, millions of people have enjoyed the view through what are now known as Caradco Wood Windows and Patio Doors.

And though, like any <u>company that's been around for over 125 years</u>, we've been through many changes, one thing remains intact— <u>our commitment to</u> providing <u>you</u> with the most artfully designed, highest quality wood windows and patio doors.

From our traditional double-hung and casement windows that are <u>a product of over a century of experience</u>, to custom designs that are the product of your imagination, we have a complete line of windows and patio doors designed to enhance the beauty of any project. In fact, <u>our product line is one of the most extensive in the industry</u>, so <u>we can be the single source for your</u> window and patio door <u>needs</u>. . . .

So no matter what style of home you're building or what size opening you have to fill, Caradco can provide you with <u>beautiful, long-lasting, energy-efficient</u> wood windows and patio doors.

Pay particular attention to the underlined words and phrases in the copy. These are the subtle ways Caradco tells prospects the things they want to know, things your copy should include, too. Refer back to the copy as you read on, to understand how the copy transmits these subtle messages.

- *How old your company is.* Everyone knows a company doesn't stick around very long without dependability, integrity, and well-received products.

- *Where your company is located.* Sometimes a geographic area helps to establish good feelings for a company. In Caradco's case, the Midwest is thought by many to have well-established values with people who are respected for their honesty and character.

- *How old your company is—again.* The line, "over a century of experience," drills home that the company has the strength of age and experience.

- *What you have to offer.*

- *A list of benefits for the buyer.* "Our product line is one of the most extensive . . ." and "beautiful, long-lasting, energy-efficient . . ." These two phrases set forth benefits every buyer wants to know about. These are exactly the kinds of words buyers look for, and they answer the question, "What's In It For Me?"

The Feature Story

The article on the facing page carries over to the following page and is headlined, "Caradco's Feature Story." It, too, boasts (without sounding boastful) of the merits of the company's products. Subheads are spaced over the two pages of double-spaced, eye-easy copy, and each of the subheads defines a benefit specific to Caradco's products:

- The Best Wood and More of It
- Old-Fashioned Craftsmanship
- Lasting Colors
- Hardware Made Easy
- Accidents Are No Problem
- Clearly More Efficient
- Guaranteed for Years to Come

Throughout the three pages of introductory information, there are small line drawings and photos, but the most prominent are the company's logo on the opening page and the warranty at the end of the three pages. The logo says:

CARADCO
Founded* 1866

Running through it is a reverse block and, in much larger type, the words:

Over 125 Years

A Catalog That Sells

Throughout the catalog are photo displays (with limited accompanying copy) of custom and non-custom windows and patio doors. Also included are specification graphs and lists, and everything is done in typestyles and layouts that imply quality, elegance, and status. The catalog is not an inexpensive piece, but when you wish to signify elite superiority, you don't offer information on telephone-book paper.

PART IV

PROMOTION: IT CAN
BE EXCEPTIONALLY
COST-EFFECTIVE

13

Direct Promotion: Hybrid of Promotion and Direct Marketing

What is promotion? How important is it to your goals? Co-op promotions and tie-ins. Kinds of promotions. Don't forget your present customers. Timing is important. Refining the MMMC message to fit the promotion. Using it to build or create an image. Logos and slogans. Value-added promotions.

Mention the word *promotion* to most people, and the first thing they think of is a job advancement. Effective promotion in marketing does advance a company, a product, or a service to a higher level. For other people, however, promotion means sales. Both are right.

No businessperson with a functioning brain would think of conducting any marketing function if it wasn't expected to increase the profit margin. But sales how-tos are not the focus of this section; promotions that will increase sales and build recognition and consumer loyalty are. Integrating the promotion message into the marketing communications mix is also a part of what this chapter is all about.

PROMOTION DEFINED

You've heard it before—now hear it again: No matter how good your product or service, people can't buy it if they've never heard of it. Advertising, direct marketing, and publicity are vehicles to get your message out to people, but promotion has additional functions. It finds ways to use

147

the message to influence attitudes and behavior, and it attracts and motivates people so they notice and pay attention to your advertising and direct-marketing messages. Yet promotion always seems to be treated like an orphan stepchild. Like publicity, it is used less often than advertising and direct marketing.

Promotion is often called *sales* promotion. Historically, efforts were directed exclusively toward selling a product or service. More recently, however, experience and investigation have proved that promotion activities are successful when they are designed to point out benefits and availability for consumers. Today, instead of selling a product or service, promotion efforts are concentrated on selling good *feelings* about a product or service. Today's marketing efforts call for *direct* promotion, which means zeroing in on niche groups of consumers and potential customers or clients and speaking directly to them. Because direct marketing, mainly direct mail, has been the most direct route to get a promotion to consumers, direct promotion has become a hybrid of promotion and direct marketing.

OFTEN-OVERLOOKED VALUES OF PROMOTION

Outside the world of marketing professionals, promotion is often tied to the entertainment industry, particularly when people see outrageous promotions carried on by movie and television personalities. There can be dignity in promotion efforts, however, when they are tied in with both large and small businesses. Direct promotion is a means by which businesses communicate with the public, and there is substantial proof that well-targeted promotional efforts do produce added sales.

The importance of promotion is growing as businesses recognize that those offering the most promotions aren't necessarily those spending the most money. Unlike advertising, direct marketing, and publicity, promotion often uses two forms of communication—words and implication. Your goals and objectives determine your need to use one or both.

Knowing Your Goal

The first step in planning any marketing activity is to decide exactly what the campaign is supposed to do. Pull out your overall marketing plan. Are the goals and objectives explicit? Do they include promotion? If not (and you now know that promotion *should* be a part of your integrated marketing plan), take your overall marketing goals, apply them to what you want to accomplish through promotion, and then construct promotion objectives to get you there.

In his book *Marketing: An Integrated Approach,* Carl McDaniel Jr. says, "The goal of promotion is to modify behavior or to reinforce existing behavior. Specifically, promotion hopes to inform, persuade, or remind." With that in mind, ask yourself:

- What behavior on the part of present and potential consumers do you hope to modify?
- By which means will you inform, persuade, or remind them? Of what?
- Is your promotion intended to correct misconceptions?
- Is it meant to build recognition and consumer loyalty?
- Is it meant to differentiate your product or service from others in the marketplace?
- Is your aim to accentuate the value of the product or service?
- Or is your purpose to merely provide information or increase demand?

The methods you use will depend on your promotion goals and objectives, but first a word of warning. Don't design a promotion that tries to do too much. Use the implied wisdom of cartoonist Bruce Hammond in his "Duffy" cartoon. Duffy is asked, "W.G. wants you to compose a company song?" He answers, "Yah. He wants it to improve morale, raise productivity . . . have a good beat and be easy to dance to." What a promotion piece that song would be if it could effectively do all that! Goals may look and sound great on paper, but be sure you make your promotion goals achievable.

COMMON-CENTS CO-OP

Co-op works for promotion as well as for advertising. Co-op promotion is helping to expand the role of promotion because (as mentioned earlier) businesses are beginning to recognize that those offering the most promotions aren't spending the most money. Funds are available from manufacturers and vendors for promotion as well as advertising, and supplies of products are available that substantially reduce the cost of sampling, bonus packs, and POP (point-of-purchase).

There are even agencies, such as Co-options and Co-op Promotions, that specialize in seeking out and offering tie-in co-op promotions that link two or more brands for marketing programs. There are peel-off labels on products that provide cross-marketing messages, as well as on-pack and in-pack product sampling. *Tie-ins* is the key word among these agencies. According to *Advertising Age,* on-pack coupons consisting of multipage booklets attached directly to products and point-of-purchase displays are ideal for cross-promotions that involve a dozen or more marketers.

Some of the more obvious co-op supplies and services include counter displays, stuffers for envelopes, and help in preparing direct mail.

Choose Your Partner

In some circles, tie-ins are called "partnership marketing." *Adweek* magazine says there is little data on how much this type of promotion has grown, but "partnering is the way to go because it moves your brands into different demographics and retailers where you could never go by yourself." *Adweek* gives an example you might be able to copycat:

> In 1994, [Herb Baum, head of Quaker State Oil Company] and his team of ex-packaged goods execs created promotional tie-ins with Prestone anti-freeze and Armor All protectants. Those were traditional brands to team with Quaker State. But 1995 [was] expected to bring even more unusual brands into Quaker's partnering plans.

Advertising Age says there are tie-in specialists that operate like dating services to coordinate co-op promotions for brand marketers. There are, the magazine says, a host of new avenues for co-op promotions that are opening up as competition among tie-in specialists grows. Among them are electronic and interactive media that are being explored as new channels for joint promotions. It would be worth your time to check out what co-op is available for your purposes.

TYPES OF PROMOTIONS

Point-of-purchase, samplings, and bonus packs have been mentioned as possible marketing promotions, and there are many others. The numbers and kinds are limited only by creativity and imagination. A general roll call might include:

- Price off and buy-two-and-save sales
- Sampling
- Refunds
- Premiums
- Trade allowances
- Point-of-purchase
- Customer service programs

- Free-standing inserts
- Bonus packs
- Contests
- Special events and trade shows

Some of the most popular promotion programs—many think they are the most effective—are special events. And, of course, don't forget the new interactive online avenues. The trick for you is to decide which conveyance will best carry your promotion goals to fulfillment.

THE TWO PROMOTION ROADS

Even professional marketers often overlook the fact that promotions designed to attract *new customers* are more costly than promotions among existing customers. Remember the purposes of promotion? To modify behavior or *reinforce existing behavior*—to inform, persuade, or *remind.* That can mean developing promotions aimed at giving you a larger share of your present customers' business or getting old customers to come back.

When you take on the job of influencing the attitudes and behaviors of *new* prospects, you face the much greater task of catching and sparking their interest; building recognition and remembrance of your company's or product's or service's name; convincing prospects that your company, product, or service is honest, reliable, and trustworthy; and reducing skepticism and the automatic tendency on the part of new prospects to put off first-time action or buying.

You can skip past all these problems by directing promotions at past or current customers, because they already know your integrity and the kind of values and service you offer. You can reduce your efforts to—as one marketer explains it—"just let them know how more will be better, and how to make better use of whatever you're selling. By making them better customers you make them bigger buyers."

This is not to say that promotions to new consumers can be completely eliminated. In today's highly mobile society (statistics show more than 5 to 7 percent of Americans move every year), great chunks of your regular customer base get erased merely because they move out of your area. You also need promotions aimed at the newcomers to your area.

THE IMPORTANCE OF TIMING

It wouldn't make any sense to time a sampling of a sauce for barbecued spareribs to arrive just before or after Thanksgiving (not unless the emphasis was on using the coating on oven-cooked ribs as a welcome change from turkey). The most productive timing for such a promotion would be during outdoor barbecue season.

Factors that influence timing can be special holidays, seasons, or special events. It wouldn't make sense to schedule a special promotion event for Superbowl Sunday when most people are indoors watching television and the streets and stores are empty of traffic. Equally problematic would be ignoring or not realizing that your planned event conflicts with an established local event. The established event will get the attention—and the people.

Seasonal buying habits should also be taken into consideration. For example, a promotion that involves cars may be best scheduled for late spring, when people are beginning to think about summer vacations and their need for safe, new transportation. And sometimes timing requires more than common sense. It goes back to your research—knowing and understanding your target group. If, for instance, you plan a promotion that requires recipients to take advantage of an offer during a limited period, and you know that your target group is retirees whose retirement income and Social Security payments arrive monthly at the first of the month, your promotion should be timed for the period when their money isn't too tight.

No one except you (or a highly trained marketing professional who has studied your specific situation) can determine the best timing for your chosen promotions. Like so much else in marketing, that's something that you must think through and decide for yourself.

WHICH MMMC MEDIUM WILL REACH YOUR TARGET?

If you decide that sampling, bonus packs, or free-standing inserts are practical means for communicating your direct-promotion message, then you obviously cannot use cable, radio, or outdoor boards as vehicles to get these items into the hands of your targeted group. Direct mail is the most frequently used method for carrying most promotions to targeted individuals. Samplings, premiums, customer service programs, and bonus packs can all be carried by direct mail. It is the most finely tuned means of reaching select groups. That's why direct promotion is a hybrid of promotion and direct marketing.

Some newspapers and magazines are equipped to handle free-standing inserts and package samplings. But they reach such a broad medley of people that targeting, other than by geographic areas, is currently impossible. (There are strong indications, however, that newspapers and magazines are gearing up for the new technology that permits delivery to individually targeted families and companies.)

REFINING YOUR WRITTEN MESSAGE

Remind yourself why promotion rather than advertising is being employed. You're looking to inform, to persuade, to remind, and to influence attitudes and behaviors. Each of these challenges shouts out for copy that is slanted to *serve* rather than to sell. And you can't serve unless you know exactly how the targeted audience wants to be served.

Play down product or service and company name. Play up what your product or service can do for the customer. Remember not only to be friendly but to play the part of a trusted friend who wants to help, to give valuable advice. No soap boxes, though! You aren't telling a friend what to do; you're *sharing:* "Look what I found. Try it. . . . I'm betting you'll like it, too." As with all marketing communications copy, say it simply and make it easy to understand.

Be Creative

A message is a message is a message, until there's something about it that attracts and convinces readers. It may be the headline, or a photo, or the way it takes advantage of new-tech ideas.

But perhaps you don't want to develop quite as creative a promotion as John McPherson's "Close to Home" cartoon idea. A couple sits in a restaurant scanning their menus. She says, "Oh, Glen. You should smell the raspberry sauce on the roast duck!" The line beneath the cartoon says, "The Candle Glow Inn introduces its new scratch-and-sniff menus."

You know, of course, that the idea isn't really very far-fetched. Fragrance companies have latched onto scratch-and-sniff technologies to the point that some magazines now offer their readers the option of no fragrances in their copies. Even though most requests for fragrance-free magazines are probably from people with allergies, if readers feel strongly enough to go to the trouble of asking for the special unscented issues, there must be some mighty feelings of resistance out there. The lesson to be learned here is to think twice before employing any creative approach.

BUILDING OR CREATING AN IMAGE

The louder a business touts its honesty and integrity, the faster people count their spoons. So, how *do* you create, build, or rebuild a desired image? Publicity is arguably the best road to take, but the right kind of promotion can do it, too.

The Wall Street Journal, in a self-selling advertisement, says that "a company would be well-advised to monitor its corporate image almost hourly . . . the image that customers, prospects, stockholders, employees and others have of a company is constantly changing."

IBM has been trying for almost a decade to change its monolithic image. It wants the public to view it as reassuring rather than boasting. One means it employed to accomplish this was to use a teaser headline that stated: "And now for something completely different." Some have referred to IBM's approach as "a strategic retreat." The approach built a whole new appeal, but never was the IBM logo changed, although by late 1991, 13 divisions had broken away from use of the IBM logo. "We don't want to be logo cops," says Jim Reilly, IBM's general manager of communications services. "But at the same time we don't want to see the IBM logo showing up in neon orange just because some unit thinks it looks good that way."

LOGOS AND SLOGANS: A COMPANY'S FRIENDLY FACE

A company's name may be its logo, so name and logo are both important in terms of promotion. Names, logos, and slogans can go a long way toward creating, maintaining, or even rebuilding a desired image. Professional marketers Stan Rapp and Tom Collins, in their book *Maxi-Marketing*, say: "Image [promotion] is simply devoted to building up, through constant repetition, a favorable impression of the likeability, reliability, or fashionability of a product or company in the minds of prospective buyers. For example, the Prudential Rock of Gibraltar." Or the IBM logo. "Corporate and brand logos are the most visible reflection of a marketer's image," states *Advertising Age*.

"It takes time for a logo to be well accepted," according to Alvin H. Schecter, CEO of the Schecter Group. He goes on to point out the contrast in performances of two logos for Federal Express. When the traditional logo was tested—with the word *Federal* atop the word *Express*, inside a rectangle as if to connote flight—the logo image outscored the name image. But when the new logo was tested—with the words *Fed* and *Ex* sandwiched together without the rectangle—the result was reversed.

Two Sides to the Logo Coin

"Why do some logos provide a warm-and-fuzzy glow to their owners, while others tarnish images?" asks *Ad Age*. "Generally," according to Schechter, "abstract logos aren't as well liked as characters, letter symbols, and other pictorial images. Sometimes the corny marks of the '20s and '30s are the most successful."

"People assume that when they do a logo, take a name and dress it up, it's going to improve their image," Schechter says. "But it's not true. In more cases it downgrades their image rather than upgrades it."

So what does all this mean? Strong evidence indicates that logos and slogans are great promotion tools. Or very bad ones. Be open to change if perception is either negative or "So what?" But don't make a change just because *you* may be tired of your logo or slogan. It takes too long to build recognition for anything new.

Slogans as Integral Parts of Logos

New York Life Insurance Company's slogan—"The Company You Keep"— is almost inseparable from its name. Absolutely inseparable are Hallmark and its slogan, "When you care enough to send the very best." The Church of God in Adamsville, Alabama, adapted (read: copycatted) a well-known slogan and made it a well-recognized part of its name: "Salvation: Don't leave earth without it." Even the United States Postal Service uses a slogan: "We deliver for you." Smuckers uses a slogan to change a minus into a plus and to build name remembrance and recognition: "With a name like Smuckers, it has to be good."

A good slogan captures an idea, an image, or a perception you want to convey, then bottles and sells it. Slogans that stick around for generations are those that say something positive that customers want to believe (and after trying the product or service, they do believe).

"The best part of waking up is Folgers in your cup," is not only memorable (and *re*-memorable) with its jingle quality, but it gets the company's name into the slogan. Getting the company name into the slogan also works for another company: "Wait'll we get our Hanes on you." "Tastes great—less filling" makes a statement that Miller Lite wants everyone to keep in mind in these days of health-consciousness. And plays on words can add power to a slogan. Think of General Electric: "We bring good things to light." And one of the telephone companies: "The one to call on."

"THE FUTURE IS NEARLY NOW"

That's the headline over an *Adweek* survey report that shows respondents were "moderately interested" or "very interested" in technologies, and they are responding to such things as kiosks, which mostly use CD-ROM technology. "These self-contained stations can do anything from sell customized greeting cards to play games to show ads," reports John Gale, president of the Information Workstation Group (IWG), a multimedia consulting and market research firm.

Record companies are able to have their videos played on its kiosks. IWG says that cross-advertising and online ordering are next. Something called Special Report Network is in more than 32,000 doctors' waiting rooms, with advertising from Chrysler, Fruit of the Loom, and Paramount Pictures, among others.

"The new media is going to be here," warns Saatchi Advertising, "and whether you define the future as two years, five or ten, you'd better prepare." "The party is just beginning," predicts *Adweek*.

PREMIUMS AND INCENTIVES

In a special section in *Advertising Age*, the lead to one story states:

> Whether it's a pre-paid telephone card with the cast of Melrose Place on the front, a t-shirt with an Anheuser-Busch logo or a gift certificate, premiums and incentives are a $28 billion industry, and there are few signs that sales growth has reached a plateau.
>
> Corporate managers view premiums and incentives as essential to inspire consumers to purchase particular merchandise and services.
>
> Approximately 50 percent of premiums and incentives are geared toward consumers, with 25 percent used as sales incentives.

So, you ask, what's so hot about premiums and incentives? It seems there's somebody marching on behalf of the effectiveness of every promotion ilk. But in the case of premiums and incentives, the answer seems to be that they work.

Eastman Kodak jumped head-first into the tempting waters with their single-use cameras. Two companies that have offered the cameras to their customers are WordPerfect Corp and Bausch & Lomb. "For Kodak, the increased distribution of the one-time cameras is a great way to gain trial usage and increase brand awareness," says Robert Kuhn of Kodak.

14

Packaging: An Important Promotion Tool

Packaging has changed ... and has become highly important. Services should be packaged, too. Designing packages and testing them. POP involves packaging and is part of the MMMC plan.

In the times before self-service stores, wrappers merely covered merchandise to keep it from spilling or leaking. Salespeople were available to help buyers make purchasing decisions. Now buyers have to make these decisions for themselves, often from dozens of choices with nothing but the look of the packages to guide them.

Many goods today are bought on impulse—particularly by people who haven't been reached through MMMC—and the appearance of a product has a great deal to do with establishing feelings about it. Packaging can send a positive or negative message, *or no message at all,* and thereby greatly affect the impulse to buy.

In an MMMC program, the package must not only heighten the sudden urge to buy but also send the same message about the product that is offered in other media. In other words, the same design features (colors, graphics, and theme) that are used in advertising and direct-mail pieces should be duplicated, consolidated, and integrated to build recognition. If potential customers repeatedly see a special graphic design or a unique dominant color in ads or commercials, they will recognize your package. Such is the case with the dominant green that Healthy Choice food products have made their own. The color almost leaps out of the

157

frozen dinners section or off the shelf to get shoppers' attention. That means that after only a few trips to the market, shoppers can recognize products from distances that don't permit reading logos. (Keep in mind that a study found that grocery shoppers seldom wear their glasses when shopping.)

WHICH COMES FIRST, THE PACKAGE OR THE AD?

Even though packaging is no longer an afterthought when marketing, promotion, or advertising awards are handed out, packaging doesn't even get invited to the event. Even professional marketers seldom seem to take packaging very seriously. But if you don't have much money for advertising or direct marketing, your package *is* your ad. If you can't afford a marketing campaign, it's your only message conveyor and your only medium for persuasion. It is promotion at its most indispensable. Packaging must come before advertising or direct marketing or publicity. Think about this: even if you have jillions to spend on all types of marketing for your product, how can you advertise it, market it, even publicize it, if you don't have a package to show? It's the most visible part of the product. It's promotion at its most basic level.

Some professionals express misgivings about the ability of packages to send marketing messages. They believe that shoppers don't take the time to read packages. That's flat-out untrue. Research shows that labels are read by between 80 and 95 percent of shoppers, *if* the packaging is strong enough to stand out from the competition and get shoppers to consider what's inside.

Knowledgeable pros recognize the importance of packaging. Remember the four *P*'s of marketing—price, product, place, and promotion? Up-to-speed marketers consider packaging a fifth *P*. It's *that* important in creating consumer recognition, acceptance, and desirability. Your package is not unlike a billboard ad, past which any number of potential buyers pass, day in and day out. As with a billboard, your message must be fast, simple, eye-stopping, and memorable.

PACKAGING DEFINED

A marketing instructor might tell you that "the package may include up to three levels of material." Philip Kotler and Gary Armstrong are university professors (at Northwestern University and the University of North Carolina at Chapel Hill) who say exactly that in their book, *Marketing: An Introduction*. Kotler and Armstrong define these three levels as:

1. *The primary package*—the product's immediate container.
2. *The secondary package*—"the material that protects the primary package and that is thrown away when the product is about to be used."
3. *The shipping package*—the corrugated box, for example, which is "necessary to store, identify, and ship the product."

The packaging shoppers see in the store, which may be either primary or secondary, rarely the shipping package, is of interest here. And packaging consists of more than just the look of a physical container. It can also be the way a product does or doesn't function. The outside of a package may attract buyers, but if the inside bag tears or won't reseal properly, shoppers may switch to the competition's product.

PACKAGING FOR SERVICE COMPANIES

The term *packaging* applies primarily to products. But in the case of services such as medical, legal, accounting, and so on, "service is the product," the operators of a Denver consulting firm point out. Laura M. Dirks and Sally M. Daniel are authors of *Marketing without Mystery.* They say that "the service package reinforces the image of the service provider through consistent use of the company name and its symbol or logo on everything from name tags in the reception area to report covers and billing statements."

For service companies—as for retailers—packaging appears as the exterior and interior appearance of the office or store. The mission is to command attention and give the user a feeling that the service being provided is different or better than competitors' offerings. A strong, positive impression builds remembrance. Call it store packaging.

The walls of waiting rooms and offices can offer the information clients want to know about experience, background, reliability, credibility, and all those other credentials that make people feel secure about medical, legal, accounting, or other service-oriented individuals or companies. Standard wall-hanging packaging includes diplomas and certificates to certify the amount and kind of training an individual has, as well as pertinent awards to further establish credibility.

A published story from any respected publication, attractively mounted or framed, can serve as a seal of approval. News or feature stories about the person or company—perhaps stories about how they sponsored a charity activity—can often indicate caring and concern. Likewise, signed photos of clients with perhaps a brief testimonial or thank-you note speak loudly about *who* is happy with your service. And symbols of membership in appropriate organizations, displayed as wall hangings or on a desk, also speak to the individual's or firm's ongoing involvement in a community or industry or profession.

THE IMPORTANCE OF PACKAGING

In addition to attracting shoppers, packaging also influences whether or not store owners will stock a product and, if they do, where they'll place it. After all, the retailer is like a direct mail route (without mailing costs) to current and potential consumers. Retailers look for certain features, and you can't afford to ignore their concerns if you want them to accept your product. They want packages that are easy to handle, store, and display. In many respects, you and retailers have identical concerns. Retailers also want packages that will stimulate sales, as well as protect a product.

From the consumers' points of view, if for any reason they don't like what they see on the outside, they'll turn to another brand, a competitor's brand. *The Wall Street Journal on Marketing* by Ronald Alsop reported the following significant survey findings:

> Although 50 percent of the packaging problems didn't affect brand loyalty, a significant number—19 percent—resulted in shoppers refusing to buy the same brand again. In another 24 percent of the cases, consumers said they'd "shop more cautiously" or "buy a different type of package."

Another survey (conducted by the Package Designers Council and also reported by Alsop) found that the four most important characteristics of packaging to consumers are:

1. Storage life of unused portions
2. Ability to recognize contents by looking at package graphics
3. Resealability
4. Ease of storage

For your purposes, there are a couple other significant advantages to remember. A new package, like a new product or service, can be material for publicity stories, either as straight news or as a feature story pointing out benefits (how the package is ergonomically or environmentally correct or how a particular family used it in a worthwhile manner).

At first, the idea of promoting your package as being environmentally friendly may seem unimportant. In 1995, *The New York Times* pointed out the mistaken belief that packaging accounts for a growing percentage of our solid waste. The fact is:

If you were to examine a dumpster of garbage from the 1950s and a dumpster of garbage from the 1980s, you would find more discarded packaging in the first one. . . . Packaging has actually decreased as a proportion of all solid wastes from more than half in the 1950s to just over one-third today.

Beyond the publicity value, it's like a posted sign, an ongoing reminder in the home or business place of having accepted and purchased your package. If it's not your only promotion, it becomes a strong extension to other promotion and marketing vehicles.

PACKAGE DESIGN

There are a number of points to consider in designing a package. Find a professional who specializes in packaging, but first know what's important so you can contribute to the process and make wise final decisions. Packaging is as personal to your product and your company as clothes are to your appearance and to the impression they give. The packaging decisions you must make are about size, shape, color, text, and materials. Some things to remember:

- The package must sell itself. There won't be anyone around to point out its features to the consumer.
- It must be original so that it doesn't blend in with all the other packages around it.
- It must be easy to handle, carry, and store.
- It must establish its identity (content and brand) and set itself apart from similar products. Find a unique quality to shout about on your package.

Use color! Ronald Alsop quotes a package designer as saying that "color isn't the most important thing; it's the only thing." Alsop goes on to state that color especially affects food marketing, because people taste with their eyes. Psychologists claim that psychological messages can be communicated with color. For example, yellow indicates sunshine and warmth, and silver gives a cold impression. Brown, the color of chocolate, often leads food buyers to taste chocolate with their eyes.

Labeling

Labeling as a promotion tool isn't technically packaging unless the label is the packaging. Well-established products may need only a label, but if a product is new (or new among a field of similar merchandise), it probably needs more than a label to be seen and heard in the crowd.

In many cases, there is a label under the packaging. In that case (or if the label is the only packaging), it is important to remember that the Federal Fair Packages and Labeling Act calls for certain mandatory information. Consumer goods must be clearly labeled in easily understood terms. For example, food products must list nutrition information. It is essential that you check the labeling requirements, if any, for your specific product.

CHANGING OR UPDATING YOUR PACKAGING

Periodically use the following checklist to decide whether updates, changes, or modifications should be made in your packaging.

- Check all aspects of your package—look, color, graphics, and text. Are they still integrated with your total MMMC plan? If there have been changes in any part of your plan, make the corresponding changes in packaging.
- Are your name, logo, and slogan *easily* identified?
- Are benefits conveyed clearly, simply, and immediately?
- Is your packaging as creative as possible, yet still within the bounds of functionality and simplicity that consumers want?
- Does your package maintain the same ease of reading and simplicity required in outdoor advertising?
- Have you checked federal, state, and legal requirements to be sure that all required information is included?
- If your product packaging is your store or office, check that the environment transmits the messages about image, ability, and dependability you want consumers to receive.

You may have a lot of information to communicate to potential buyers, but don't tell them so much that you confuse them. The education process can't be handled exclusively on the carton. Remember, the package is like a billboard. With a billboard, however, you have up to seven seconds to get your message across. With your package, you may have only one or two seconds.

TESTING YOUR PACKAGING

Anything that can be tested, should be tested. Package pre-testing, like direct-mail testing, can save you lots of money. It's usually much more economical to produce a few samples for a test than it is to order a large quantity of the projected packaging and *then* find out that people don't react the way you thought they would.

Of course, the broader the test, the more accurate the reading you'll get. If funds are tight, a marketing instructor at a local college may have students who can carry your product into the field and tape-record reactions of people at a store where your product would most likely be sold. (Of course, you must first get permission from the store owner or manager. Smaller stores are more likely to work with you on this kind of project.) Keep in mind that, to accurately test shelf appeal, your product must actually be displayed on a store shelf, with someone standing by to note customers' actions and reactions.

If there is any way you can squeeze out the funding, hire a small research company to do package testing for you. Some research firms are able to set up simulated stores, call in a cross-section of people who are likely buyers, and conduct simulations.

Make sure you investigate all testing means available in your area.

ON-PACK PROMOTIONS

On-pack promotions by candy bar marketers have really been taking off recently. For example, Hershey's Bar None has gone all-out to tempt teens with on-pack promotions for what they call "The Coolest Stuff"—freebies such as basketballs and boxer shorts—for mailing in ten or more wrappers.

M&M/Mars has an on-pack offer for a watch depicting the M&M peanut figure skateboarding. Free CD players, movie passes, and trips are also offered, along with chances to win a portable stereo if the candy bar buyer finds a wrapper that says "It'll make you go crunch."

Notice that word *free* again. There are no figures available, but for on-pack and point-of-purchase offers, "buy one, get one free" seems to work better than "two for the price of one."

POINT-OF-PURCHASE PROMOTIONS

Would you call the sign on the wall in a John McPherson "Close to Home" cartoon point-of-purchase promotion? The sign says, "July Special: Earn 5,000 airline miles with each Hip Replacement Surgery!" and the drawing shows three doctors performing surgery. Beneath the drawing are the words, "More and more businesses are teaming up with airlines to offer frequent-flier miles to their customers."

In-store, point-of-purchase (POP) merchandise displays aren't exactly a *packaging* technique, but they can get people to stop and notice your package. And, for this reason, they are growing in popularity. POP displays have two intents: to catch a consumer's attention and to cause impulse buying. They are direct response at its most direct.

POP promotions may be in the form of signs and banners; on-shelf, on-counter, or in-aisle displays; or freestanding units that hold collections of a product, along with information about it. One of the most seductive forms is the posting of messages on shopping carts.

In a supplement to *Advertising Age* devoted exclusively to POP, the headlines over one story wisely advise:

PLAN P-O-P at the start
Integrate it in the total creative approach

Integrated marketing that embraces POP materials and displays should convey a shorthand version of the main marketing message, the article says. It should be something that takes advantage of the space available at retail and reinforces what the consumer sees in other media.

15

Wanted: A Few (More) Good Promotions

Promotions that are interactive—trade shows, expos, and events. Package the event booth. When entertainment works. They can build your data bank. Sampling. Tie-ins. Contests and sweepstakes. Premiums and incentives are value-added promotions.

Sometimes a promotion works beyond expectations. Other times it works, but not up to expectations.

It's possible that none of the promotion ideas set forth so far are the best for your purposes. You have a need, you believe, to meet people face-to-face, to have them receive your message from a real person they can see, hear, and question. It's your contention that to achieve full impact, people need to see, touch, taste, or smell your product or see your service in operation. But salespeople ringing doorbells don't have many doors opened to them these days. So you'll have to substitute.

Perhaps a special event would be a better way to get your information directly to niche groups of people and generate new customer leads. An event such as an expo, a trade show, or a state fair may very well provide potential customers with a better sense of the value of your product or service, because personal contact gives people the opportunity to get answers to their questions and make their own judgments. Given a choice, people almost always prefer to rely on their own appraisals.

SPECIAL EVENTS

Now that *interactive* isn't just a marketing buzzword but an edict, the popularity of special events has soared—from 5,600 trade shows in the mid-1980s to almost double that number now, with some 100 million people attending. Events offer opportunities to be interactive, with direct inter-play between business and customers and business and prospects.

Beyond the obvious promotional advantages, an event is also an ex-cellent opportunity to conduct some market research without the cost of hiring a research firm. And where else but at a trade show is there such broad opportunity to observe the competition? Also, don't forget that the media cover events, so an event is an excellent opportunity to gain pub-licity, too.

What's in a Name?

If an event is strictly a medium to reach manufacturers, suppliers, or dis-tributors, it's called a *trade show.* Otherwise it's called whatever fits the occasion. Perhaps it's a "Photo Phanatics Expo." If you're offering a new, do-it-yourself, difficult-to-explain photo-developing process, this kind of event could be a true blessing. People can experience hands-on the ease with which the task is performed and witness first-hand how to control color and light and dark in each photo. And you get the opportunity to learn what confuses people and make adjustments in future advertising, direct mail, publicity, and promotions. Events also provide you with an opportunity to compile a priceless contact list for future mailings and pro-motions.

Are Events For You?

Trade shows, expos, and state and county fairs are best for products and services that must be explained and demonstrated (or at least seen) to be sold. Fairs attract mass audiences, but trade shows and expos (which can be national, regional, or even local) appeal to special-interest groups. Even so, they might not necessarily be fine-tuned to the target level you'd like. They do, however, offer a way to reach and influence large groups of people with similar interests, and they offer an excellent opportunity to educate the industry.

An excellent source of information about specific trade groups and trade shows is the *Encyclopedia of Associations* (available from Gale Re-search Company, Book Tower, Detroit, MI 48226; 800/223-GALE).

Booths

Most events, but trade shows in particular, call for renting a booth (or space) that is staffed by your own people. Your staff's role is to meet people, hand out information (about your product, service, or company), demonstrate products, answer questions, and acquire names, addresses, and phone numbers for future contact purposes.

Special displays dress up an event booth, but more important, they grab interest and present some information. They get people to stop, look, and listen. By the time people reach your booth, they may be tired or even bored from all the other information they've had tossed at them. Your booth requires packaging just as your store or office does. Employ the same principles you used earlier (in Chapter 14) to design packaging for your store or your office.

Keep the packaging of your booth as similar as possible to the packaging of your product, store, or office—to build recognition and remembrance. If you have consistent, dominant package colors, use them as a central feature in your booth. Or use some of the wall displays from your office to establish your honesty, integrity, and image.

Dress up your booth with attractive graphics and visuals that identify your company and its product or service, and use enough creativity to stop traffic. If people keep passing you by, and you never have the opportunity to show and convince them one-on-one, you might as well spend your money on advertising or direct mail.

If the show has a dominant central theme, try to adapt your display to fit in. After all, that central theme was probably used in pre-event advertising and publicity and is what helped bring the people in.

Portability of your displays is an important cost factor to consider. How easily can they be dismantled and used again at other events? Try to estimate how many times the same display equipment will be used for other events and the number of people you expect to stop and receive a personal explanation, demonstration, or sales talk. When you take these things into consideration, the cost of a display that is exciting enough and sufficiently attractive to create interest and stop traffic probably isn't as high as a direct-mail or direct-response campaign.

Display: A Word with More Than One Meaning

The word *display*, as it is used here, means "decoration"—booth adornment. Some businesspeople use the word *display* to mean the way they present their product, as in "Just lay it out there—put it on display—and they will come." Forget that interpretation of the word.

Showing your product doing its work is the best display there is. It is not only a stopper, but it's like a picture—worth a thousand words. When casual strollers see a group of people watching something work, curiosity makes them want to stop and watch too. From that point on, it's your responsibility to involve them, get them to touch it, try it, whatever is called for. It's your job to talk *with* them, not *at* them, and to listen—to their questions and to what they think and feel.

A word of caution is called for, though. If you just want people to stop, put a standup comic out there, or a puppet show. Entertainment will stop almost everyone, but not one of the people who stop to hear a comic will learn a thing about your product or have the slightest incentive to find out about it. Entertainment may stop traffic, but the minute the light turns green, traffic moves on. Unless . . .

When Entertainment Works

The New York Times tells the story of a Lutheran pastor in suburban Phoenix who recognized the value of entertainment. It hit Walt Kallestad like a bolt one day at a shopping mall when he noticed a particularly long line of people waiting to see a movie. He remembers asking a friend, "How in the world could we ever create something so exciting in church, where people would wait four and a half hours to get in?"

Well, he did create something so exciting that great numbers of people now attend his Community Church of Joy. The church features "electric bands playing contemporary music, dramatic skits and sermons that focus on the tough issues of everyday living." And this entertainment factor draws more than 2,500 adults and 1,500 children a week "—which places it in the ranks of the United States' megachurches."

Making Sure Entertainment Is Appropriate

Entertainment does work as a marketing tool—*when it's relevant.* If you can't tie the entertainment in with your message (and, as a result, people walk away the minute it's over), then forget it. But even if entertainment per se isn't appropriate, that doesn't mean your presentation or demonstration should be deadly dull. No one will stick around for a monotone recitation of facts and figures, even if every one of your facts and figures answers their question: "What's in it for me?" You might as well put your presentation on a 78 record and wind up the old Victrola.

Make your facts and figures interesting. Make them come alive just as a newspaper story takes the facts—the answers to *who, what, where, when,* and *why*—dresses them up, and makes them interesting to read. In your case, you have the opportunity to do an original news story to fit the personal interests of every individual you talk to. This is an excellent opportunity for you to practice using those 5 W's, which you'll be using later, in the fourth section of the book, on publicity.

How long should your demonstration last? Like good advertising copy, it should be concise and packed with information. Two or three minutes—five at the most—is about all the time people will stand still and listen to a speech. On the other hand, if yours really is a one-on-one demo of what a product or service will do for the customer by letting them try it, then you can play it by ear. You'll know when interest lags.

Signing Them Up

If you want an event to increase your database of potential consumers for follow-up mailings or your direct-mail list, you may want to offer a remembrance or souvenir to those who register. To be effective, a souvenir should be something that won't be tossed, and it should make them remember your company, product, or service each time it's used. Some restaurants are starting to use a souvenir that serves as a replacement for the matchbooks that were everywhere a few years back. It uses the same kind of artwork as a souvenir matchbook, but in place of the matches, each book contains about 20 small sheets of paper. One restaurateur described them as "about the size to write a phone number." Like matchbooks, they fit easily into a pocket or purse.

A handout should be given only after you've talked to a person and found out that he or she actually is interested in what you have to offer. Or you can screen people by having them fill out a card that asks questions such as "What kind of film do you use?" or "Do you plan to buy photo-developing equipment within the next year?" Perhaps a more revealing question might be, "How old is your darkroom equipment?"

Obviously, something that people will use on a daily basis is the best kind of souvenir. But try hard to come up with something more imaginative than a keychain or a calendar.

SAMPLING

You don't hear the word *sampling* much anywhere but among marketing types. It's a form of one-way research and communication that puts a product in people's hands but doesn't reveal whether they tried it, if they liked or disliked it, what they thought about it, or how they'd change it. It merely puts the product close to a potential customer. Whether that potential customer ever picks it up and uses it is never known.

There probably isn't a person in America who hasn't received a packet of coffee, a bar of soap, a single-serving box of breakfast cereal, or a travel-size tube of some kind of cream. Samples arrive in the morning newspaper, in magazines, and in the mail. They are meant to demonstrate a product's superiority over similar products, to introduce it as something new and unique, or merely to induce recipients to try it and then buy it. There may be a coupon on or in the package that offers a full-size container at a reduced price.

You should know up front that sampling is the most expensive sales promotion tool in the entire toolbox. Its costs include not only the price of the product itself but also the expense of special-size packaging, plus distribution expenses. How to distribute a trial-size sample depends on its size and its perishability. A single-serving packet of coffee is much easier to package and distribute than cereal, dishwashing liquid, or laundry detergent. Distribution methods include enclosure with a newspaper or magazine, direct mail, door-to-door delivery, POP giveaways, or handouts at promotion events.

Not all samples are free. Sometimes a sample is attached to an introductory-size package that let's the consumer sample the product before opening the full-size container. There's a ploy here. Marketers know that people are almost sure to try something they've paid for.

Not only is sampling costly, but it requires substantial planning. If you feel that sampling is essential to the success of your marketing plan, then take the time to consider all of the special packaging and distribution costs, and think through in advance the complexity of carrying out a well-planned program.

After you've considered all this, if you still believe that sampling is necessary, consider using a company that specializes in samples distribution. That may make more sense than doing it yourself.

TIE-INS

Goodie bags aren't new. You find them at every trade show. But a few promotion agencies are doing something new with goodie bags. And it's a technique you may want to copycat. A descriptive name for it might be "tie-in promotion." It trades special goodie bags for the purchase of a product or data about consumers' tastes. According to *The New York Times*, it works like this: "It combines elements of product sampling with so-called place-based marketing—media created for sites like hospitals, classrooms and airports—and data based marketing, compiling lists of consumers to address one to one."

For example, ticket buyers at General Cinema theaters filled out cards answering demographic information about their ages, moviegoing habits, and tastes in music. In exchange, they received bags containing audiocassettes, coupons, and other items meant to stimulate their interest in recordings by rock, rap, and country musicians signed with labels owned by the companies seeking the information and offering the goodies. "The concept," says *The Times*, "is indicative of the unconventional promotions capturing the attention of marketers as they increasingly focus their sales pitches on narrower audiences."

CONTESTS AND SWEEPSTAKES

Contests are hot again. On the one hand, people love lotteries, and they love to win prizes, whether its money at a casino or a trip to a tropical paradise. On the other hand, businesses love promotions that directly involve the consumer in the promotion. Contests and sweepstakes are win-win promotions. The downside is that the worth of sweepstakes and contest prizes has climbed so high that a million-dollar lottery or sweepstakes is almost commonplace—but still far beyond the reach of most businesses.

Prizes are the common denominator in contests and sweepstakes. Sweepstakes are merely random drawings and require no skill by the entrant. Contests, however, require entrants to show ability in the designated contest category. Contests can serve a double promotional purpose. At the same time that they are awarding prizes to winning contestants, contests can earn a prize for the sponsoring business in the form of a slogan, drawing, graphic, or photo that can be used in future advertising or direct marketing. And essay contests may provide quotes or testimonials that can be used in future marketing materials. Such a contest might also provide material that could be used later for a publicity feature story directed to newspapers or appropriate magazines.

Why a Contest?

The reasons for promotional contests are unlimited and vary according to the needs of individual businesses. Some generic purposes include:

- *To check consumer understanding of advertising messages.* This can be done with an essay contest: "I prefer the XYZ service because . . ." Without providing much information about the service on the entry form, this kind of entry reflects the effectiveness of previous or current advertising.
- *To find a new name or slogan* to go with an established name, product, or service. When this is the purpose, don't neglect to describe tie-breaking procedures, because several entrants may come up with the same idea.
- *To spice up ads or other message vehicles and increase readership.* Headlines that carry the word *CASH* are proven attention-grabbers. Readers are likely to read through the piece to find out what the giveaway is all about, even though not all will enter the contest.
- *To increase the number of unit purchases.* You might, for example, require a specified number of proofs-of-purchase, such as three bar

code symbols or any designated package identification, in order to enter the contest.

Keep The Rules Simple

The more complicated the rules, the fewer entrants you will attract and the greater the number of misunderstandings and misinterpretations. Be sure to specify the following:

- Closing date of the contest
- Entry requirements
- Provisions for breaking ties
- Where to send entries
- Who is eligible (and ineligible)
- Prize structure
- Description of judging methods
- Who the judges will be
- Statement that judges' decisions will be final
- How and when winners will be announced
- Statement that no entries will be returned and no correspondence will be acknowledged
- *Most important:* Be sure to include a notice that all entries become the property of the contest sponsor so that you can use all or part of entrants' submissions in the future.

PREMIUMS AND INCENTIVES ARE VALUE ADDED PROMOTIONS

In a special section in *Advertising Age,* the lead to one story states:

> Whether it's a pre-paid telephone card with the cast of Melrose Place on the front, a t-shirt with an Anheuser-Busch logo or a gift certificate, premiums and incentives are a $28 billion industry, and there are few signs that sales growth has reached a plateau.
>
> Corporate managers view premiums and incentives as essential to inspire consumers to purchase particular merchandise and services.
>
> Approximately 50 percent of premiums and incentives are geared toward consumers, with 25 percent used as sales incentives.

So, what's so hot about premiums and incentives? The answer has to be: *They work!*

REMEMBER THIS

Promotion means finding ways to get your product or service recognized and remembered. If you use an 800 number as a direct-response means to connect with consumers, and the phone doesn't ring—don't call the telephone company to fix the phone. Sit down and ask yourself why it doesn't ring. What's wrong with the promotion avenues you're using to establish recognition and remembrance? Remember the acronym that stands for the four jobs that are the ultimate goals of all marketing: *AIDA*. Get *A*ttention. Hold *I*nterest. Arouse *D*esire. Motivate *A*ction.

16

Case Studies: How the Pros Used Direct Promotion

Crossovers among marketing disciplines. Six of the nine copycat cases plus an extra case used promotions: Fast-Signs, the UnInstaller, TU Electric, KPDX *No News*, Caradco Windows, It Takes All Kinds, and Bank of America.

By now you see that marketing disciplines don't often have sharply defined boundaries. Ads in newspapers and magazines and commercial spots on TV and radio are clearly recognizable as advertising. But then video from those commercials or repros of the ads, or testimonials from them may be used as a part of direct mail, promotion, or publicity. There are many kinds of crossovers, as well as frequent, definite overlaps—as you will see when the pros explain their marketing strategies.

The pros used advertising for all nine of their campaigns. Direct marketing was used in only five cases, and promotion in six.

Gary Salomon says FastSigns stumbled into its first promotion almost by accident. Rick Wemmers plotted the use of promotion for the UnInstaller as an attention-getting tactic at retail stores. EvansGroup adopted a new angle for TU Electric's booth at the State Fair of Texas. The booth was changed in order to generate awareness in a way that was fun and unique. Promotion by the McKinney Johnson Amato agency was used to rework an image and build awareness for KPDX's NO NEWS campaign. The 180-degree image change that was achieved for Caradco Windows by Lindsay, Stone & Briggs was accomplished with promotions that included sales aids and trade shows. And promotion was a major force used by Lindsay, Stone & Briggs in their anti-racism campaign directed at teens.

An extra case—Bank of America—is added to this discussion to provide ideas for relocations and grand openings.

CASE 1: FASTSIGNS SAW OPPORTUNITY AND GRABBED IT

Gary Salomon says:

> Our first national promotion came about almost by accident. It was the fall of 1990, and the first American troops were heading out for Saudi Arabia from bases across the country.
>
> A military wife in Phoenix asked one of our stores there to donate a Good Luck banner to be signed by citizens and sent off with local troops as a morale-booster. That first banner quickly filled up with signatures, and the rest of our Phoenix stores stepped in with additional banner contributions.
>
> Word of the project reached us [at FastSigns' Dallas headquarters] at 10:00 in the morning. By 11:00 we were making plans to take the idea nationwide.

Instant Communication for the Price of a Fax Modem

> Time was of the essence. In order to communicate the concept to our network of about 100 stores as quickly as possible, we immediately bought a fax modem, which would automatically send the information to all our franchisees overnight.
>
> The next morning, our franchisees began responding by phone and fax. They loved the idea, they were already working on their banners, and they were proud to be part of a company that cared enough to organize such an outpouring of support for our troops.

Promotion Tumbles Over into Publicity

> Luckily we already had a relationship with a public relations company that was able to assemble a list of over 600 media contacts nationwide and get a press release mailed out to them in just a couple of days. [This was a significant crossover into publicity as a part of promotion.]
>
> Response was excellent. Countless newspaper articles were run, most with photos of people signing the banner at the local store. Many radio stations promoted the project with public service

announcements. And many of our stores received coverage on their local television news.

Press involvement was vital to the project, since only through the media could we spread the word that the banners were available for signing in each of our stores.

A secondary benefit of this coverage was an enhanced national and local awareness of the FastSigns name. But we had to tread a fine line in promoting the project—we wanted to take advantage of the opportunity to draw attention to FastSigns, but we wanted the primary focus of that attention to be on the project rather than on ourselves. To overemphasize our involvement would have been ungracious and, ultimately, counterproductive.

To tie the whole project up on a national level, I traveled to Williams Air Force Base near Phoenix and presented a special banner to the woman who had started it all.

In the end, FastSigns' stores provided over 200 signature-laden banners to the Pentagon for shipment to units stationed throughout the Persian Gulf area.

Good Timing and an Extra Benefit

Our spontaneous banner project managed to make just the right statement at just the right time, when most people were eager for a way to lend moral support to our troops. The simple act of signing a banner took on profound symbolic meaning.

Yes, we hoped the project would encourage a feeling of goodwill toward FastSigns. But our primary motivation was a sincere desire to encourage respect and appreciation for the dangerous job our servicepeople were doing in Saudi Arabia. And in retrospect, I can honestly say that I think the most valuable effect of that project was not our exposure in the media but the sense of pride and commitment it sparked among our own franchisees.

CASE 2: THE UNINSTALLER'S UNIQUE PROMOTION

Wemmers Communications classifies itself as an agency that conducts marketing, advertising, public relations, and promotions. The agency actually conducts promotion campaigns, whereas some advertising-only agencies rely on sister agencies to handle promotions for them. Although Rick Wemmers says that advertising was the primary tool used to raise sales for UnInstaller in the initial launch stages, he also says they kicked off that ad campaign with a very unusual magazine insert that was a promotion piece.

The insert was the first of its kind ever produced to be run in computer magazines. It presented a number of production challenges, but the impact was tremendous. The insert was a magazine-size four-pager on heavy stock. The first page was a drawing of a computer monitor with the name *UnInstaller* under it. But the monitor's screen was actually a see-through plastic *window,* through which you could see the copy on page three:

UnInstaller
Cleans
Windows

As you opened this plastic window (turned the page), a concise, two-column, ten-line selling pitch became visible beneath the drawing of the computer monitor. On the facing page, the page that was the other side of the see-through window, the company's 800 number was printed under the window. The back page (page four) was a roundup of information computer users would want to know, all under a double-meaning headline:

ALL WINDOWS MUST BE CLEANED.
UNINSTALLER CLEANS THEM COMPLETELY

There was also some information meant to convince readers of their need for the product:

> Sooner or later, all Windows must be cleaned. The reason for this is that, whenever a program is installed in Windows it automatically modifies your system, making changes to your configuration files, sometimes adding its own files, and always placing bits and pieces of itself in places you don't know about. UnInstaller keeps your Windows clean and running smoothly by removing all traces of an unwanted application—new or existing—without hassle. It does it easily, and it does it completely.

Following this intro to the individual pieces of information beneath is the user-friendly "suggested retail price" of $69.95.

Impact: Tremendous!

Rick Wemmers' says:

> This was the first [promotion piece] used by our agency to kick the awareness up for UnInstaller. It was used as an insert to draw maximum attention and support to the product's display at the 1994 Spring Comdex Show in Atlanta.
>   More than 1,250,000 of these inserts were used in two magazines—*Windows* and *Windows Sources.*

Noise Level at the Shelf

In software retailing, says Wemmers, there is a great deal of noise level at the shelf.

> Many shoppers walk slowly down the aisle, looking for something new, which is often noted in the box design and copy. If a box or headline catches their attention, they usually will stop and pick it up to read the back for details.
>
> This [Exhibit 16.1] was the second box design for UnInstaller. The first was white with blue type and had a "window washer" on the front. We felt the box needed more attention-getting power at retail, so we designed the red color with the product benefit screaming on the front.

A Shelf Talker

Another UnInstaller promotion piece (see Exhibit 16.2) was used on store shelves to draw attention to the product. The first point-of-sale piece

Exhibit 16.1   UnInstaller packaging: white type on attention-getting red with the product name in a lighter red.

Exhibit 16.2   UnInstaller's plastic shelf-hanger
that bounces as a result of the circulation of air
and attracts customers' attention as they walk by.

used, it was plastic, with white type on a red background, and was attached to the shelf where the product was stocked. When someone
walked past the shelf, the piece would bounce, thereby grabbing the
passerby's attention.

Trade Shows

Trade shows were also used to draw customer attention to the product. But
free goods and special discounts or premiums were not used. Wemmers'
reason? "There doesn't seem to be a need to motivate customers beyond
stating the simple benefits of the product loudly and clearly."

CASE 3: TU ELECTRIC AT THE STATE FAIR

George Arnold is president and CEO of EvansGroup, the marketing agency that represents TU Electric. He explains how the promotion plan for TU evolved and the methods used to put it together.

TU Electric makes it a point to be represented every year at the Texas State Fair. Historically, TU has merely had a booth staffed by company representatives who handed out informational brochures. In 1994, however, TU managers decided to adopt a different angle for the booth. Focus group testing and telephone surveys had shown that customers were feeling powerless about the size of their electric bills, and the managers decided that the state fair would be the ideal forum for educating customers on ways to lower their bills.

Getting customers' attention while they were having fun was the direction EvansGroup decided to take. An improv comedy troupe was enlisted to customize a script that would not only educate fairgoers but also entertain them.

Promotion Objectives

Building traffic to the booth was necessary in order to:

- Generate awareness of energy-saving tips in an entertaining format.
- Build TU's image as community-minded, caring, and concerned.

Execution

The comedy troupe was commissioned to script a 30-minute show that would communicate energy-saving tips in a fun format, and video clips of the show ran between the live shows for additional exposure. Articles appeared in the entertainment section of *The Dallas Morning News* (another overlap of marketing disciplines—promotion and publicity), and a performance schedule appeared in the state fair program. Finally, an LED (light-emitting diode) display on Dallas Area Rapid Transit buses was programmed to give TU Electric information to riders.

Results

Due to a local radio promotion, articles in newspapers and other print media, and word of mouth, there was heavy traffic to the booth on a daily basis. Most shows were standing-room-only. Four to five shows were scheduled each day, and fairgoers commented positively throughout the run of the show. For the first time, customers were in the TU Electric booth laughing and having fun—not complaining about high bills.

CASE 4: "NO NEWS" WAS BIG NEWS FOR KPDX VIEWERS

The NO NEWS campaign was planned to rework an image and build awareness for the one television station in Portland with no news programs on its schedule. McKinney Johnson Amato, the agency representing KPDX, developed a summer promotion that would gain exposure at events and get some memorable hands-on contact with viewers. Liz Johnson explains it this way:

> The traveling KPDX NO NEWS set was patterned after the sideshow scenery set-ups where people stick their heads into cut-out backdrops, putting their faces on the painted body of a muscular beach hero or a curvaceous bathing beauty.
> Our backdrop was a news set complete with faceless NO NEWS anchors. It gave eager bystanders a chance to be instant celebrities.
> This promotion also had a charity tie-in. People walked away with a framed Polaroid photo of their shot at fame, and all the profits went to Tri-County Special Olympics, whose people staffed the booth at all events.

Collateral promotion items included "I ♥ NO NEWS" buttons for general distribution and "NO NEWS Team" watches for the station's clients.

A Survey That Was "Just a Lotta Fun"

To gather information about the effectiveness of the campaign, a person-on-the-street promotion was used as an informal survey that kicked off the KPDX fall campaign. Liz Johnson describes it:

> We had a man walking the streets of Portland, Salem, and Vancouver for four weeks, giving away $490 a day. To win $49, all a person had to do was answer one simple question: "What Portland television station has no news, just a lotta fun?" An amazing 70 percent of the people asked knew the answer without prompting.

The agency recognized and used to its client's advantage the public's growing insistence on being entertained. The integration of all marketing communication avenues was accomplished with the graffiti-like addition to transit and outdoor advertising of the "Just A Lotta Fun" message.

CASE 8: CARADCO WINDOWS

Promotion was a support component rather than the foundation of the Caradco Windows vertically integrated communications campaign. A trade show booth was used, along with catalogs and sales aids, and all were integrated to have the same brand image—an image of Caradco as being 180 degrees different from its leading competitor.

Sprinkled throughout the factual information in promotional materials were smile-producing subheads. One dignified brochure is entitled *Windows of Opportunity.* A section on patio doors is headed "Slide Over Here." Another reads, "There's a Lot Hanging on This." And still another is subtitled "Raising Your Expectations."

But as lighthearted as these headlines may be, the information presented under them is solid, useful, and concise. And all promotion pieces feature photos that include the pencil drawings exclusive to the integrated Caradco campaign. These Caradco-style photos give the pieces instant recognition.

CASE 9: IT TAKES ALL KINDS

Promotion for the teen-targeted "It Takes All Kinds" campaign by Lindsay, Stone & Briggs was in the form of a teaser campaign begun two weeks before the beginning of the actual campaign. Marsha Lindsay explains:

> Using card stock paper, posters were printed on a photocopier and put in high-teen-traffic areas. Our rationale behind this teaser campaign was to build excitement and gain attention from an "alternative" source rather than from traditional media, authority figures, or other institutions.

BONUS CASE: BANK OF AMERICA GRAND OPENING

When Bank of America was scheduled to open in-store branches in Kroger supermarkets, grand opening promotional plans were needed. The information that follows about the Bank of America promotion might generate ideas and help you if or when you open a new business or relocate an existing one. The promotional plan comes from EvansGroup.

Background

In 1994, Bank of America was opening in-store branches in Kroger super-markets, nine in the Dallas area and four in the Houston area. Openings were scheduled throughout the year at the rate of approximately one a month.

Objective

To open 100 new checking accounts at each in-store branch during the two to three day grand opening periods.

Strategies

- Develop appropriate product offerings to encourage account openings.
- Hold a grand-opening event at each Kroger store.
- Utilize promotion and advertising co-op opportunities with Kroger.

Target

Primary: Adults 25 to 54 years, current primary shoppers at Kroger stores, with household incomes of $30,000+.

Secondary: Adults 25 to 54 years, residing or working in primary trade area of each Kroger store, and current secondary shoppers of each Kroger store, with household incomes of $30,000+.

Tertiary: Other audiences, including local opinion leaders, news media, Bank of America employees, Kroger employees.

MMMC Avenues

- Use of in-store signage, point-of-purchase, in-store radio, and public address announcements to reach primary and secondary Kroger shoppers.
- Use of exterior store signage and exterior grand-opening activities to reach primary and secondary Kroger shoppers, as well as drive-by, non-Kroger shopper traffic.

- Use of in-aisle selling to reach Kroger shoppers prior to and during the [preliminary] soft opening.
- Use of radio remotes to reach non-Kroger shoppers and to reinforce messages to primary and secondary Kroger shoppers.
- Participation in Kroger advertising supplements to reach primary and secondary Kroger shoppers.
- Use of door hangers to reach non-Kroger shoppers and to reinforce messages to primary and secondary Kroger shoppers with the primary trade area of each individual store.

(Take note of the several MMMC crossovers.)

Tactics

- Hold grand-opening event on second Saturday and Sunday following soft opening of branch, or for new Kroger stores, in conjunction with Kroger grand-opening activities.
- Promote the Alpha account and "free checks" benefit.
- Provide an added value with any checking account opening of approximately $50 in Kroger coupons.
- Prior to and during soft opening, bank employees hand out fliers promoting grand-opening offers and activities.
- Offer sweepstakes drawing throughout grand-opening days, offering one week of specific groceries (eggs, milk, or bread) every other hour and one month's supply of groceries at the end of each day.

Results

In the first six months following the grand openings, 11 stores showed $10 million in deposits and a total of 10,000 accounts. The most recent grand-opening event generated more than 200 accounts in one day.

PART V

PUBLICITY: LEAST EXPENSIVE MARKETING TOOL MONEY CAN'T BUY

17

Publicity: Advertising That Money Can't Buy

Publicity builds image. Integrating it into the marketing mix. PR and publicity are different. Benefits of publicity. Photos as publicity tools. Three parts of a news release. It's always a story. Features are excellent means to acquire publicity ... but they have a style of their own. Ideas for publicity stories and where to find them.

It looked like a news story on page two of one of the country's largest circulation newspapers. It had a two-column photo, a headline, and a reporter's byline. It was actually a *sidebar* to a 33-column-inch news story about a father who had invented a device to limit his kids' TV viewing.

The sidebar read like an ad even down to the final paragraph that gave the price and an 800 number for placing orders.

The news story alone was a marketer's or publicist's dream come true, but the sidebar was like having a 14-column-inch ad placed smack-dab in the middle of a solid-news page. And this was in a major metropolitan newspaper 2,000 miles away from where the father and his kids lived and the device was sold.

Now consider this: publicity in the form of straight or feature news in established, reputable media is more readily accepted by the public as being true and reliable than the same information in ads, direct-mail pieces, or any form of promotion.

PUBLICITY TO BUILD OR ENHANCE AN IMAGE

A *Wall Street Journal* ad emphasizes the importance of not letting others define the impression of a company—or a person—and of maintaining an untainted image:

> A company would be well-advised to monitor its corporate image almost hourly. Even in less revolutionary times, the image that customers, prospects, stockholders, employees and others have of a company is constantly changing. Prudent companies diligently track these blips and wiggles, then counter or adjust them with a steady stream of corrective communication. . . .

In this particular ad, *The Journal* suggests advertising as the means to accomplish this task, but its people know as well as those in any communications medium that advertising isn't always accepted as unbiased fact, whereas publicity in established, credible media is. If asked to compare, they undoubtedly would acknowledge that advertising is good, but publicity is better.

This chapter will discuss the ingredients necessary to create or re-create the image that adds up to profits. Let's start with a look at publicity in terms of its relationship to marketing.

SLEEPING UNDER THE SAME BLANKET

Marketing is a customized, fit-the-customer mix of advertising *and* direct marketing *and* promotion *and* publicity. As never before, this mixed media marketing must be integrated. Advertising and PR consultant Thomas L. Harris says that he thinks of this integration of publicity and PR in the marketing mix as an engagement, "a pledge to marry sometime in the future . . . and recognize the benefits of integration before we are forced into a shotgun wedding."

Actually, all four components of the mix sleep under the same marketing blanket. However, if you have separate agencies or segregated departments within your company that handle individual marketing functions, don't count on any one of them to jump in and lead the others in the integration process. You're the official matchmaker who must initiate their courtship and walk them through the engagement and marriage. You're the leader who must take responsibility for coordinating your integrated marketing communications program.

PUBLICITY OR ADVERTISING?

The terms *publicity* and *advertising* are often thought of as being synonymous. Or even worse, publicity is often called "free advertising." The simplest explanation for the difference between the two is this: With advertising, you're saying good things about yourself in media space you've paid for, whereas with publicity, someone else is saying those good things about you in space that can't be bought at any price.

Publicity can rightfully be considered advertising that money can't buy, but if a newspaper editor or a television news director ever perceives your publicity release to be a bid for free advertising, it will be slam-dunked into the nearest wastebasket. After all, *paid* advertising underwrites editors' and news directors' salaries.

You might have a hard time finding publicity pros who call themselves marketers. Most will firmly declare, "We're communicators and PR people, not marketers." If they'd only think about it for a minute, they would realize that communications and PR together (with publicity being the most visible part of PR) make up one of the biggest components of marketing. Publicity and PR practitioners need to recognize that they are part—a very large part—of the marketing process. And they are capable of substantially increasing marketing returns by increasing the value of the publicity attained. But they can only do this *if* their client's message is as fully integrated throughout publicity efforts as it is throughout all of the client's advertising, direct marketing, and promotion operations.

PUBLICITY OR PUBLIC RELATIONS?

Also confusing is when publicity professionals give publicity the alias of "public relations" and vice versa. Publicity is the *information* activity of public relations. But PR plays a part in advertising, promotion, and all forms of communication. PR is a great deal more than publicity. It is employee relations, community relations, sponsorships, the tone of an ad or a direct-mail letter, the attitude portrayed by a business, and the way a company's people greet the public in person and on the phone. But even though publicity plays a major part in both PR and marketing and can be one of marketing's most effective tools, it is an entity unto itself.

You may want to post the following notice anywhere marketers for your company operate:

Publicity is a distinct discipline with distinct abilities and accountabilities and should not—must not—be confused with public relations, advertising, promotion, or direct marketing.

Public relations is an important part of doing business, but publicity is the tool, the vehicle, the fourth element that rounds out the MMMC circle.

BENEFITS OF PUBLICITY

Although the process of integrating MMMC uses a variety of techniques, its central characteristic is focus on a single message—a specific benefit, for example. When that message is spread across the mix, the value of publicity noticeably increases. Returns from publicity can come in the form of a boost in sales, a hike in name recognition and remembrance, a heightened or brightened image, and improved public attitude and opinion—all of which increase revenue. Beyond these advantages, publicity has the power to gain the public's attention in a much less intrusive way than other marketing channels. But perhaps the most significant advantage of employing publicity as a marketing tool is that it can do much the same job as advertising for a lot less money.

MORE BENEFITS

Colonel Sanders said in one of his commercials; "One thing you gotta remember when you're dealing with people. They're all different." Businesses are like people. No two are exactly alike. And no two companies can design and conduct their publicity campaigns exactly the same way either. The same goes for their advertising, direct marketing, and promotion efforts.

Their reasons for using publicity may be very similar, however. For a substantial number of businesses, publicity is used to provide information—about a product, a service, or a company. As discussed earlier, publicity is sometimes used strictly to promote image—although all publicity, advertising, direct marketing, and promotion projects some kind of image—warm and friendly or cold and aloof, high-priced or discount, good or not so good. Whatever the reason, most businesses that use publicity do so because it adds a dimension of legitimacy that can't be found through other avenues.

One of the most welcome benefits of publicity is that it adds additional media weight without added expense. (Yes, there are limited preparation and distribution costs, but there are absolutely no space or time charges and only minimal production costs.) Unlike purchased communication instruments, however, there is no guarantee of placement and no control over how the information will be used. There are some things you can do to substantially increase use, however.

As you did with each of the other marketing techniques, review or establish what you want a publicity campaign to achieve and how to go about achieving it. In other words, outline a plan, set goals and a budget, and decide who will be your organization's publicity representative.

WAYS TO ATTRACT PUBLICITY

When a funeral home in Altus, Oklahoma, offered to discount the funeral costs of two slain gang members by one hundred dollars for every firearm turned in, they literally reaped a bumper crop of publicity. The story was picked up by The Associated Press and distributed nationwide. Before deciding on the action, the funeral home talked with the local police chief who said something that made an excellent quote for their news release: "Enough's enough. This has got to stop. We're just killing each other. Talk is cheap—action will tell the tale. All they've got to do is put a gun down." The publicity made those attending the funerals leary of relinquishing their guns at the funerals themselves, but weapons were turned in before and after the services.

Motel 6, the Dallas-based chain of budget motels, took a major news event and used it for its own publicity purposes. A national radio spot used their well-known "leave the light on" slogan and promised to leave the light on for striking baseball players and team owners. The spot encouraged "cash-conscious players and owners to stay in its no-frills rooms in the hopes that the two sides will meet at the ice machine, watch movies together and settle their differences right then and there." Media promptly picked up on Motel 6's "light" pitch and played it out across the country. One of the publicity stories, in *The Dallas Morning News*, quotes a Motel 6 executive as saying: "I think most people have a hard time with baseball players who are whining over salaries that start at six figures. And that's really what Tom [Bodett] is poking a little fun at."

In both of these cases, businesses took events of concern to the public and creatively used those events to attract publicity on their own behalf. In the first case, the publicity had a serious twist—funerals are no time to be lighthearted. In the second case, the events were somewhat serious, but the treatment could be—and was—lighter in application. (A list of ways to attract editors' attention and space in their newspapers appears at the end of this chapter.)

No one can tell you the best way for your company, product, or service to attract publicity, but keep your eyes on the news and your creative hat on your head, and be ready to launch a news or feature story according to news or developments of the moment.

PHOTOS AS PUBLICITY INSTRUMENTS

Photos with captions sometimes make it into print when an accompanying news release doesn't. A good example that appeared in the first section of a major newspaper publicized both a business and a nonprofit group. The headline over the photo of a girl having her hair styled read, "With a fine-toothed comb." The caption beneath the photo read, "Christine Carson, 16, waits patiently while Amphon Boen, co-owner of Jon Scott Salon, combs her hair Sunday. Ms. Boen, her husband, Ron, and three other stylists donated their time to style the hair of about 15 girls from Buckner Baptist Children's home."

WHAT'S PUBLICITY COMING TO?

It's coming to every business of any size that wants it and is willing to change its mindset against traveling the digital and electronic route. You may not need to know how to use a camera to shoot a publicity photo, but no matter how flexible your mindset about high-tech, you'd better know the basics of how to construct a hard copy publicity release or it won't matter which back road you take: it will be long and very rough. In other words, you're out to climb a big mountain, and learning how to produce publicity can be your climbing gear.

If you haven't been collecting news and feature stories as copycat examples, you're strongly urged to begin immediately—to even dig out past editions of print media and clip from them. And *The New Publicity Kit* by Jeanette Smith (John Wiley & Sons, 1995) has an entire chapter of publicity releases and examples from professionals that can be copycatted. Your copycat stockpile may include stories about new products or services, improvements on old ones, expansions, relocations, special events, and new executives, department heads, or board members. You may have collected stories about awards received by a company or its employees, bad press stories that reflect on your industry and can translate to fallout for your business, and good stories that build image, recognition, and name remembrance for a company or industry. There are dozens of other possibilities, but only you can recognize those that might directly or indirectly work for you.

STYLE

Russell Baker, a columnist for *The New York Times,* states the most important rule in publicity writing style:

> Today's reader is too busy to read long sentences.
> Or long paragraphs either.
> So.
> Keep paragraphs—
> —short!

NEVER MIND THE ANSWERS— WHAT ARE THE QUESTIONS?

Everyone who made it through sixth grade knows at least two things about newspapers:

1. They're black and white and read all over.
2. Their stories answer the five W's—*who, what, where, when,* and *why.*

The first statement isn't exactly true any more—color has come to newspapers. But the second rule is as important as it ever was. Take any possible news about your organization—a new service being offered, or a revamp of a previous service, a new executive or member on the board of directors. Any of these can be effectively told as a publicity story by answering those five W's.

Following is an example that just about any straight-news editor would probably welcome and use—if an earth-shaking news story doesn't lock up every inch of extra news space and knock your chances off the page. All five W's—*who, what, where, when,* and *why*—are answered in just four paragraphs.

FOR IMMEDIATE RELEASE
Boulder Builders Names New Chief Executive

Boulder Builders, which has been a well-known construction company in Denver since 1971, named its president, John J. Jones Jr., as its chief executive, completing a management succession plan begun a year ago.

Jones, 47, fills the post left by his father, Johnny Jones, who founded the company and will retire as chief executive but remain as chairman.

The younger Jones has been with the company since its inception and worked his way through various positions, including vice president of operations. He was elected to Boulder Builders' board last year.

"I hate to see my Dad relinquish his spot as president. He started this company and it's served our clients well," said John Jones Jr. "But he deserves some time to travel and enjoy life a little more. And he'll still be around, on the board, for us to lean on."

If this were sent as a publicity release, it would be double-spaced and follow other format requirements, which will be discussed later in this chapter.

Rick Lanning, writing in *Supervision* magazine, tells readers who are seeking publicity to put themselves in the editor's shoes and recognize that the following ingredients are looked for:

- *News value.* Is this information that is different, exciting, helpful, productive, or entertaining to the public?
- *Photo possibilities.* Does the story lend itself to good photo coverage?

The bottom line is that editors are always looking for a good news story. If it is properly presented and has a local angle, it will be welcomed above others. An eye-catching photo with a human-interest angle and a publicity-winning caption may be used to dress up a page even when there's no room for the story itself.

A NEWS STORY IN THREE PARTS

There are three main parts to a straight-news story: the headline, the lead, and the body of the story.

The Headline

The purpose of the headline you write for your release is to catch editors' eyes, to tell them what the release is about, and to entice them to read the entire story. The head that actually appears over the published story will be written by a newspaper staffer, and your release may be rewritten or edited to fit space restrictions.

The mountain of releases an editor receives every day is staggering, so the headline you write must catch an editor's attention and include the most significant point of your story. Try to include something that will interest or benefit the editor's readers, but keep it short and concise.

The Lead

The lead is a one- or two-paragraph summary of the facts in the rest of the story. It answers those five *W*'s and may also answer *How?* (And there are two more *W*'s—*who says?* and *why not?*)

Your lead should always be short, no more than 50 words, but if that doesn't get the job done, use a second, *brief* paragraph. The head and the lead are the most important parts of every straight-news story because they are what must first catch the editor's eye and later, in the newspaper, lasso readers' attention and tease them into reading the rest of the story. Your head and your lead may be all an editor or a reader has the time or desire to read.

The Body Text

The body of your story puts flesh on those five *W*'s with the most important information presented immediately after the lead. Each paragraph that follows decreases in importance in what is called the "inverted pyramid" style of newspaper writing. There's an important reason this style is used—so that editors can cut a story at any point to fit space allocations, without cutting the thrust of the entire story.

TIMELY: ANOTHER ESSENTIAL WORD IN YOUR VOCABULARY

"News is history shot on the wing," shouts *Adweek Magazine* in one of its own ads. Gene Fowler, American journalist and author of such books as *Good-Night Sweet Prince* and *Beau James,* said it, and it's a much catchier way of saying what anyone who's spent any time in a newsroom has heard repeatedly: "Yesterday's news is history." Newspapers (and television and radio) aren't in the business of publishing history. Release your information before an event happens if possible, or immediately after. *Timely* is a word that's even more important than *local* in your new-found publicity vocabulary.

WE INTERRUPT THIS WORKSHOP FOR AN ANNOUNCEMENT

Have you noticed how often the word *story* is used in talking about straight news? There's a reason. News is about facts, but facts alone don't make a story. Facts alone are pretty dull reading. Your job is to flesh out the facts, make them interesting and engaging. Human interest is what most readers—and *all* editors—look for, so load your stories, both straight-news and feature, with human interest.

FEATURES AS PUBLICITY RELEASES

Feature stories require more time and effort to write than straight-news stories, but they are an excellent, no-cost way to build or reinforce image, and they stand a far better chance of being used than a straight-news story. Readers love them, and editors are depending on them more and more to attract and hold readers. Features editors need them to fill space in oversized weekend editions that have sections with deadlines days, even a week, in advance.

Newspaper features are, at heart, news stories. They report facts, but they can also include opinion, something that no true straight-news story can do except when hidden within quotes. What's more, straight news must be printed *now*, not tomorrow or when space permits. Even though a feature story reports facts, its timing is not vital. Features often provide background information about events in the news, but they can be printed days or even weeks and months later.

Feature Style

Feature stories, like fictional short stories, are *not* written in the inverted pyramid style. They start with an attention-grabber and build to a strong, often surprising close.

Straight-news stories must be objective. The reporter's or publicist's opinion may not be included. A feature, on the other hand, may offer a decided point of view and present only one side of an issue. And finally, straight-news stories are never written in the first person, whereas features sometimes use *I* or *we*.

Forget Haystacks—These Needles Are Everywhere

Readers love features because they're loaded with human interest. People love to read stories that give little-known information about famous (and infamous) people or about little-known people who are interesting. Material for features is everywhere—in the experiences of your company, your employees, and your customers. "How-to" information is always a favorite with readers. Even a history of your company can provide fascinating reading if you use anecdotes and quotes that make it come alive.

EDITORS' SELECTIONS CRITERIA

The following is from *The New Publicity Kit* by Jeanette Smith. It lists the things editors consider and check in every news and feature story.

- *Interest value.* If you are deeply interested in the subject, chances are that your enthusiasm will show through and intrigue the reader.
- *Exact facts.* The more facts the better, but be sure they are interesting facts or at least are presented in an interesting way. Statistics are facts, but they are seldom interesting until you put them in context.
- *Strong, moving verbs.* Use as many verbs as you can, and limit adjectives.
- *Basic newspaper style.* Follow standard news-writing rules.
- *Anecdotes.* Use an amusing story to help flesh out a fact, an incident, or a personality.

LOOKING PROFESSIONAL

Whether it's a straight-news release or a feature-news release, the way it looks—the first impression it makes on an editor—may be its death sentence. The first pass through the stack of releases an editor receives each day is based almost solely on appearance. There just isn't time to bother with anything handwritten, typed with a faded ribbon, or printed in an exotic, difficult-to-read typeface.

The New Publicity Kit's appearance guidelines will at least delay a release's death sentence until the headline and perhaps a sentence or two are read.

- Neatness counts. No typos, misspellings, or cross-outs.
- Use standard-size, 8½ × 11-inch paper. Do not use onionskin, colored, or erasable paper.
- Print the release on your business letterhead or, even better, on special "News Release" stationery.
- Use only one side of the paper.
- Leave ample margins: 1½ inches for the side and bottom margins. (Copyeditors use the blank space for corrections and notations.)
- Address your release to the appropriate editor. Even if you deliver it personally, address it to the proper person so that it can be left if he or she is not available at the time you are there.
- If possible, give each newspaper in the same geographical area a release with a different lead, and try to include a local angle in the lead.

- *Never* doubleplant. (*Doubleplanting* means giving the same story to two editors on the same newspaper.)
- Better never than late! Whether your release is used could depend on its timeliness.
- Use paper clips, not staples, to fasten pages together.
- Be sure to keep a dated copy of the release in your files.

A sample of a newspaper release is shown in Exhibit 17-1 to show placement of information that must be included and an acceptable format. Other examples included in Chapter 21 show how professionals set up their releases.

Figure 17.1   Sample format for a newspaper release.
(When no letterhead is available, use plain white business-size paper.)

AAA NETWORK SERVICES
4321 East South Boulevard
Archer City, Nevada, 00001
Telephone 123/098-7654   Fax 123/456-7890

NEWS RELEASE

Contact: Allen Brown   For Immediate Release

AAA Network Services shops for merger partner
Move could make it easier to attract bigger customers

ARCHER CITY, NEVADA—AAA Network Services announced today (date in parentheses) it is exploring a possible merger that will boost the company's ability to sell its interactive network services to larger businesses over a broader geographic area.

The announcement was made at a meeting that included city officials, company executives and employees.

"When Senator Robert Dole said, 'The best way to cope with change is to help create it,' our executive board decided we'd look into creating a change that would help us attract bigger customers," said Joe Johns, AAA Network's president and CEO.

— more —

Figure 17.1 Continued

AAA Network shops for merger partner—2-2-2

"After a great deal of research and study we recognized that a merger would benefit both partners by expanding our sales area and giving us both a greater number of salespersons to attract more and larger consumers."

A company interested in such a merger could come from almost any industry interested in technology, Johns said.

AAA Network Services specializes in advertising, media services and interactive marketing. It is well known throughout southwest Nevada for its annual drive to collect computers to give to area schools, which then distribute them to needy students.

# # #

EXPOSED!

As your company's publicity practitioner, you needn't be a photographer, but you do need to know the requirements that photo editors place on the pictures they use in their newspapers. You need to understand how to stage photos and pose people, because publicity photos *are* staged. They have to be, because publicity is seldom a spontaneous news development. But don't repeat that out loud in a newsroom. Editors lump staging photos in with making up quotes for a story.

There are only a few simple rules for arranging publicity photos:

- Don't place people in front of windows. The backlighting will wipe out their faces and features, making silhouettes of them.
- Choose attractive but simple backgrounds. Put a dark-skinned or dark-clothed person against a light background. Don't place people who are wearing busy prints in front of busy backgrounds.
- Choose the right format for the medium—vertical for newspapers, horizontal if cable might also use a stillphoto.
- Make your shots visually interesting. Try to have people doing something—anything except eating, that is. A lineup of people looking into the camera or watching someone sign something is an absolute taboo. And keep the number of people in a single photo to one or two—three at most. And be sure to give your picture a local twist. For newspapers in particular, but for any

medium that attracts only a narrow geographical audience, *local* is the most important word in publicity.

25 WAYS TO ATTRACT PUBLICITY

1. Restructure the company so that an early retirement program is available.
2. Announce a hiring policy, and cite the number of local layoffs in a recent time period.
3. Hire a well-known individual.
4. Hire a little-known individual with unique qualifications.
5. Conduct a contest—the best way your company can help a local school, for example.
6. Acquire a contract for a new account, an installation, or construction job.
7. Open an operations hub in conjunction with current operations.
8. Develop a new way for your company to cut back expenses.
9. Do a profile of your oldest employee—either in age or seniority—with his or her ideas about ways to retain a job.
10. Conduct an employee survey about the best attributes of companies as employers.
11. Name a milestone and cite its significance.
12. Install new equipment, the use of which will benefit customers.
13. Solicit the public's advice about ways to_____ . (Fill in the blank.)
14. Offer to provide the three *A*'s—advice, advocacy, answers—to business majors at a free seminar.
15. Announce a job-sharing plan for your employees who wish to work part-time.
16. Launch a new service.
17. Conclude an old service.
18. Move to a new location.
19. Complete a merger.
20. Announce substantial sales increases.
21. Announce a plan for increasing security for clients or shoppers while they're visiting your business.
22. Team up with a competitor to _____ . (Fill in the blank.)
23. Declare a new use for an old product or service.
24. Create an enjoyable, pleasant use for your product or service.
25. Include the mayor on your board of directors.

18

Broadcast and Narrowcast Publicity— The VNR

Narrowcasting versus *broad*casting. Publicity in the electronic age. The five VNR fundamentals. Elements of a VNR, including billboards, briefing, feed menu, anchor lead-in, anchor tag, keys, secondary menu, and b-roll. Notification, distribution, and use reports.

"For every reader who dies today," says Edward A. Morrow, "a viewer is born." In other words: *There goes the printed word*. Morrow is a past president of the American Booksellers Association, and he made the remark at the annual meeting of the Association of American Publishers in 1995. He also said that, yes, electronics will replace the book. Scary, huh? Scary enough that *The New York Times* reported that several of the book publishers at the meeting were visibly dismayed by Morrow's comment. One closed his eyes wearily, another shook his head, and another dropped his face into his hand. Even more disconcerting was the remark Morrow made that was meant to reassure them. According to *The Times*, "Printed books won't disappear, he said, but, like vinyl records, they will become collector's items in just a few years."

BACK TO THE PRESENT

Guess what? Like books, printed news releases haven't disappeared yet, either—except in television news rooms. This chapter is about getting you up to speed in producing television news releases, and you'll learn a whole new language. In this chapter we stop using words and talk in letters of the alphabet—telling you that if you want good VPR on HDTV, you'll have to use VNRs, EPKs, perhaps hold an occasional SMT, and then use a VMS or ETS to check them out.

Actually, don't sit around and wait for HDTV—High-Density Television—it, like the demise of books, may not happen for awhile. But you can get excellent publicity returns on narrowcast cable stations, and in many cases on commercial *broad*cast TV.

The meanings of the alphabet soup above: VPR = video public relations; VNR = video news release; EPK = electronic press kit; SMT = satellite media tour; VMS = video monitoring services; ETS = electronic tracking service.

IT'S NARROWCASTING TODAY—*BROAD*CASTING WAS YESTERDAY

To unconfuse you a little, programming on cable channels is *narrowcast*, according to the narrowly defined interests of each channel's audience, much as magazines and radio stations have come to focus on the narrow interests of highly vertical audiences. But commercial and public television *broad*casts to the broad interests of its mass audiences.

And about SMT—that's short for satellite media tours, and there are also satellite news conferences, as well as video conferencing. We'll explain and compare these procedures, strategies, and techniques later in the chapter.

PUBLICITY IN THE ELECTRONIC AGE

High tech really slammed down on publicists seeking television and radio publicity, but many professionals and small-business do-it-yourselfers haven't fully awakened to the fact yet. No longer can publicists sit down at a keyboard and bat out a newspaper news release, then circulate it to broadcast news departments. Television news just won't use it. It's the equivalent of junk mail, and some television newspeople are insulted by the appearance that they play second fiddle to newsprint.

VNRs (video news releases) and RNRs (radio news releases) are more complex and more costly than the old way, but with cable's narrowcasting there are substantial indications that small businesses *can* afford to circulate their publicity messages via television and often with such great success that the cost becomes incidental.

VIDEO NEWS RELEASES

A VNR is the television equivalent of the long-standing press release. To get the attention of television newsrooms, VNRs must closely resemble locally produced news stories, not commercials—exactly as is the case with print publicity releases to print media. VNRs can provide a variety of visual elements, ranging from full reports to just interviews and/or supporting video. A good VNR can satisfy the needs of the business submitting it, the station receiving it, and the audience viewing it.

That explanation, and much of the information that follows, comes from VNR-1, a Dallas-based company with offices and production facilities in Los Angeles, New York, Chicago, Tampa, Atlanta, Washington, D.C., and London.

Newsrooms want and need clear-cut storylines. Complicated storylines with too much detail will be passed over in the daily rush. The preferred length of a VNR is one and one-half minutes, and the chances a newsroom will shorten the report and remove recognition of the business's name and message increases almost proportionally with every second over the minute-and-a-half mark. Since the only purpose for a VNR is to get your company's message on the air, it pays to pay attention not only to length but to all the components required to make acceptable VNRs.

VNR Fundamentals

Television newsrooms demand five fundamentals of their reporter's stories—and they demand no less in a VNR. These fundamentals are:

1. Topicality
2. Localization
3. Timeliness
4. Humanization
5. Visuality

The first four are also demanded in newspaper and radio newsrooms as well. The fifth fundamental is required exclusively by television.

1. *Topicality.* Topicality is by far the most important element in your VNR. VNR reports that may fail every other means of good construction may be aired simply because they offer new material on a "hot subject."
2. *Timeliness.* A VNR's usage can be greatly enhanced by timeliness. Stories timed to seasons of the year, government rulings, new

laws, new social trends, and spot news can all play a positive role in airings.

3. *Localization.* A television newsroom is dedicated to covering local news. In terms of a national release, your story needs to be relative to audiences both in Bangor and Biloxi. TV news management has long instilled in reporters, producers, and assignment editors the need to find a local angle for every story.

4. *Humanization.* If your VNR is distributed beyond the local market, you cannot produce a separate report for every market. However, by humanizing your VNRs, you can achieve a great degree of localization because *as an audience, Americans have a lot in common as people.* Any news story—in either video or print format—is irrelevant if it cannot show how the story affects people. Newsrooms want people stories. Slick graphics, aerial shots, and incredible statistics mean very little without a human angle.

   The best VNRs start and end with people. Using people to "bookend" the story helps frame the point of the story. The logic is simple. Viewers in Bangor and Biloxi do have one thing in common—the need to know what the story may mean to them. That point is best made by showing viewers real people they can relate to and be affected by.

5. *Visuality.* Sometimes, based only on the fact that it is strong visually, a television news department may choose to do a story.

Tell the Truth

The rule that applies to all other publicity efforts also applies to VNRs. Unsubstantiated facts, opinions expressed as facts, exaggerations, paid actors or endorsements, falsely portrayed video (accurate and identified reenactments are not included), and false interviews have no room in your VNR.

Keep It Absolutely Basic

Cover only two to three points. It's a natural desire to give viewers *all* the points in a story, such as all nine things to check when choosing a pharmacist. But television news people know it's impossible to hold viewers' attention or their memory beyond one or two (at the most three) issues or points.

There's an old joke about television news reporting. If Moses had come down from the mountain with the Ten Commandments today, TV news would report it this way: Today Moses came down from the mountain with the Ten Commandments. The three most important are . . .

Elements of a VNR

The Written Release
The first element in a VNR tape or feed is a written release, says Jack Trammell of VNR-1. The word *release* in this case has a completely different meaning, however, than when prefaced by *news* or *press*.

This written piece is a statement that releases—that is, gives permission—for the video and interviews within the VNR to be used by television newsrooms without restriction. It is placed at the front of the VNR production or feed and is the first thing the editors see. It tells stations that the following video news release is for their free and unrestricted use and is produced by ABC Public Relations on behalf of its client the Acme Company.

Stations have come to expect such a written statement as part of their agreement to use the VNR. It assures them that they will not be legally bound to pay for or notify anyone of its use. Restrictions within the permission-to-use release may cause the station to disregard the VNR altogether rather than to conform with what they construe as tampering with their freedom to make their own decisions.

The station must be told clearly which organization(s) produced and/or backs the VNR. Listing your company's name or the name of the publicity agency is not enough.

On occasion, a VNR may have a specific life span. In those instances, the release should include a recommended air date. However, be aware that such recommendations could restrict potential airings later. Newsrooms are well known for waiting weeks before airing stories they perceive as "evergreen" or timeless.

A contact name or number should be given in the release for newsrooms to call if they have questions or problems. If your VNR has a wider than local or regional distribution, you should remember that many stations may be several time zones away from your office. So, be sure to include an after-hours number since the VNR may not be aired until evening hours.

Written Release Example
The following VNR is provided for your free and unrestricted use by the Acme Corporation/Dallas, Texas.

For information concerning the content of this report, contact:

Jody Johns
Acme Corporation
214/123-4567
214/456-7800 (after hours)

The Billboards
In the world of VNR production, the word *billboards* has a different meaning, too. They are electronically typed or "keyed" messages used to quickly

explain and identify video elements to a reporter or producer who often scans the videotape at a high speed. Billboards may require more than several "pages" of screens. However, the shorter, the better. Specific types of billboards are discussed later.

Editor's Note Briefing

The editor's note briefing (also known as a "storyline briefing" or "producer briefing") is your first and best opportunity to get the interest of the reporter or producer viewing your VNR. In that respect, you might compare it to the headline on your print news release.

It is here that it is most important to explain the following:

- Reason or "hook" for the story (for example, newly released study)
- Sources (authoritative statistics and interviews)
- Content (how information will be illustrated, including human angle)
- Direction (what is the point of the story and what is the practical benefit to the viewer)

Editor's Note Example

Editor's Note: "VCRs are changing the way Americans live"

The latest National Consumer Poll shows VCRs are now in 83% of American homes and sales are expected to increase 50% in the coming Christmas season. The poll also shows VCRs have already greatly changed American lifestyles. This report explains the practical effects of VCRs revealed by this study and explains the straight facts every American family should know. The first interview is with Mr. John Smith, a Homeowner League researcher who argues that most Americans are VCR-ignorant.

The second interview is with Henry Hart of the American VCR Makers Association who believes this lack of consumer awareness can be cured in five easy steps. Our report also visits the home of Frank Lee, an average American father who demonstrates his new knowledge of VCRs and shows new footage of the latest high-tech VCR.

The point of this story is to give the viewer practical information he/she can use with their VCRs. With the growing number of VCRs in homes, we believe this information is invaluable, particularly during the Christmas season.

Feed Menu

The feed menu quickly lists the reports and their length as well as support elements to be included on the VNR feed. News editors will use the feed menu to quickly locate and time the video they need.

For tape distribution only indicates separate audio channels to aid the editor. This is not necessary in satellite feeds since the actual transmission usually merges the two channels into a monaural signal.

Feed Menu Example

This file or tape contains:

1. Full track report (1:21)
   (FOR TAPE DISTRIBUTION ONLY):
   Narration track—Channel 1
   Natural sound track—Channel 2
2. Natural sound report (NAT SOT) (1:21)
3. Additional b-roll
   A. Average American family with VCR
   B. VCR manufacturing
   C. VCR in use
   D. National Consumer Poll Study
   E. VCRs being sold
4. Additional interviews
   A. John Smith deplores VCR ignorance
   B. John Smith details how survey was conducted
   C. Henry Hart of the American VCR Makers Assoc. describes five steps to understanding VCRs
   D. Henry Hart on impact of VCRs in American life
   E. Jim Lee explains frustrations when operating VCR
5. Additional animation/graphics
   A. Computer animation of VCRs at work
   B. Logo graphics
      1. National Consumer Poll logo
      2. Homeowner Research League logo
      3. American VCR Makers Assoc. logo
   C. News graphic chart showing rising sales of VCRs from 1986 to present.

Suggested Anchor Lead-in

A lead-in is simply what the anchor says to introduce the VNR in its report form. It will not be used if the newsroom decides to use only some of the pictures or interviews.

Almost every station newsroom will rewrite whatever is submitted. However, it does give you the opportunity to form the story. (And in the case of some cable systems and syndications and smaller market broadcast TV newsrooms, which usually are short on newsroom personnel, your lead-in may be used as presented.)

Lead-ins generally run no more than ten to twenty seconds in length. Any good producer knows that only crisp, impactive, and active writing gets and keeps the attention of the viewer. The suggested lead-in should include the most effective facts in the VNR, written in simple declarative sentences.

Suggested Anchor Lead-in Example

83% of American homes now have VCRs. A new national study says that most of us do not understand what to do with them. James White reports consumer confusion has prompted one VCR company to issue a consumer advisory that can offer you some practical help.

Suggested Anchor Tag

Anchor tags are designed by newsrooms to allow greater "anchor involvement" in news stories. These on-camera summaries immediately follow the package. Anchor tags can help provide phone numbers (often toll-free) and addresses for more viewer information. Stations prefer telephone numbers over addresses because they do not want to be involved in forwarding mail.

Verbatim Text of Report (Optional)

On occasion, the entire text of the VNR can be printed, including the verbatim text of any interviews within the report. Styles may vary but the purpose is the same—to give the producer the greatest flexibility to edit the report and to give the reporter an ability to record his own narration in place of the original VNR reporter.

Verbatim texts can also be used to phonetically spell difficult-to-pronounce words. They also help reinforce your central message to reporters and producers, who will often use the text to create simple voice-over tape or teasers within the newscast.

Suggested Identification Keys

An often neglected detail in VNR production is the creation of "keys" or the electronic type used to identify interviews or pictures. These keys are also known in many stations as "Chyrons," "supers" (superimpose), or "teles" (tel-ees). *Chyron* is a registered trademark of a key computer manufacturing company.

Again, productions that have keys already on the video, in an attempt to force their use, are virtually never aired because the font style does not match the local station's font. This only contributes to the appearance of an externally-produced report, which is unacceptable to most stations.

Rather than placing the keys on the video, VNR-1 supplies a list of what should be typed below interviews and locations. If used sparingly, keys can not only give proper identification but also can be a discreet way to air the name of your company and/or reinforce the company's message.

Many VNRs never mention the company they are trying to promote but depend totally on the use of keys for identification with the report.

Station newsrooms have been more accepting of this form of accreditation than any other production element. Generally, newsrooms believe revealing the name and title of the company interview is part of *their* job and journalistic responsibility in fully identifying the source of their interviews. There are two basic rules for keys:

- They must be simple.
- They must use correct spelling.

If you provide keys, list them as they would appear on the report in chronological order. Each key is usually identified with the label *KEY*.

```
Incorrect:
    KEY:  VCR Making
          Anderson VCR Plant
          VCR Division
          Acme Manufacturing
          Anderson, NJ
Correct:
    KEY:  Acme Manufacturing
          Anderson, NJ
```

Keys can be used to identify locations, individuals, and the name of the reporter. Keys appear on screen long enough to be read slowly. The exact times in which the key is to be used and the length of time is determined by the producer once the report is finished.

Be careful not to have too many keys in the report. Graphics, or art/animation with nomenclatures, which may be included in the report, do not count as keys.

Key List Example

```
KEY:  Acme Manufacturing
      Anderson, New Jersey

KEY:  Dr. John Smith
      Researcher
      Homeowner League

KEY:  Frank Lee
      VCR Owner

KEY:  Henry Hart
      American VCR Makers Assoc.

KEY:  James White Reporting

(Total Report Length: 1.21)
```

Other VNR Elements

Billboard for Pre-tracked Report
This type of billboard simply advises the editor, reporter, or producer that the fully tracked (reporter and natural sound), ready-to-go report is about to appear next.

Included on this advisory is the total running length of the report. In the instance of *tape distribution only,* it is important to designate which channel of audio contains the reporter track and which contains the natural sound track.

In tape distribution, audio channels can be separated by the newsroom editor and a full natural-sound-only re-feed is generally not needed.

> Billboard for pre-track report example:
> (satellite, standardized)
>
> Full track report to follow:
> Total running time: 1:21
>
> Billboard for pre-track report example:
>
> Full track report to follow:
> Total running time: 1:21
>
> Channel One: reporter track
> Channel Two: natural sound track
>
> *(The digital countdown for the report now begins)*
>
> Billboard for anchor tag example:
>
> For more information (or a free brochure) about VCRs, call the American VCR Makers Association, at 1-800-NEW-VCRs. That's 1-800-NEW-VCRs.
>
> Billboard for natural sound-only report example:
> (standardized)
>
> This billboard is used for satellite-only distribution of the VNR
>
> Natural sound only report to follow:
> Total running time: 1:21
>
> (The digital countdown for the natural sound report now begins)

Secondary Menu
The secondary menu is an additional reminder to the editor or producer or reporter of what is still to follow on the VNR feed.

Secondary Menu Example

To follow:

1. Additional b-roll
2. Additional interviews
3. Additional animation/graphics
4. Contacts for more information

Billboards for Additional B-roll

The billboards for additional b-roll follow the secondary menu billboard and details what raw footage pictures are covered. (B-roll will be explained later in this chapter.)

Billboard for Additional B-roll Example

Additional b-roll

A. Average American family with VCR
B. VCR in use
C. VCR manufacturing
D. National Consumer Poll Study Graphic
E. VCRs being sold

Billboard for Additional Interviews

This type of billboard outlines the interview points that are not included in the original report. These interviews should be short and to the point. The general rule is that the shorter, more pointed, and more animated the interview segment, the more likely it is to be used.

Some organizations use the additional interview segment at the end for interviews that may have more political than practical value in the VNR. This allows more open use of company spokespersons without the danger of damaging the full report.

Billboard for Additional Interviews Example

Additional Interviews

A. Dr. John Smith deplores VCR ignorance.
B. Dr. John Smith details how survey was conducted.
C. Henry Hart describes five steps to understanding VCRs.
D. Henry Hart explains Association's Impact on VCRs in American life.

At the beginning of each interview, a short separate billboard should fully identify the interviewee. This is another opportunity to reinforce your organization's identity with the producer or reporter. Some businesses add a one-line explanation of the gist of the interview or the actual question.

Billboard for Graphics/Animation

Not all VNRs have or need graphics or animation. If graphics are offered, a short explanation of what they show and each one's source is helpful. If animation is offered, a short explanation of what the animation reveals is needed. A total running length is often helpful to editors.

Billboard for Graphics/Animation Example

VCR graphics/animation
> Total Time: 33 sec (for animation only)
> (This <u>animation</u> shows the inner workings of a VCR in operation <u>OR</u> this <u>graphic</u> shows the rising national sales of VCRs based on statistics from the National Figures Assoc.)

"For More Information" Billboard

Often reporters have additional questions about the information presented in the VNR. Jack Trammell says VNR-1 highly recommends that your organization duplicate the data provided earlier in the written release and provide two primary media contacts with telephone numbers at the end of the feed. Since many VNRs are reviewed after business hours, it is especially important to leave night numbers. Your personnel should be ready to receive calls and be prepared to work quickly for reporters on a deadline.

"For More Information" Billboard Example

FOR MORE INFORMATION CONTACT:
Sarah Smith, Spokesperson
American VCR Makers Association
(212) 123-4567
(212) 456-7890 (after hours)

Dr. John Doe, Researcher
Homeowner League
(613) 765-4321
(613) 098-7654 (after hours)

One of the first questions a reporter asks of a VNR is whether it can be localized. This is a great opportunity to get the reporter fully involved by providing information on how to quickly and easily reach local contacts. Advise these contacts in advance and list them with local phone numbers (including after-hours numbers), or provide a single media contact who has a list of those numbers readily at hand.

Localization Billboard Example

LOCAL VCR CONTACTS
> If you wish to further localize this report, contact those listed for more information or check the following list for a contact nearest you:

VCR CONTACTS
Fred Smith   (312) 765-4321
VCRs Int'l   (312) 098-7654 (after hours)
Chicago, IL

Cindy Brown   (918) 123-4567
Former President   (918) 456-7890 (after hours)
American VCR Makers
Los Angeles, CA

"For Technical Information" Billboard

On rare occasions, VNR satellite feeds and distributed videotapes have technical difficulties with audio and/or video. Because of this possibility and the possibility of technical questions from a station's engineering department, VNR-1 recommends a final billboard that lists the transmission site, telephone numbers, and contact personnel. Contact personnel are often engineers at the VNR uplink site from which the tape is being played. You can easily obtain this information in advance.

"For Technical Information" Billboard Example

FOR TECHNICAL INFORMATION REGARDING THIS FEED, CONTACT:
Frank James, Chief Engineer
Central Satellite Uplink Company
Telephone: (212) 123-4567

End of Feed Billboards/Standby for Re-feed (Standardized)

This final billboard advises engineers who are rolling the recording tapes at television newsroom satellite downlinks that the feed is complete.

End of Feed Billboard Example

END OF FEED

The last billboard simply advises stations that the entire VNR production is to be re-fed. This allows stations that are aware they began recording the feed late to know they can still catch the first part of the feed.

Standby for Re-feed Billboard Example

STANDBY FOR RE-FEED

B-roll

It's essential for you to understand a term that's a very important part of all of television's alphabet language. It's often a key add-on to a VNR. It's called *b-roll*. Here's VNR-1's explanation:

B-roll is literally any video in the story which is not graphics or an interview.

It is an old term from news-film days when interviews were edited to a roll of film marked "A" and pictures were edited to a roll of film marked "B."

The films were played simultaneously to complete the news report on air.

Complete VNR productions often give additional b-roll following the package to stations to assist in re-editing or to supply video promotion or "teases" often aired just before commercials to promote the upcoming story.

NOW YOU KNOW THE PATTERN FOR A VNR . . .

Now that you know the basic pattern for a VNR, you must ask yourself if you have the "goods" to cut it.

Jack Trammell, who heads VNR-1, makes some absolutely essential points. He says, "Producers, writers, photographers, and editors should all have one thing in common—recent *broadcast news experience.*"

He also points out that as VNRs have come more in demand by television newsrooms, and VNR production has increased to meet the demand, so have the number of companies claiming to be able to produce them. The danger is that many production companies are commercial groups that do not know the news business or understand the curious logic of what makes news "news" for television news producers, or they are industrial video groups (now calling themselves "internal audience" producers) who have never worked in a newsroom and therefore are unable to produce broadcast-quality material. Both groups have produced disastrous VNRs that often result in a company's reluctance to try VNRs again.

A VNR production company must have newswriters, producers, photographers and crew, an editor, and access to actors if necessary (although 99 out of 100 times, actors are not used in VNRs). Most importantly, *they must have broadcast news experience.*

What you can contribute is your presence at the shoot—and a bottle of aspirin! Actually, you probably will want to bring along a portable telephone, a stopwatch, and a microcassette recorder to co-record interviews for references back at the office.

COUNTING YOUR VNRS AFTER THEY'RE HATCHED

After all that effort and work, you distributed it and saw it on a local station. But you also sent it to stations across the region that your business serves, and you want to know—how did it play in Peoria? And Bloomington, and Springfield, and Decatur—as well as New York City?

Exhibits 18.1 and 18.2 are consolidated charts to give you helpful information about various methods of notification and distribution, including both positives and negatives about specific methods. (Thanks, again, to VNR-1 for the information in these charts.)

ELECTRONIC "CLIPPING SERVICES"

Remember when we warned you back at the beginning of the chapter that we planned to teach you to talk in letters of the alphabet? *ETS* and *VMS*

Exhibit 18.1 VNR-1 roundup of pertinent information about ways to notify television stations, including positives and negatives.

Notification

	Facsimile Machine	Telephone	Mail	Newswire
Guidelines	1 sheet	Keep brief	Keep brief	Keep brief
Distributor	Producer/ Agency	Producer/ Agency	Producer/ Agency	Producer/ News Agency
Positive	Immediate Simple to use	Immediate May gain rapport w/editors	Simple to use	Immediate Monitored routinely in newsrooms
Negative	May irritate stations due to overloaded fax machines	Regular or continuous calls may irritate news personnel	Slow. Requires more advanced planning. Easily misplaced. Client cannot make last-minute changes.	Risk of being lost in the masses of incoming newsroom wire

Exhibit 18.2   VNR-1 classifies distribution methods
with their positives and negatives.

Distribution

	Satellite	Hand Delivery	Mail	Overnight Delivery
Distributor	Producer/ Satellite Distributor	Local Reps	Producer/ Agency/ Client	Producer/ Agency
Positive	Immediate Virtually all stations have satellite capability	One-on-one delivery may further localization of story	Can be handled by agency or client. Can be kept & aired at a later date	Immediate
Negative	Stations often have high satellite traffic	Cumbersome Imprecise delivery may stifle reg- ional launches	Often mis- placed or delayed. Can not be up- dated. Time consuming Expensive Labor intensive	Very Expensive

are other terms you may want to know and use if you want to check where your news was used. Yes, there are electronic "clipping" services just as there are clipping services that check print coverage.

ETS stands for electronic tracking service, and VMS is short for video monitoring services (which is also the corporate name of a company that offers VMS).

"Introducing NewsAlert. The electronic clipping service for the 21st Century," says a direct-mail piece from Burrelle's/VMS NewsAlert. As the flyer says, it's a service that allows you to "access news about your company, your products and about your competitors, every business day by simply turning on your computer."

"Based on your specifications, NewsAlert does all the searching for you, delivering a customized press and broadcast clipping report right to your PC."

The flyer goes on to advise that "not only is NewsAlert a comprehensive clipping service but also an 'early warning' device, alerting you to important news stories that can affect your company or organization."

There is also another system called VeriCheck.

THEN THERE IS MEDIALINK

Medialink, the world's largest provider of video public relations, actually monitors the exact times, stations, station affiliations, number of seconds your VNR ran at each station, and the audience numbers for the news segment in question. All this information is compiled and sent to you in a report. Medialink's president, Larry Moskowitz, tells how it's done:

> "SIGMA," Nielsen's electronic tracking system, stamps a custom code onto the invisible portion of your [VNR]. Once the encoded video has been distributed to stations via satellite or cassette, Nielsen de-coders nationwide search local and national newscasts for your project's code and reports back any findings.

Exhibit 18.3 is an example of a report showing not only the list of stations where the VNR was used, their locations, and dates and times it was used, but it also gives each station's rank and data about its audience.

There's another way to locate usage information. You can attempt to round it up yourself. This is definitely not recommended. There is no reliable method to do this, and each means for gathering the information will be strongly resented by busy newsroom personnel who probably don't even have the data about when your VNR ran. The positives and negatives are shown in Exhibit 18.4, which was compiled by VNR-1.

MORE ABOUT TV'S ALPHABET SOUP

Yes, there's an industry-wide alphabet soup, but it's important that you understand that each newsroom may also have its own language that is completely different from the language used in the newsroom across town. You may have to ask from time to time what is meant by a certain alphabet designation. Only widely used and widely understood expressions are explained here.

Exhibit 18.3 A report showing use of a VNR
for "Vespa" Flying Insect Sting Shots

Project Station Specifics					Project: "VESPA" Flying Insect Sting Shots
STATION	**MARKET**	**RANK**	**DATE**	**TIME**	**AUDIENCE**
SCI & TECH SATELLITE NEWS	JAPANESE CABLE		10/1/95	Varioius	300,000
WNBC (NBC)	NEW YORK	1	7/27/95	5:00 PM	620,000ETS (:06)
KABC (ABC)	LOS ANGELES	2	7/28/95	4:00 PM	614,000 ETS (:56)
KCAL (IND)	LOS ANGELES	2	7/27/95	3:00 PM	200,000 ETS (:26)
KNBC (NBC)	LOS ANGELES	2	7/25/95	4:00 PM	482,000 ETS (:05)
KTLA (WB)	LOS ANGELES	2	7/25/95	10:00 PM	514,000 ETS (:55)
KTLA (WB)	LOS ANGELES	2	7/25/95	12:00 AM	87,000 ETS (:42)
WMAQ (NBC)	CHICAGO	3	7/25/95	4:00 PM	145,000 ETS (:26)
WFMZ (IND)	PHILADELPHIA	4	8/4/95	7:00 PM	10,000 ETS (:38)
WFMZ (IND)	PHILADELPHIA	4	8/4/95	10:00 PM	7,000 ETS (:40)
WMGM (NBC)	PHILADELPHIA	4	7/28/95	6:00PM	3,000 (Phone call confirmation)
KGO (ABC)	SAN FRANCISCO	5	7/25/95	11:30 AM	65,000 ETS (:36)
WHDH (NBC)	BOSTON	6	7/25/95	6:00 PM	376,000 ETS (:24)
WHDH (NBC)	BOSTON	6	7/26/95	5:00 AM	66,000 ETS (:53)
WUSA (CBS)	WASH, D.C.	7	7/28/95	6:00 PM	320,000 ETS (1:17)
WJBK (FOX)	DETROIT	9	8/1/95	7:00 AM	70,000 RTV
WSB (ABC)	ATLANTA	10	7/25/95	5:30 PM	216,000 ETS (:38)
WSB (ABC)	ATLANTA	10	7/26/95	5:30 AM	87,000 ETS (:09)
WSB (ABC)	ATLANTA	10	7/26/95	6:30 AM	91,000 ETS (:24)

Exhibit 18.4   Verification-of-Use Methods

Verification

	Telephone	Mail Response Cards	Nielsen VNR Survey	Burrelle's
Positive	Immediate verification	Inexpensive	Structured Tested National Standard Survey	Neutral Gives broad- transcript summary
Negative	Often irritates newsroom On duty personnel may not be aware of airing	Stations rarely return cards and often mistake data	Polls give sample of total U.S. news directors surveyed	Several days for first con- clusive data

			Luce Press Clippings	Video Moni- toring Serv.
Positive			Neutral	Can provide taped air checks Quick response w/ air times
Negative			Takes sev- eral days for first conclu- sive data	More expensive Limited detailed information

For example, there are SOTs. SOTs (or sound on tape) are also known in radio as *actualities*. SOTs are the interviews in your VNR. SOTs included in a story must be short and to the point. SOTs are often the only time a company representative may appear in the story.

Additional SOTs following the actual report are often provided in VNRs for several reasons, one of which is that they give news stations an additional option in editing.

One major opinion is that an SOT can help get your story aired as a simple voice-over graphics or interview only, rather than being scrapped entirely because the news producer may have interest in the story but no time for a fully packaged report.

19

Press Conferences: In Person or by Satellite

Hometown business news conferences don't mirror those in Washington. When to hold one. Advice from a pro. Practice makes better. The spokesperson. Make a list; set the day and hour. Invitations. Handouts. Photogs. Room setup. Satellite conferences and media tours. Satellite costs. News conference press kits.

Anyone who's ever been part of conducting a press conference knows the feeling: If we have it, will they come? And if they come, will it turn into head-to-head combat?

A lot of our concepts and fears of "them"—the news media—are Washington based and Washington generated. Not many weeks go by when there isn't a televised press conference, shown in all its splendor, emanating from the White House.

Apparently the sweat and fears reach even to the presidential level, according to a cartoon by Doug Borgstedt that appeared in *Editor & Publisher* magazine. Unnamed likenesses of President and Mrs. Clinton are shown in their bed. He's sitting, eyes wide. She's tucked in and presumably abruptly awakened. He says, "What a terrible dream! I dreamt I held a press conference and nobody showed up!" She replies, "That's no dream dear—that was a prediction."

Washington news conferences, widely reported and picked apart in and out of the media, are what has formed beliefs about the manner in which *all* news conferences take place.

THE REAL WORLD IS A DIFFERENT WORLD

That, however, is not at all how it is in the real world of hometown business news conferences. And a person whose company is paid to train businesspeople in how to conduct themselves at news conferences verifies this fact. Former television news reporter and producer Jack Trammell, now production supervisor for VNR-1, says that 90 percent of media interviews are not hostile at all, that in most cases "all they [reporters] really want to do is a kind of 'how-great-your-company-is' story."

But, because of false impressions acquired from television about the media and about news conferences, what might be a positive experience turns out to be "an irritating, exhausting, nervous nightmare for the executive," says Trammell.

Of course, not all executives' fears come from watching televised news carnivals. Some of it comes from what most people carry around inside themselves—a fear of failing to look good and act with confidence in front of an audience. They become what TV news people call "deer in the headlights" when a camera is turned on them. In other words, they lack media skills.

But luckily, anyone and everyone can learn the necessary skills. No talent is called for, only the ability to learn a few skills that improve as they're practiced. That's why it's imperative that you hold your own media training sessions for your own people. Later in this chapter we'll go into more detail.

FANTASY REALISM

The technology revolution has changed the *look* of news conferences. It hasn't changed when or why they're called. There still are on-the-ground, in-person press conferences. (Sorry! We should call them *news* conferences in deference to those in the broadcast field.) Then there are the new-tech variety.

The first kind pretty much follows the years-old standard format, except for such things as the equipment provided for reporters if a nearby press room is furnished (computers replace typewriters, for instance). But the second—the new-tech kind—appears to be a whole new ballgame. In actuality, however, the same basics apply to both types. We'll look at those basics and then examine new-tech applications as they presently exist.

First, though, you should know *when* and *if* a news conference is called for. If you hold one that doesn't offer a lot of meat—with potatoes, and gravy, and perhaps a little dessert—your publicity story not only won't make the evening news or the morning newspaper, but you won't make a single media friend.

SIT DOWN WITH A PRO

We've asked Joseph B. McNamara, executive vice president and general manager of Edelman Public Relations Worldwide, to sit down with us and tell us some of the most important aspects of deciding when, where, how, and *if* a news conference is called for. His experience and credentials make the information he offers essential, indispensable, and invaluable. (Edelman Public Relations Worldwide has offices in nine U.S. cities and 11 countries—from England to China to Australia.)

Is It Time to Call a News Conference?

You learned as a kid not to cry wolf if you wanted people to continue to believe you. Don't cry wolf now, either, by scheduling an insignificant conference. Your credibility—and the future acceptance of you and your company by the media—is at stake.

Don't ever ask the media to spend their time (they'll say it's wasting their time) attending a session the content of which could, and should, be presented in a news release or a VNR.

As McNamara says, the decision about *if* a news conference should be called depends upon whether it's newsworthy enough to justify calling reporters together from across town, through traffic, with all the expense involved, to attend something that they supposedly won't be able to really understand the full impact of without being there.

McNamara also stresses that this is something strictly for reporters, so "don't pack the audience with employees and well-wishers to make it a love fest so that no matter what the spokesperson says, everybody thinks and indicates this is just wonderful. This gathering is strictly to give *reporters* information, the chance to ask questions, and opportunities to do one-on-one interviews afterward that will maximize their understanding of that message."

Times when news conferences are appropriate include when a demonstration or a viewing is required in order to understand it, or an individual(s) is best questioned in person, or when your company, product, or service is or has become the source of an important news story. Some times when a news conference can attract the interest of newspeople include providing an opportunity for viewing and experiencing the way a new product or service works, introducing a well-known personality who will be used in upcoming advertising (newspeople love personalities even when the advertising itself isn't exactly newsworthy), introducing a newly appointed or elected executive who really has something worthwhile to say or is highly quotable, describing and explaining an expansion program, showing newly acquired property, presenting a progress report that is better understood with visual aids or when questions and answers are allowed, or making company head(s) available to reporters—as in the case of an unfavorable situation that could result in "bad press."

Checklist Questions

Unfortunately, every one of these *appropriate* times can also be *inappropriate* if the event turns out to be dull and boring or trivial. Here are questions you can ask yourselves in a meeting with your staff to determine whether a news conference is in order for your company.

- Will a news release or videotape—accompanied by an operation manual and perhaps a press kit, b-roll, or fact sheet and backgrounder—give reporters all they need to produce interesting stories in terms of their medium's viewers or readers?
- Will a hands-on look at the product or use of the service *add* anything to a standard news release or VNR? What will it add?
- Will appearance(s) by executives and/or board members improve the company's level of integrity and reliability and gain credibility for the company's position?
- Does this avenue give reporters the news and/or information they couldn't get otherwise?
- Is there another, perhaps more effective way to handle getting this information to the media? Perhaps with an editors' workshop, a press breakfast or lunch, or a press party?
- Can the company spokesperson(s) present the information effectively and stand up to a question-and-answer period? (Don't give an unqualified answer to this question until you've tested it with at least one practice session.)
- Would a face-to-face meeting with reporters give them an opportunity to question other aspects of the business that we do not wish to make public—aspects such as policy, a long-range program, or employee attitudes?

Put It in Perspective

"Normally, to do any announcement," says Joe McNamara, "a lot of preparation is needed. The message must be crafted and developed so that it is specifically designed for the intended audience that it is being delivered to; the proper channels of distribution must be selected; and the target audience(s) [as determined earlier in the planning process] must be selected to their smallest common denominator."

All of the above are required, whichever communication channel is employed. When the channel is a news conference, however, "a little extra preparation" is required, advises McNamara.

PRACTICE MAKES PERFECT—YOU WISH!

Practice makes *better.* And practice tells you who among your people can go before the cameras without becoming, as Jack Trammell describes it, a deer in the headlights. Practice in this case *never* makes perfect!

So before you make the decision to have a news conference, hold a practice session or two. This kind of advance preparation tells you a great deal about whether you should even attempt such an event and whether or not you have a spokesperson(s) who will be a good representative for the company. But don't hold so many practice sessions that they become rehearsals so that when you finally appear in front of reporters and cameras you sound like a prerecorded message.

Gather all the key people you know who aren't afraid to speak their minds and have them sit as an audience where reporters would sit. Give these people two kinds of questions—those you would like to have asked and those you hope nobody asks. Have these substitute reporters ask the questions. Then, if necessary, repeat them two or three times until you discover the best way(s) and manner in which to respond.

Also include among your audience the people who know and understand the technical aspects or the engineering features to check that answers offered give correct information (but in nontechnical language). And if there is any chance the questions involve legal considerations, include the company's legal experts, too, to anticipate or warn of any potential legal problems that could come from any answers.

If you videotape the session for replay later, you can let your spokespersons see how they looked and the effects of their body language. Over time, this will give them greater comfort in playing not only to an audience but to cameras. The tape also will allow everyone to critique answers and make suggestions for changes.

Training by professionals and practice sessions can set you right about what really happens in these sessions. Trammell says there are about a thousand companies in the United States that do this type of training, and the cost is roughly $1,000 to $1,500 a day. At least check it out.

Most believe it's worth the cost for the person(s) who represents the company to get adequate media training beyond in-house practice sessions. Joe McNamara says that even among clients who say they don't need it, who consider it a waste of time and money, he doesn't know one who has said after the training that it wasn't useful.

Even if you sincerely believe that you'll never hold a news conference, you never know when, seemingly out of nowhere, the news conference opportunity of the century will appear on your doorstep, or a bad news happening brings reporters flocking. And if either situation happens, there won't be time to get training or to conduct practice sessions.

CHOOSING THE RIGHT SPOKESPERSON

By now it should be obvious that the person(s) who appears on behalf of your company has a mighty influence on the impression the public—through the media—receives of your company. Recognize that your spokesperson(s) is the figurehead—the hood emblem, as Trammell so graphically describes it. And if that person doesn't look good, the whole event and even the company itself doesn't look good.

On the other hand, it can be a great help for the head of the company to get to know the media—and for the media to get to know him or her. This can mean big returns over years to come when a one- to two-page news release or a minute-twenty-second VNR may be the only contact the media has with the company. It can also mean the difference between preconceived good or bad reactions by the media, and ultimately by the public, if or when an unexpected, unpredicted, undesirable situation arises.

Qualifications for the Spokesperson

Joe McNamara recommends the following list of abilities and capacities—requirements, if you will—for choosing the person who will speak for your company when you call a news conference.

1. The ability to communicate effectively is of course the first requirement, and that involves a number of things, such as knowledge, the ability to speak clearly and simply, the ability to think, listen, and react under pressure with positive results, the ability to know how much to communicate and when to shut up, and appearance—including positive body language.
2. The ability to adapt and follow instructions is essential.
3. Title is also important—the spokesperson should be someone with sufficient stature in the company and who is authorized to speak for the company.

FIRST TAKE A CHILL PILL . . . THEN DRAFT YOUR CONFERENCE PLANS

Planning is essential for a successful news conference. And unless there is some kind of crisis that demands immediate action, relax and give adequate time to the process.

Making a List

Before you make a list of media people to invite, decide who will be interested in the content of *this* conference. If, for instance, the news is of interest only to business publications and business page reporters, invite only those people. If it's medical news, list medical publications and cable channels, medical news services, and medical reporters. If there are reporters who regularly cover developments in your overall industry or who have reported news of your company in the past, include them. If you're not sure who should be invited from specific news groups, send the invitation to the newspaper's city editor, the managing editor of a specific publication, and/or to the assignment editor at a television station.

Setting the Day

"The time of day and the day of the week are very, very important because of deadlines as well as publication and broadcast times," says McNamara. In making these decisions, Edelman professionals start by targeting a certain segment of the population. An example might be young professionals, white collar workers. "We ask ourselves, 'What is the best day of the week to get news and information to them, and what method is best?' " That, they say, dictates which day of the week to hold the press conference. In other words, if Thursday is the best day to reach your target audience, you call the conference in accordance with the media getting the news to the targeted group on a Thursday.

Try to stay away from Mondays—things are pretty hectic around newsrooms following weekends. And Fridays shouldn't be a top choice either, because many people's minds are seduced a little by upcoming weekend activities, and they're not as willing to stick around to ask questions or do a photo session or a special interview.

Tuesday through Thursday usually brings the best attendance. *Usually* is the operative word. Check before scheduling *any* day to be sure there is nothing of news importance scheduled elsewhere in the area. And hope that no sudden news event happens—such as an earthquake or tornado in the area—to draw media to its coverage rather than to yours.

Setting the Hour

Choosing a time of day for a conference may be the most difficult decision. Morning and evening newspapers have totally different deadlines. And a morning paper may have three, four, or as many as six editions. Television stations may have as many as nine news broadcasts over a 24-hour period.

Take a little extra time to call each newspaper and/or station and find *their* best time of day. Then choose the time according to the medium you most want to attend your news conference.

It's obvious that a news conference should be timed for the convenience of newspeople and for the widest coverage, except in the unlikely case of a developing crisis when the time to call it is as soon as possible. No matter how big your company or how important your news, please remember not to time the news conference for the convenience of your own people.

If only morning newspapers are to be included, mid- or late-afternoon is probably the best time. If you want your news to appear on early evening cable or local television news programs, the conference is probably best set for 9:30 or 10:00 A.M.—10:30 at the latest. With this timing, it might even make noon news programs.

Check the times that best fit the targeted media *in your community* and then schedule accordingly.

THE INVITATION

A letter on your company's letterhead describing the purpose of the conference is a standard format. Never, *never* telephone an invitation. Exhibit 19.1 shows an example of an invitation from Edelman Public Relations Worldwide.

The RSVP number is important. Notice that in the Adelphia invitation there's no contact name and number, only the name and number of a person who will accept responses. Edelman Public Relations Worldwide says that there are strong reasons for this—so reporters can't try to do advance interviews or get advance information about the announcement or the reason for the news conference. If some reporters succeed in getting advance information, they may break the story ahead of other media, which would create bad feelings among other reporters. Telephone operators and anyone with information about the purpose of the news conference should be told in advance not to give out any information.

Hand deliver or send the invitation so that it doesn't arrive so far in advance that it gets lost or buried in the onslaught of other mail but still gives the recipient sufficient time to assign someone to cover it. Follow the delivery of the invitation with telephone calls to confirm that the invitation reached the right people and to check whether or not they will attend.

Exhibit 19.1

Cordially invites you to attend a

Press Conference

that's

Not Just Another Basic Cable Announcement

The Western Show

Wednesday, November 30

1:50 to 2:20 p.m.

Room A 1415
Anaheim Convention Center

R.S.V.P.s encouraged but not required

Call Veronica at 214-443-7572

We look forward to seeing you there.

HAVE NEWS RELEASES
AND PRESS KITS FOR HANDOUTS

The News Release

Every news conference should offer a written news release that gives the five *W*'s of the information to be presented at the conference. The news release in Exhibit 19.2 is for the news conference announced by the invitation in Exhibit 19.1.

Exhibit 19.2   This three-page news release for Adelphia's news conference is longer than most releases because—as a handout at the conference and later to send to reporters who were unable to attend—it is meant to give reporters as much information as possible, information that undoubtedly will influence the kinds of questions the reporters will ask.

PAGETIME   **NEWS RELEASE**

Two Forest Plaza
12201 Merit Drive
Suite 100
Dallas, Texas 75251

Tel   214. 233 8812
Fax 214. 233 1619

MEDIA CONTACTS: Laurie Pennino, Allison Ellis, Reba Russell
                         Edelman Worldwide
                         214-520-3555

ADELPHIA LAUNCHES PAGETIME™,
THE INDUSTRY'S FIRST CONSUMER PAGING SERVICE
FOR CABLE SYSTEM OPERATORS

ANAHEIM, Calif. (Nov. 30, 1994) -- Adelphia Communications Corporation
(NASDAQ:ADLAC) today announced the formation and launch of PageTime™, the cable
industry's first personal communications service (PCS). Adelphia Communications,
headquartered in Coudersport, Pa., has opened an office in Dallas, Texas, to offer personal
paging services as a premium cable service to multiple service operators (MSOs) throughout
the U.S. beginning in early 1995.

PageTime is a unique cable industry approach to PCS in that it will utilize existing
paging infrastructures to deliver paging services to consumers, augmenting these established
networks with its own infrastructure as it comes on line over the next five years. PageTime is
working with AirTouch Paging, headquartered in Dallas, Texas, on its initial market roll outs in
the Southwest, Southern Florida and Southern California regions.

Jim Boso, president of PageTime, noted that the new premium service offers cable
operators an unprecedented opportunity to enter the wireless communications market without
waiting for future networks to be built.

- more -

Exhibit 19.2   Continued

PageTime Launch/2

"PageTime will provide cable affiliates with a low-cost, easy market entry into the consumer paging business without tying up channels or requiring any capital investment on their part to enter the business," said Boso. "Consumer paging is a great way for system operators to increase unregulated revenues as they prepare for the coming competitive environment."

John Rigas, president and chief executive officer of Adelphia, pointed to the growth of consumer paging as a key reason for Adelphia launching this new cable service.

"Consumer paging is a rapidly growing personal communications service," said Rigas. "Last year, for the first time in the paging industry, new "consumer paging" subscriptions outsold new "business paging" subscriptions, making it the fastest growing segment of the market. PageTime brings a strong capability to address this expanding opportunity through a well-thought-out consumer paging strategy."

PageTime intends to create national brand recognition for its consumer paging services by using several strengths that cable operators bring to the personal communications business, including direct access to consumers through underutilized local cable advertising spots, ongoing direct mail marketing, and cross channel promotions. Cable operators also have in place extensive subscriber tracking, billing, customer service and technical support infrastructures that can easily be applied to consumer paging operations.

PageTime is currently arranging a national in-bound call center to handle sales orders and service, a national telemarketing center to upgrade subscribers to its new premium service, and a national pager distribution center to drop ship pagers directly to subscribers within one day of their order. The company also is developing software to interface paging head-end sites throughout the country with local cable billing systems to fully automate the paging transaction process.

- more -

Exhibit 19.2   Continued

PageTime Launch/3

Motorola, the leader in business and consumer paging equipment, will produce the pagers, offering stylish, colorful models currently on the market as well as new pagers labeled specifically for PageTime and its cable affiliates. PageTime will manage all pager procurement and sales activities for cable affiliates, thereby reducing product cost, inventory and maintenance requirements for local cable operators.

Adelphia is a 49.9 percent owner of Page Call, Inc., which was a successful bidder on three regional narrowband PCS licenses covering 62 percent of the country's population, and expects to begin construction of its infrastructure shortly after the award of its licenses by the Federal Communications Commission (FCC) in 1995. PageTime will take advantage of this infrastructure to ensure long-term availability of transmission capacity as the market expands.

"I am looking forward to working with Adelphia to provide PageTime subscribers with unique personal paging services," said Lisa-Gaye Shearing, a financial executive in the communications industry and the 50.1 percent owner of Page Call, Inc.

"We've developed a strategy and business plan that will make it extremely attractive for MSOs and local cable operators to enter the consumer paging marketplace," said Boso. "With nationwide brand recognition, broad-based economies of scale, long-term access to transmission capacity, and extensive service and support capabilities, consumer paging is now an attractive new business opportunity for cable system operators."

Adelphia owns or manages cable systems serving more than 1,370,000 subscribers in 12 states. Adelphia is actively involved in the construction of SONET-based (synchronous optical network-based) competitive access networks and will provide switched telephone service in four New York cities within the next six months.

###

The Press Kit

Have on hand a supply of press kits that provide an abundance of additional information from which a reporter can draw to extend and expand the limited news presented at the conference and in the release. Both a release and a press kit can be delivered immediately following the conference to members of the media who were unable to attend.

Press kits? This seems to be a term that is accepted among all branches of the media. You also sometimes hear the term *electronic press kit*, but these aren't kits at all. They're videotapes containing added interviews, background action and sounds, and interior and exterior shots that can be played with a television anchor's or reporter's voice-over commentary. A supply of these should be available if television reporters are present. Be sure they're on Betacam recording tapes.

How to construct press kits is explained later in this chapter.

AN ADDED WORD FROM JOE McNAMARA

Reporters at news conferences should have sufficient understanding of the topic to ask meaningful questions, advises McNamara. Providing information for this kind of understanding is the job of those calling the conference. There are different ways of achieving this, but McNamara favors giving them everything up front. That means handing out news releases and press kits as reporters arrive, in spite of the risk that they may be too busy going through the materials to pay strict attention to the speaker.

Edelman counsels its clients not to worry while they're speaking if they see only the tops of heads as the reporters read the materials given them earlier. "Professional reporters are used to listening while they browse through information," says McNamara. However, "Materials should be designed for a quick read," he adds. "They should be concise summaries and not big long texts to wade through, that are difficult to grasp."

When detailed materials within the press kit are called for, McNamara recommends that you add a summary cover page that presents sufficient information reporters can use to ask relevant questions.

HAVE PHOTOGRAPHERS ON HAND

You'll hope reporters bring their own still or video photographers. But don't assume they all will. Have professional photographers on hand, not only to provide file photos and videotapes for your own records and to include with the releases and press kits you send to reporters who weren't able to attend, but also for use by reporters who show up without a photographer.

THE SETUP OF THE ROOM

The way the conference room is set up, even the size of the room, should depend largely on the photographers who will attend. Television cameras require more room and a different seating arrangement than newspaper reporters and print photographers. (If television crews will be on hand, be sure to have plenty of heavy-duty extension cords and electrical outlets available.)

When TV cameras are lined across the rear of the room, your speakers must be seated across the front of the room, whereas when only newspaper reporters and photogs are present, the speakers can sit among the reporters and be called to the front of the room to speak. Then the still photographers can roam the room for the less formal, action shots most newspapers prefer.

Choose the size of the room as carefully as the manner in which you set it up. If it's too large, the impression is that only a few people are attending and therefore the content of the conference must not have much significance. It's far better to have a room that's a little overcrowded (remember those presidential conferences?), every seat filled, with a few people standing, giving the impression that wow! this must be really important!

Newspeople are highly aware of the "us-and-them" feeling among so many businesspeople. So, a word of caution about seating speakers behind a table or standing them behind a podium, which only reinforces the appearance that your people are donning body armor to protect themselves from anticipated combat. The less formal the seating arrangements and the less protective the body language of the speakers, the greater the feeling of friendliness and harmony there will be between your people and the media.

About body language. It's a PR tool that no one thinks about when the language is friendly, but it's something everyone unconsciously reacts to and resents when the protective armor—such as arms crossed across the chest—is evident. Make recognizing and learning the right body language a part of your practice sessions.

And of course don't seat your people in front of windows, mirrors, or a reflective background. Otherwise photographers will throw up their hands and walk.

UP IN THE AIR ABOUT SATELLITING?

If a news conference is strictly a local affair, there's no need for it to be carried by satellite. Also, there are several elements to consider before you decide to spend the kind of money required to organize and conduct the satellite variety.

First you must ask yourself: Does the effect of this story go beyond our local community? If the answer is yes—let's say you're a regional power company covering a couple of states and you're raising rates for your service—it's time to consider satelliting.

Next you must shop for the best and least expensive means of presenting a satellite media conference. Local production companies as well as local television stations are the place to shop. The stations or production companies must have an *uplink* capability. These days they all undoubtedly have *downlink* capacities—you see downlink satellite dishes in many people's backyards—but few have uplink capability.

Many television stations with uplink capabilities are also willing to rent out their production facilities and staff to independent groups. Smaller, independent local stations are the places to call first. The principal difficulty is that many of the commercial stations are not always excited about having other members of the press show up at their facility.

Don't rule out cable stations, particularly those at colleges and universities. They may not only have the equipment you need, they may also probably use student staffers, which reduces charges and may bring production costs within your budget limits.

You will tell them you require a closed, quiet studio with uplink capability, a speaker's microphone, a camera operator, plus whatever else is required to conduct and transmit a news conference to the areas on your list, and you need it all for an hour or so.

When you finish your "shopping tour," you must decide whether you'll conduct your conference at the uplink point for both local *press* as well as for broadcast media. The question is: Would there be better results from holding separate news conferences for print and broadcast media, or would you prefer to call them all in and get the whole thing over with at one time?

Satellite Media Tours from the Ground Up

Every day, executives of corporations, trade associations, nonprofit organizations, and government agencies stand before audiences gathered at sites across the United States or around the world. They stand before cameras at electronic meetings that link private audiences gathered in different locations. Both the executives and the audiences are able to see and hear each other on high-quality television monitors or large projection screens. They can interact as easily as if they were all in the same room.

All this may be done for either a satellite news conference or a videoconference. The difference?

- A satellite news conference allows the participants in a videoconference to interact with news media.

- A videoconference is an electronic meeting that links private audiences (such as your headquarters staff and employees around the country) in different locations by television and satellite technology.

And then there are satellite media tours. If you look up the term *media tour* in a marketing glossary, you may get the wrong idea about what a *satellite* media tour is. For example, *Webster's New World Dictionary of Media and Communications* states that a media tour is "an itinerary of cities or markets in which a spokesperson or other publicity representative is sent, generally for a day or two." In the satellited version you send only the *video image* of the spokesperson, seldom for more than an hour, and it's possible for the person to visit all the cities on the "tour" at one time.

Usually, however, a satellite media tour is a series of one-at-a-time, prescheduled interviews conducted via satellite between your spokesperson and television station reporters across your area, across the country, or around the world. You or your spokesperson speak from one location but are switched electronically in sequence from one station interview to another, conducting on-air, one-on-one discussions, either live or pretaped for use in later news segments. For example, visualize your company spokesperson on-screen, being interviewed by selected television reporters. That's a satellite media tour—called an *SMT* within the industry.

SMTs also give you the means of appearing from appropriate and more exciting locations than a local studio set. For example, the setting could be a research hospital when you wish to announce a medical breakthrough procedure or your manufacturing plant when a new product is being introduced. The latest technology even allows for a really high-impact setting—under water—if the appropriate tie-in with your news can be made.

And how do television stations and cable systems react? Both are insatiable consumers of live and taped interviews, and they particularly favor those that lend credibility to their news segments and extend their electronic reach to anywhere in this country or the world.

Medialink, the world's largest provider of video PR services by means of satellite and taped videos, is currently the only transmission network in the country just for satellite media tours, video news releases, and public service spots. Medialink is able to transmit satellite news conferences not only from a studio set or corporate headquarters but from remote locations, such as an offshore oil platform or the floor of a major trade show.

Medialink points out that this can be a cost-effective means of generating television exposure, because you can accomplish in hours from one location what would require days or weeks on the road.

Exhibit 19.3   Most "Satellite Alerts" are sent by fax, as was this one. It's not a news release. It tells where, when, who, and what about a video package that is presented as a news conference—but with no opportunity for questions and answers. It includes enough information to catch the attention of news producers, assignment editors, and entertainment reporters.

Attn: News Producers, Assignment Editors, Entertainment Reporters

S A T E L L I T E   A L E R T
Friday, January 13, 1995

RUDOLF NUREYEV'S ART COLLECTION AUCTIONED TODAY

Dancer Rudolf Nureyev, who gained international fame for cat-like leaps and fast spins, also collected art and the old masters from his collection will be auctioned this morning at Christie's, New York.

His shoes and costumes went on the auction block last night.

We will be satelliting a TV news package, which includes a cut piece about his career and art collection, and B-roll and soundbites from the auction, this afternoon.

Satellite Times & Coordinates - Friday, January 13, 1995

2:30 to 2:45 PM EST
2:45 to 3:00 PM EST(refeed)

Telstar 302 - Transponder 11H - Channel 22 - Audio 6.2 & 6.8

The package will include footage of Nureyev dancing some of his most famous roles and appearing with the Muppets; shots of his huge apartment in New York's legendary Dakota; shots of his paintings, sculptures and costumes; auction footage, brief interviews with people bidding on his costumes and shoes, and an interview with Christopher Burge, chairman, Christie's New York.

If you would like any additional information or if you would like a hard copy, please contact Maria McCarthy at DWJ Television, 800-766-1711.

One Robinson Lane, Ridgewood, New Jersey 07450   (201) 445-1711   Fax (201) 445-8362

Satellite Costs

To transmit a signal by satellite one way is relatively inexpensive. Sending a telephone signal back to the sender so he or she can hear your comments or your questions is a little more expensive. But to send a satellite signal with a satellite picture with the sender also receiving a satellite picture with sound is still very expensive. Although cable companies are working to make this latter method affordable, it's still prohibitive for most small and mid-size companies.

The first, the simple one-way type, is called when a situation exists where you don't want questions, you just want to say something and make sure everybody gets the word as soon as possible, and then you get out of there. It's done with the hope the stations will glean from your "speech" the responses they're looking for.

NOW, ABOUT PRESS KITS

Whoa! Let's stop right here and recognize—again—that broadcast people are somewhat allergic to the word *press,* allergic to its use in *press* conferences and *press* rooms. *Press* refers to hard copy and print reporters, to people whose end results, whose finished product, appears after having been printed by a printing *press* of one kind or another.

The word *press* has hung on over the years, just as we say we *dial* a telephone number at a time when dial phones are as rare as a town that receives no broadcasted news.

In deference to broadcasters, most PR people have tried to alter their language and change *press* to *media* wherever and whenever possible. When referring to a press kit, however, *press* is a far better word than *media* because *media kits* are provided by media to potential advertisers, not to newspeople.

Quel confusion! Maybe someday someone will come up with a replacement name that actually describes what we now know as a press kit. In the meantime, everyone in any way connected to news, publicity, and public relations recognizes what a press kit is and what it's for. Until then, it appears the term must remain.

Kit Contents

A concise list of the appropriate, recommended contents, as well as all the necessary details about how to develop a press kit, is included in *The New Publicity Kit* by Jeanette Smith (Wiley, 1995). Here's an abbreviated list of recommended contents:

- News release giving major points (presented at the conference) for reporters to flesh out and use or to draw on for their own stories.
- Fact sheet for those reporters who wish to write or produce their stories from scratch.
- Backgrounder about your organization.
- Concise history of your organization (or if it's an announcement of a merger, include separate histories of both organizations).
- Bios of celebrities or special personalities who appear at the conference as well as company executives in whom the media would be interested.
- Quotes sheet of quotable remarks by conference participants.
- Operating manual, if the event's purpose is to introduce equipment or a product.
- Photos for print and b-roll for television of the product or equipment and people using it, speakers or participating personalities, and any other appropriate subjects.
- An attractive, well-prepared brochure, such as an annual report, that gives additional background information.

It's a Cover-Up

Of course, it's what's inside that counts most. But there should be a cover, a "holder" of some sort for the kit's contents. It can be an elaborate, custom-designed folder with your company's name imprinted or embossed on it. Or it can be a very simple folder, depending on the impression you wish to relay.

Two things every press kit should have on its cover:

1. The company's name, using a distinctive logo (if one exists) to build recognition, plus the address and telephone and fax numbers. Don't count on the fact that this information is probably on each piece enclosed, because some or all of those pieces may be used and then tossed or mislaid.
2. A business card, for the person who is trained and qualified to reply to any questions media may have, should be attached to a pocket on the inside of the cover. (Some folders have slits built into the inside pocket.) If you already have a telephone Rolodex-type card, include it, too, as a courtesy and in the hope it will be held for future use. (Many editors and beat reporters keep press kits on file.)

YOU GAVE IT—NOW WHAT?

You gave it and they came. Well, at least a few showed up. Not as many as you'd hoped, but that's not a calamity. Actually, it can be an *opportunity*, if you act quickly.

You may already have a list of reporters who told you they wouldn't or couldn't attend the news conference but requested information from it. Get a press kit and a news release (video news release with b-roll for television reporters) that summarizes what took place at the news conference to each of these reporters as quickly as possible. Use a personal or a special delivery service.

Immediate is the operative word here, not only because of the old cliché that yesterday's news is history, but more importantly because those who did attend undoubtedly will use the information immediately, and few journalists want to appear to be scooped by their competitors.

Attach to each a colored sticky note or a note-sized memo that is a flagged, *personal* reminder to each individual, to jog his or her memory about the event and to get it past anyone assigned to process the editor's or reporter's mail.

20

Crisis Communications: Turning Bad Happenings to Good Press

Three authorities share their expertise. Expect the unexpected and have a plan. How to treat media in a crisis. Best ways to get news to the AP. Visual reports provide greatest impact. How Pepsi handled—and trounced—a crisis. Video- and teleconferences. Tracking VPR. Tips from a pro.

In this chapter you're going to meet three "VIPCs"—very important professional communicators—who know their way around in today's vastly different publicity and public relations worlds. They will give you answers to questions you've always wondered about—and to questions you'd never even know to ask.

The three authorities are Tom Geddie, an MMMC pro; Bob Wieland, of The Associated Press; and Laurence Moskowitz, founder and president of Medialink, which provides communications services to PR, corporate, and governmental communities.

MEET A REAL, LIVE SPIN DOCTOR

Yes, Tom Geddie is a real, live spin doctor. As the owner of Strategic Communication in Dallas, Texas, his job is to put the right spin on any kind of publicity opportunity. It is what he does for such mega corps as E-Systems, EDS, Perot Systems, and Texas Instruments. Previously he worked for Parkland Memorial Hospital and other organizations and was a journalist for United Press International and *The Dallas Times Herald*.

As Geddie tells it, he's been involved in crisis communications since he first set foot in the communications world as a 20-year-old intern at UPI. It's important to remember that in news communications there are two sides that must be considered and remembered when a crisis hits your business. The two sides are the media's side and yours—and Geddie knows both.

Therefore, for the best possible results, it is important to take an intense look not only at your own position but also at the media's viewpoint. When you understand what both sides are looking for, then, like any good doctor—spin or otherwise—you can accurately assess the ailment and the health condition and prescribe the proper treatment to cure the disorder.

EXPECT THE UNEXPECTED

Disasters can happen to the biggest, most sophisticated and knowledgeable companies, such as when Pepsi had its syringe crisis and Intel Corp. discovered a flaw in its premier Pentium computer chip. Big or small, sophisticated or not, how a company responds to a crisis tells a lot about its ability to weather the ultimate bad press that results.

Follow the "Doctor's" Advice

"Doctor" Tom believes that most reporters try to do their jobs fairly. Still, when you face a crisis your primary objective is to solve the problem and to let everyone who is important to you know that you are solving it. A cliché, "tell it all, tell it fast, tell it accurately," really is the best advice, he says.

First impressions count in responding to a crisis. The first hours and first contacts set the tone for the duration and aftermath of any crisis. *Never*, warns Geddie, pretend the problem does not exist, because it will not go away. The more accurate the information you share, the more accurately the story will be told.

Before a crisis ever happens, though, you need to build consistent, credible relationships with everybody who is important to you—customers, employees, regulators, the general public, and the media.

You need to have a written crisis communication plan in place, and you need to rehearse it like a fire drill so that key personnel know exactly what to do during a crisis. You need to anticipate as many potential crises as possible, knowing that your plan must be broad enough to help you through the unexpected. (We recommend that you gather staff for a brainstorming session to help you foresee all crises that could possibly be expected for your company.)

You also need to know what you wish to accomplish during a crisis and to focus on long-term outcomes rather than on just stopping the bleeding.

Follow these steps if you find your company in a crisis:

- Do not try to manipulate the facts.
- Do keep your basic messages simple and clear.
- Express your genuine concern for any people involved.
- Be positive. In nearly every instance, you can show what you are doing to solve a problem.

How to Treat the Media

It's important to recognize that the media are not your primary audience; rather, they are one of the pipelines—probably your most effective and efficient—through which you can reach your primary audience.

So make these rules a primary part of your crisis plan:

- Make time for the media, whether you want to or not.
- Anticipate the questions reporters will ask and make sure you know the answers in advance. Or, if you don't know the answer to an unexpected question, say that you will do your best to get it and you will get back to the questioner ASAP. Then be sure you do get back as quickly as possible.
- Remain calm and assertive at all times.
- Return phone calls.
- Respond to requests as fully as you are able to.
- Don't play favorites among the media. Treat everyone equally.

Once the crisis is past, follow up with all of your important audiences. You want to repair any damage to relationships. Evaluate your response(s), and be objective about it. Make any changes necessary in the plan or in your implementation of the plan.

Be prepared! Be able to walk into a news conference as Henry Kissinger once did, and ask, "Does anyone have any questions for my answers?"

CLIMB THE FENCE

Now it's time to hear advice from the media, who are your pipeline to reach the public, including your customers. Meet Bob Wieland, who truly knows and understands the terrain on media's side of the fence. He's in his 20th year as a newsman with The Associated Press, a career that has included directing the Texas Sound statewide audio news service in Austin and supervising the broadcast wire for Texas radio and television stations. He got his start at 19 as a news writer in New York City for radio station WINS.

The Associated Press is a little different from what most people think. Its a news *cooperative*. That means that when a newspaper is voted into membership, its members are required to share their news with AP without pay. The agreement is that AP can pick up their stories, rewrite them, and retransmit them.

"We don't have the huge cadre of reporters that everybody thinks of when they picture the AP," says Wieland. Instead, "we've got a bunch of people in little rooms like in North Dakota sitting there rewriting the local newspaper." The AP is staffed 24 hours a day and its reporters do go to the scenes of major disasters.

The Best Way to Get News to the AP

On an everyday basis, when you, as your company's publicity "agent," wish to get in touch with the AP to discuss a story, you probably send a press release through the mail, send a fax, or send some other sort of dimensional mailing to call their attention to a story.

"The best—and easiest—way to get the news to the AP is to get it in a local newspaper, get a good spread there, and then call it to our attention," says Wieland.

Tell AP, "Hey, the [local newspaper] has already done this. . . . They did a feature . . . and you might want to pick it up."

"We're not insulted," says Wieland. "We don't mind doing a story that somebody else has already done." Often in broadcast you hear, "Well, Channel 4's already done this. We're not going to pick it up; we're Channel 8."

If, however, you want to bypass the local media, or you think that they're ignoring a story, then go directly to the AP. And, as with other news media, they have special contacts for different types of stories, for example, a sports editor and a business editor.

"We May Doze, But We Never Close"

What time to call isn't a concern. Who to call may be. Always ask for the supervisor on duty, Wieland says. If the supervisor determines that what you have is a business story or a sports story or something a reporter can handle, the supervisor will pass you off to that person who will then ask you questions and put something on the wire.

"The main problem from AP's stand," according to Wieland, "is getting somebody to pick up the telephone and call us—or being there when we call you."

But who do you contact when there's a disaster? Bob Wieland says, "You get in touch with whomever you can if you're on a proactive stance. If you're on a reactive stance, you'll hear from us. If you call us, we'll be glad to hear from you first."

Designate a Spokesperson

In support of Tom Geddie's tip about being sure there is a designated spokesperson who can answer the who, what, where, when, why, and how that journalists will be asking, Wieland says, "That cannot be stressed enough because that designated spokesperson adds the extra 'W' to the mix—the 'who says?'

"We need attribution on a story. We need somebody's name. We cannot take unattributed material on a major story because the general desk in New York is going to call down to get the name of that spokesperson. And in some cases they're going to want to know the middle initial and the person's age, so readers don't confuse him or her with somebody else.

"What we want is very simple," he says. "We want the five *W*'s, the *H*, and who said. We can get the information about what happened from the fire department, from the police department, from going outside the building and interviewing people. But in order to get the inside word we have to have something from inside."

In a Crisis, the AP Wants Word from *You*

Confirmation from you is what Bob Wieland says a news organization must have. "Even if it is a 'No comment.' And sometimes that can serve you just as well—if it's artfully done—as a full explanation."

Wieland gives an example of a "no comment" that was exactly the right thing to say. A couple of years ago an engine fell off one of American Airlines' aircraft over New Mexico, and a radio reporter called to ask, "What can you tell us about the engine that fell off your airplane?" AA's spokesperson took about a second to think about it, then said, "We don't know what happened, but we damn sure are gonna find out."

"It was perfect," says Wieland. It showed concern. It showed that they were aware of it, that they took responsibility for it, and that was all the radio station needed. And it was the perfect sound bite for the AP to pick up and quote."

Later, Wieland says they reported about the shear bolts that sheared as they're supposed to when they encounter turbulence, and the engine fell away—just as it's supposed to—as opposed to having the wing fall off, which certainly no one wants to have happen.

TV versus Print and the AP

You undoubtedly heard ABC News' PR campaign that boasted night after night that more Americans get their news from ABC than from any other source.

Just the facts, sir, about that claim. The facts come from Bob Greene, writing in *The Chicago Tribune,* who compared CNN and the AP during the Gulf War. According to CNN, between 1.5 and 2 million American households were tuned to CNN. During a single 24-hour period CNN is seen at least momentarily in 20 million American homes. The AP, on the other hand, is subscribed to by more than 1,700 newspapers in the United States, 6,000 U.S. TV and radio outlets, and 8,500 foreign media subscribers. This adds up to about a *billion* people per day who are exposed to AP reports.

There's another interesting fact: ABC gets more of its news from the AP than from any other single source.

Impact Is Another Matter—Visual Images Have It

What happens when you have a story so big and so memorable and so important that there are certain things from it that the public will remember forever? asks Wieland.

Impact is perhaps greatest from visual "reports." Who can ever forget Joe Rosenthal's Pulitzer prize–winning AP photo of the flag-raising on Suribachi at Iwo Jima?

Still photos remain important, says Wieland. Recognizing this, the Associated Press has a vast network of still photographers. But video clips also have huge impact on viewers. So the AP is setting up to shoot and move video clips around the world.

To illustrate the impact of video images, Wieland recalls a day in February 1993 when the Bureau of Alcohol, Tobacco and Firearms thought their assignment about nine miles north of Waco, Texas, would be a piece of cake. But it didn't work out that way. "Remember what the video looked like from that event? The federal agents being literally blown off the roof by withering gunfire from within Mt. Carmel?

"For 51 days the Feds controlled that story. They tried to mold public opinion to support the reasons behind the aborted raid. It didn't work," says Wieland, "because 51 days later there were images that may never leave people's minds—flames engulfing Mt. Carmel as tanks poked holes in the wall and pumped tear gas inside. Did the tear gas injections knock over lanterns? Were the fires set by the Branch Davidians? Gradually information about the raid is being released so that eventually we may know the entire story. But the flames from that video cancelled the impression of ATF agents being ambushed as they tried to storm the Branch Davidian headquarters."

BACK ON YOUR SIDE OF THE FENCE AGAIN

Now meet Larry Moskowitz, founder and president of Medialink, the world's largest distributor of VNRs for use by local and network television newsrooms. Moskowitz is a cum laude journalism graduate from Penn State who has an impressive background that began with serving as a reporter and editor for United Press International and with PR Newswire.

With his credentials established, Moskowitz makes a statement that gets a publicity seeker's attention fast. "I believe that television is the most maleable medium that we've ever known—as long as you know how to use it. I don't want to sound like I'm calling television journalists something less than print journalists, but they are different and their jobs are very different."

Print journalists have time and a weapon called the telephone, he explains. Their medium is words. The way to deal with print reporters is to give them words. On the other hand, television moves so quickly there isn't time to work the phones, and phones don't get pictures for broadcast journalists. They don't have time because television isn't one edition a day—it's up to nine editions each day. "So if they receive the pictures, the temptation is to use the pictures," says Moskowitz.

How Pepsi Handled a Crisis

Pepsi had a crisis that could have been a disaster for any company. Instead, they conducted a damage control campaign that did exactly what was needed. What they did can serve as an example to copycat.

The problem came out of nowhere, as Larry Moskowitz recalls it. It began when, all of a sudden, Pepsi began getting calls that people were finding syringes in their Pepsi cans. The first story popped up somewhere in the upper Midwest. The next story came out of California. The stories were picked up basically by radio and didn't enter the television arena until about six to eight hours after the first report. Then it did make a network newscast. Boom! Crisis!

"What made it a crisis? Television," says Moskowitz.

After it hit television, the AP picked it up, and it ran on their major national news wire.

Moskowitz says that Pepsi learned that this absolutely could not be something that was happening as part of the bottling process. The FDA became involved because all of a sudden the safety of American consumers was involved. The FDA understood Pepsi's position, that there was no way this could happen in its bottling process.

That's when Pepsi decided to fight fire with fire. They realized that they had a national crisis on their hands. And stock prices started to plummet, while sales of Diet Pepsi fell off like a rock. The crisis reached tremendous proportions as reports continued to come in.

The fire Pepsi used to put out the fire was called Medialink, which brought a crew into the Pepsi bottling plant to shoot a video of the cans being inverted milliseconds prior to being filled. The video, transmitted to stations across the country by satellite, established that there was no way anyone could throw foreign matter into those cans. It also proved that there was no way a medical plant next door could have heaved the things into their bottling arena.

Twenty minutes after receiving the video, CNN ran the clip. Within an hour and a half it was on all three networks. Basically it shut the hoax down.

But then came the big, lucky break. The video ran on television, and somebody running a convenience store in Oklahoma saw the footage on CNN and said, "Wait a minute. Let me go check my surveillance camera . . . that lady [the accuser] was in here yesterday."

Sure enough, when the convenience store owner delivered his black and white surveillance footage, there was the woman literally putting the syringe in the can after she'd made sure the clerk behind the counter had turned around to get her a cup so she could fill it with the Pepsi from the opened can.

That footage put the nail in the coffin of the hoax. Sales rebounded and the stock price actually exceeded the level it had been at prior to the initial reports of the crisis.

But that's not the end!

Don't Just Leave It for Dead. Bury It!

To ensure that the story wouldn't be left at this point, Pepsi continued to put out yet two more video news releases. The final one was merely a video of a full-page newspaper ad with a headline that said "Pepsi is pleased to announce . . . nothing." The accompanying text explained that this had been purely a hoax and now it was over.

Results, based on electronic usage monitoring: Pepsi's VNR campaign was seen by an aggregate of 500 million viewers on 3,170 television news program airings.

Terminology! It's Important!

Moskowitz believes it's important to recognize that the so-called generic term *video news release* implies different things to different people. As he explains, "In one case we'll put out a prepared statement—a spokesperson making a statement—and some footage of the product itself. That isn't a package. No narration goes with it. It is just footage that allows stations to go to their local store, shoot the aisles and show the product on the shelves, and then fashion their own stories. What they need is a statement [a quote or a brief interview] and some generic footage."

Another term that can be misconstrued is the word *crisis*. It doesn't necessarily mean something horrible is happening. Sometimes a crisis can just be a big or breaking story.

Moskowitz says that in Chinese the word *crisis* is represented by two conjoined characters that stand for danger and opportunity. Smart public relations people are turning former crises into opportunities.

"New-Fashioned" Conferences

A videoconference, when coupled with a teleconference to the media, allows a company to announce to the press and to chief analysts across the country what is about to happen before it is actually transmitted to television stations. (See Chapter 19 for detailed information about holding news conferences.)

There are ways to reach one station or every station in the country—to hold a "new-fashioned" electronic or satellite news conference—or to merely announce some internal news within a company. They can be done for any group from the White House to small companies, says Moskowitz.

As an example, when two companies merge there can be two reactions, says Moskowitz:

- Any number of *negative* results, such as speculation that thousands of jobs may be on the block or that the consolidation indicates one or the other company couldn't make it alone.
- Or it can have a *positive* spin through an integrated campaign.

"When I mention 'integrate' I think it's very important to not just focus all your attention on television, but to recognize the power of getting your story out on the wires, and to recognize the importance of the analysts' community," says Moskowitz.

VPR Is Now Trackable

For many, many years advertisers have had scientific analysis of payback available to them. They are able to determine that when x number of advertising dollars are spent here, there are x number of dollars of benefit as a result. In VPR (video public relations) there is no such volume of research. There has been no way to determine payback; video publicity wasn't measurable.

About five years ago, Medialink, Nielsen, and Radio TV Reports began searching for a way to come up with a measuring method. Together, they devised two systems to electronically track video once it's been transmitted. Nielsen's system is called SIGMA. Radio TV Reports' service is called VeriCheck.

"So when VNR-1, for instance, gives Medialink a VNR to be transmitted to stations on a regional basis, nationally, or around the world, we now *encode* it. With encoding we know instantly how many seconds aired on precisely which stations wherever it was transmitted," says Moskowitz.

The interesting thing, according to Moskowitz, is that "the committee of three" that came up with the technology has proven that 100 percent of all stations in the United States that have their own newscasts have from time to time used VNRs. Furthermore, about 60 percent commonly use them, and those are not necessarily small stations as was formerly believed.

(There's more about tracking video releases and use reports in Chapter 18.)

HOW TO GET ALONG WITH THE MEDIA

Are there "rules" for establishing good relationships with newspeople? Yes, and an old-timer in the publicity business put them in the form of five simple "commandments:"

1. *Integrity.* Thou shalt not prevaricate, nor shalt thou exaggerate.
2. *Immediacy:* Thou shalt not procrastinate.
3. *Accessibility.* Thou shalt not build walls.
4. *Familiarity.* Thou shalt do thy homework.
5. *Honesty.* Thou shalt learn to say, "I don't know."

Your role then with media is:

1. To be helpful
2. To be obliging
3. To be honest
4. To avoid being a "suppress agent"

And what all this adds up to can be condensed into three short sentences:

1. Know your organization; really know it.
2. Do the publicity job efficiently, reliably, and credibly.
3. Make the reporter's or the editor's job as easy as possible.

TOM GEDDIE'S CRISIS COMMUNICATION TIPS

Almost as a summary to all the information presented in this chapter are the following tips (condensed for purposes of space) offered by Tom Geddie and his firm, Tom Geddie Communication Planning & Evaluation. You may want to copy and post them, because many of them also work for times when things seem to be running normally.

Before Something Happens

Build credible relationships with every audience that is important to you, including the media (which are in many cases your primary conduit to reaching your other audiences).

Put a basic crisis plan in writing, knowing that you will never be able to identify every potential crisis.

Rehearse.

Develop background material to have available during a crisis to support your position.

Study how other organizations deal with crises; apply what you learn to your situation.

Respond to potential crises before they develop.

Focus on long-term outcomes.

Educate team members to speak with a unified voice.

Identify objectives by looking at each of your audiences.

Identify outside experts, as well as staff, who can provide technical expertise about any problem you are able to anticipate.

Putting the Plan into Action

Help your organization manage the crisis, rather than watching helplessly as the crisis manages the organization.

Promptly notify all individuals and organizations who will be affected by developments. Promptly provide accurate information to journalists or they will look elsewhere, and what they find from other sources may not be accurate.

Stick to the known facts. Do not speculate.

Do not develop a siege mentality.

Be aware of media deadlines; follow through with timely updates.

When the crisis is over, summarize the resolution, and when appropriate, summarize steps you've taken to prevent future problems.

Communicate thoroughly with employees during and after the crisis.

Draw your crisis-planning team from among the public relations staff, senior management, the organization's legal representative, and key line people.

Assign specific duties. Make someone responsible for each duty.

The Media

Anticipate and answer basic journalistic questions: who, what, where, when, why, and how. (And, as AP's Bob Wieland recommends, tell them "who says.")

Remain calm and assertive at all times.

Speak with one voice. To ensure consistent, accurate information, all employees should know that any media request or question should be forwarded to the primary spokesperson.

Share and enforce predetermined and fair ground rules for media access to areas of your facility or the site of the crisis.

Use your primary spokesperson and qualified, enthusiastic technical experts who are involved in the situation for your news conferences.

Cooperate with reasonable requests; if you cannot, explain why. Offer alternatives.

Fill requests for individual interviews as rapidly as possible, because interviews with people solving the crisis will help you tell your story.

Sharing facts, but not speculation, may help keep media from overreacting.

Be on call to the media 24 hours a day during a crisis.

Follow-up

Survey primary audiences to identify the status of relationships after a crisis.

Develop and implement, rapidly but thoroughly, actions to overcome any damage by emphasizing the organization's response and its continuing strengths.

If changes are necessary, implement and share the changes with all affected audiences.

Use local op/ed and letters columns and other resources to communicate with audiences after the crisis passes.

Evaluate your response and make any changes necessary in the plan and/or its implementation.

21

Case Studies: How the Pros Used Publicity

If at first you don't succeed ... Tips for conducting a grassroots campaign. Different markets lead to different results. Publicity gave credibility to a new product—with enormous results. Certain research was a key to returns.

Who says honesty is the best (publicity) policy? *Advertising Age* reports that this fake, but comical, "news" release was found floating on the Internet:

> In a joint press conference in St. Peter's Square this morning, Microsoft Corp. and the Vatican announced that the Redmond software giant will acquire the Roman Catholic Church in exchange for an unspecified number of shares of Microsoft common stock.

Microsoft's plans, according to the story, include making the sacraments available online through the Microsoft Network and appointing Pope John Paul II as senior VP of a new religious software division. If the deal goes through, according to *Ad Age*'s report from the fictitious Internet release, "It will be the first time a computer software company has acquired a major world religion."

Perhaps this publicity release didn't make the networks' nightly news, but it did get inches in *Advertising Age* and undoubtedly a number of other publications. And perhaps it even built a bit of regard for Microsoft's sense of humor and thus made the company seem a little more human, a little more friendly.

Our copycat pros believe that communicating by means of publicity—real publicity, not the Internet kind—was good marketing for four of the nine copycat cases: The four were Case 1: FastSigns; Case 2: MicroHelp and the UnInstaller; Case 7: Oregon BFA Assn.; Case 9: It Takes All Kinds. So, let's hear what our pros have to say about these four cases.

CASE 1: FASTSIGNS ON THE FAST TRACK

The original thought behind asking professionals to tell how they used the four marketing avenues to reach particular goals for their clients was to give you the benefit of professional marketers' advice and counsel. But Gary Salomon, president and CEO of American FastSigns, Inc., is a *businessman*. If you've checked his experiences in chapters 3, 8, 12, and 16, however, you undoubtedly agree he has become the equal of a fullfledged marketing professional the do-it-yourself, learn-by-experience way. Here, in his own words, are the ways he used publicity.

If It's New, It's News . . . Isn't It?

When my partner and I started FastSigns in 1985, we knew it would be expensive to give our idea a fair trial in the marketplace. To get the most for our money during the start-up period, we decided to avoid paid advertising as long as possible and to pursue free publicity as our primary promotional tool. After all, FastSigns was not just a new business, it was a whole new concept. Our story was newsworthy! Surely we could get mentioned in some of the leading business magazines without too much trouble.

We targeted a half-dozen publications, ferreted out some contact names, and distributed a well-produced press release emphasizing our inventive use of computer technology and our unique focus on professional customer service in a traditional industrial field. Then, as every publicity handbook prescribes, we followed up with personal phone calls to each of our media contacts.

And we got *bupkis*.

Back to the Drawing Board

In our first foray, we had worked hard to present an image of absolute professionalism. It was an important point of distinction between FastSigns and the rest of the sign industry: we were much more service-oriented and customer-conscious than the traditional sign manufacturers, and we had tried to communicate that through our textbook-proper approach to the media.

But professionalism had gotten us nowhere; it was time to try another tack. During a brainstorming session, my partner suggested that we draw upon our own internal resources. "We're a sign company," he said. "Let's send 'em a sign!"

So we designed some small banners that pictured a crawling baby with the caption, "We'd Get Down On Our Hands & Knees For A Little Attention." We rolled the banners up in mailing tubes and sent them off to our targeted publications. And when we called our contacts to follow up, they actually remembered us: "Oh, you're those guys with the cute banner."

Success at last!

But three months later, we still hadn't gotten any ink.

If at First You Don't Succeed . . .

Despite our growing frustration, we decided to give it one more shot—and we went loaded for bear. Our next banner was 4 feet tall and 15 feet wide. It pictured, a big, burly construction worker with his arms folded and a menacing look on his beard-stubbled face. The caption read, "Bruno Is Getting *Very Angry.*"

We sent the Bruno banners off to our magazine contacts. Then I flew to New York for a long weekend with my family, intending to make my follow-up calls the next week. But on Saturday, the phone rang at my parents' house.

"I love your banner," said a woman from one of the nation's top business magazines. Somehow, she had managed to track me down through three cities and two states. On a weekend!

"We hung the banner up in our office and everybody's gotten a kick out of it," she continued. "In a couple of months, we're planning to do an article on the top 40 fastest-growing franchise systems, and I wonder if you'd be available for an interview."

Oh boy, was I ever *available!*

We did the interview, FastSigns was noted in the article, and the calls began to roll in. What's more, the right people were calling—people with professional backgrounds, good business sense, and start-up capital. Clearly, we had found a pipeline to our target market.

And once we had been validated by that first magazine, other publications began to take notice. Our name started to show up on their lists of hot new ideas and up-and-coming franchises. FastSigns had gained instant credibility.

The Power of the Word . . . the *Editorial* Word

This experience taught us the astonishing power of the editorial word, and we successfully focused our national efforts on the pursuit of editorial coverage for some time.

In 1989, we decided to test the waters of paid advertising with a full-page ad in a national magazine that had given us good press—and our franchise sales *exploded*.

Another lesson learned: Together, editorial and advertising create a powerful synergy.

As described in the copycat chapter on advertising [Chapter 8], we carried that idea still further by designing our ad in "advertorial" style and running it in the same issue with a listing or survey that also mentioned FastSigns. The ad spelled out the details of our story; the editorial piece lent third-party support to that story.

The Right Angle

Publicity is all about angles, and in those early years, the obvious angle on the FastSigns story was "new concept . . . fast-growing company . . . building a whole new branch of the sign industry."

But we soon became too big and too successful to present ourselves as innovative mavericks with a ground-floor opportunity to sell. It was time to define a new angle, a new stance from which to address our prospective franchisees.

Based on industry research, business trends, and a gut feel for where we stood in our own development, we began to speak of FastSigns not as an exciting newcomer, but as the proven leader of the fastest-growing segment of the sign industry. We emphasized our track record of success and alluded to our vision for the long-term future of our business. But because the competition was always watching, we were careful not to tip our hand too far.

The bigger you are, the less attractive it is to blow your own horn. Today, FastSigns is clearly dominant in its industry, and we have to tread a fine line—always working to get good press, but always careful not to act like a 400-pound gorilla.

That's an important difference between publicity and advertising: In publicity, modesty is becoming.

The Big Leagues

In 1990, we decided to try using an agency to pursue media placement for our publicity stories and help us plan our publicity efforts. And for the next four years, we learned from our mistakes:

The first agency we tried was sophisticated, reputable, and completely ineffectual. It took only a few months for us to see that they didn't have the media contacts we had hoped for.

The second agency was an out-of-town franchise specialist that did a pretty good job getting us placement but had no one on its staff who could write a simple declarative sentence. We had to do all the writing ourselves, and as our needs grew, that became a burden we could no longer carry. A still greater problem, though, was that no one in that agency ever developed any real understanding of our business, despite a half-dozen visits to our headquarters and attendance at two of our conventions. We needed greater depth than they had to offer.

The Number Three [agency] was the sister company to one of our major suppliers, and we hoped that the relationship would inspire a greater commitment to our interests. We invested a lot of time in educating that agency on our business. We described in detail our plans for several major projects, asked for their input, and told them exactly how we would like them to help us implement those plans. They nodded sagely, took a lot of notes, and appeared to be working hard on our behalf—but the results never appeared.

Finally, we turned to a freelance public relations professional who agreed to help us with our national publicity on a contract basis. Over a period of several months, she developed a good understanding of our business, and we became comfortable with her style and her abilities. She succeeded in getting good placements for us, and when the opportunity arose to create a staff position for her, we did so with the confidence of familiarity.

I don't mean to suggest that it's impossible to build a productive relationship with an agency—but for a company like ours, which is so strongly marketing-oriented, the closer, in-house relationship seems to work best.

Grassroots Campaigns

Because FastSigns is a franchisor, we're involved not only in promoting our franchise but also in promoting each of our stores. Our first project for a new store is to work with the franchisee to help get some local publicity about the grand opening—and we've found that if the press release reads like an ad for FastSigns, chances of seeing it in print are slim. Instead, we tailor each grand-opening release to the individual franchisee.

Here are a few examples:

- For a franchisee who retired from the military and returned to his hometown to open a FastSigns store, we focused on his roots in the community, how happy he and his family were to be back home, and how they were looking forward to making their store a valuable resource for local business. We made sure to send a copy of this release to the military newspaper at a nearby Air Force base, as well.
- For another franchisee, we wrote about how much she enjoyed the creative nature of the business and how delighted she was to be building a business with the power to serve the community in some

very meaningful ways. In addition to the usual media targets, we also sent this release to local and regional women's publications.

- For a franchisee who had made a complete change of professions and was new to the area, we mentioned his experience as a commercial real estate agent, how it helped him develop an understanding of the concerns of small-business owners, and how he and his family had moved halfway across the country to settle in their new city because it was such a wonderful place to raise children. We also created a special version of this release that included a paragraph about the franchisee's unique expertise in effective real estate signage and submitted it to all the area's real estate publications.

Gauging the Marketplace

We've found that different markets hold different potentials. As a rule, the smaller the market, the better the response from the local media. For example, in secondary markets like Beaumont, Texas, and Greenville, South Carolina, where the communities are small and close-knit, we can probably get the mayor and half the city council to attend our grand-opening party . . . with a newspaper photographer in tow.

But in a city like Chicago or Los Angeles, we're lucky to get a one-sentence mention in the newspaper's Business Briefs column. So how do we get publicity in larger markets?

First, by narrowing our focus. Although we do contact the major newspaper and business journals, we focus our attention on the suburban publications in the immediate area of the store. To a suburban weekly, our new store may be a hot story.

Second, we look for a way to "open up" the story—to broaden the focus and make it relevant to more people. For example, the Americans with Disabilities Act became effective in 1992, bringing with it some complex new signage requirements for almost every type of business. During that period, we shifted the focus in our press releases to emphasize the basic facts about the new law and to state that the experts at FastSigns were available to conduct on-site ADA surveys at no charge, with no obligation. That gave the press a much stronger reason to run our stories.

But Is It Working?

Only by closely tracking the results of your efforts can you determine how effective your choices have been. In advertising you can use a bounce-back mechanism (such as a reply card or discount coupon) to flag the sales that result from a particular campaign, but publicity offers you no such device. So how can you tell whether your publicity efforts are worthwhile? The short answer is that you can't.

The pursuit of publicity is largely an act of faith: You simply have to trust that your efforts will be rewarded. And if they aren't, you can take comfort in the fact that you invested much less hard cash in your bid for publicity than you would have had to spend on paid advertising.

But beware of carrying that theory too far. If you don't budget adequately for paid advertising during a crucial stage in your company's development, you'll set up a dangerous dependency on publicity stories that may never materialize. You've got to have a backup plan—and the funds to implement it.

If my partner and I hadn't managed to attract the attention of that first magazine when we did, we would have had to reach out to our target market through paid advertising far sooner. Eventually, awareness would have spread through word-of-mouth—but by that time, our cash flow would have become so sluggish that FastSigns might never have gotten off the ground.

On the other hand, you *can* get a general feel for how well your publicity is working. A clipping service can capture your print and broadcast placements for you, and it's safe to assume that every such placement has some degree of positive impact on your business.

And for every customer who mentions that he or she saw that article about you in the local business journal, there are probably 20 more who noticed it but will never think to say so . . . plus hundreds (or even thousands) of others for whom it served as one more reminder of your company's name. And that's valuable—because research has shown that it usually takes six impressions to get a customer in the door. If you can use publicity to get some of those impressions for free, you're ahead of the curve.

An example of a successful press release used by FastSigns is shown in Exhibit 21.1. It shows not only news content but format and how their logo is used for their release letterhead.

CASE 2: MICROHELP AND THE UNINSTALLER

Rick Wemmers seems almost to underplay the publicity results Wemmers Communications was able to produce for its client MicroHelp Inc. on behalf of the UnInstaller.

He says that "the integrated use of several marketing communications tools proved to be a great combination for this product." And he goes on to say that publicity gave the new product both credibility and sales support from experts in places where customers sought news and advice on purchases.

Exhibit 21.1   A Two-Page News Release for FastSigns

Contacts: Carol Kerns
             214/447-0777, ext. 247

                                                   For Immediate Release

             Mary Ryan
             214/447-0777, ext. 230

**One-day turnaround proves key
to sign franchise's success**

DALLAS, TEXAS — The FASTSIGNS® chain of one-day sign and lettering stores continues to increase its extraordinarily high per-store volume, while reinforcing its leadership position as the world's largest and fastest-growing sign franchise. With over 270 stores now open in the United States and several foreign countries, plus over 150 more sold, the FASTSIGNS network is clearly on the fast track — and gathering momentum.

Gary Salomon, the 39-year-old entrepreneur behind the FASTSIGNS phenomenon, has risen to the forefront of the one-day signage industry with remarkable speed. Based on his background in finance, marketing, and small business development, Salomon founded the company in 1985 with a test store in Dallas. That store used state-of-the-art computer systems to create precision-cut vinyl lettering, logos, and custom graphics for virtually any signage application in just one day. The selling advantages of high-quality one-day signage were readily apparent to area business owners, and the first FASTSIGNS store quickly established itself as a vital resource to the business community it served.

Success was so immediate that the test store was closely followed by two more company stores, which served as further proving grounds for the FASTSIGNS concept. Franchising began the following year. "We did a lot of research to be certain we had a valid, fully-developed concept before we took the first step," says Salomon. He attributes FASTSIGNS' remarkable record of success to two factors:

— more —

American Fastsigns, Inc. • 2550 Midway Road, Ste. 150 • Carrollton, TX 75006 • 214/447-0777 • FAX 214/248-8201

Exhibit 21.1   Continued

One-day turnaround — page 2

the high-quality, high-profit product, and the extremely thorough business

planning, operational training, and ongoing support provided to franchisees.

"What FASTSIGNS has to offer is very timely, and very much in demand in

today's competitive marketplace. We're in the business of helping other businesses

to succeed, and to build on their success."

The FASTSIGNS success story hasn't gone unnoticed: FASTSIGNS appears

consistently on the Inc. 500 list of the fastest-growing private companies in

America; Entrepreneur magazine has honored FASTSIGNS as the Number One

sign franchise every year since 1992; Success has named FASTSIGNS the Number

One Business-To-Business Franchise (1991) and Number One among sign

franchises (every year since 1991); and in 1994, Gary Salomon was personally

honored by Ernst & Young as the Retail Entrepreneur Of The Year in his region.

But perhaps the most important evaluation of all comes from Signs Of The

Times, a leading sign industry trade journal, which has twice surveyed sign

franchisees nationwide (1991 and 1994). Both surveys confirm FASTSIGNS as

the leading franchisor in virtually every area of measurement, including training,

post-investment support, and marketing.

Market leadership is a responsibility the franchisor takes seriously,

anticipating the needs of current and future franchisees and gearing up to meet

them. The FASTSIGNS support staff includes experts in franchising, business

management, computer operations, marketing, advertising, communications,

training, and personnel management, all dedicated to the franchisee's success —

"Which is, after all, the true measure of *our* success," Salomon points out.

# # #

What he doesn't mention are the size and amount of publicity that
news releases, along with certain preplanned strategies, were able to generate.

Efforts That Paid Off—BIG

As you read this section, note the news release shown in Exhibit 21.2. Your
jaw may drop more than a trifle when you realize the amount and kind of

Exhibit 21.2   This is a much different news release than most. All pertinent information is presented almost as a fact sheet and is contained in only 1¼ pages.

MicroHelp,Inc. 4359 Shallowford Industrial Parkway Marietta, GA 30066	Tel: (404)516-0899 Fax: (404)516-1099 Sales: (800)922-3383

MicroHelp News Release

For more information contact:

MicroHelp, Inc.
Customer Service
(800) 922-3383 or
(404) 516-0899

For release 9 a.m. EDT
October 15, 1993

MicroHelp Ships UnInstaller™ for Windows™

MARIETTA, Georgia -- October 15, 1993 -- MicroHelp, Inc. of Marietta, GA announced today that it has upgraded UnInstaller, its best selling utility for Windows, to version 2. This new version provides the following features:

- The ability to find and remove orphaned files
- A new System Cleanup option that removes fonts, video drivers and unneeded Windows components
- An MDI interface that includes an optional status bar, a button bar and 3-D effects
- An Undo option that will restore an uninstalled application
- Support for Norton Desktop for Windows and other popular shells
- The ability to find and remove duplicate files
- A built-in File Viewer that displays most popular file formats
- An INI editor to assist with .INI file maintenance
- Enhanced support for tracking entries in Win.ini, System.ini, Autoexec.bat and Config.sys

"UnInstaller 2 incorporates those features most requested by our customers," said Mark Novisoff, president of MicroHelp, Inc. "We are excited about this new release and confident that it will become an integral part of every Windows user's toolbox."

Availability and System Requirements

UnInstaller 2 is available immediately and can be ordered directly from MicroHelp at (800) 922-3383 or from better software resellers. Suggested retail price is $69.95. Upgrades from version 1 are $29.00 and are available directly from MicroHelp. UnInstaller 2 requires Windows 3.1 or higher, 4MB of RAM and 3MB of free disk space.

About MicroHelp

Founded in 1985, MicroHelp, Inc. is a leader in the rapidly expanding tools and utilities market. The company offers a wide range of tools for users and programmers of the Windows environment.

##########

Microsoft is a registered trademark and Windows is a trademark of Microsoft Corporation.
UnInstaller is a trademark of MicroHelp, Inc.
All prices listed are U.S. suggested retail prices. Reseller prices may vary.

publicity that early releases—along with follow-ups, of course—are generating today.

Initial Strategies

First, though, let's look at how Wemmers initially handled publicity. "Product reviews are the most powerful publicity tactic in software," he says. "A good review in the right magazine can really affect product sales positively.

"MicroHelp had already received some positive product reviews in early 1994, but this alone did not accelerate sales. It was the addition of advertising and retail promotion that seemed to make the difference."

Wemmers Communications went further than merely sending out news releases. Editors of various high-tech magazines, both vertical and horizontal, were contacted and briefed on the features and benefits of UnInstaller. Magazine articles and product review columns began to appear extolling the unique and helpful benefits of UnInstaller. "The phones began to ring and the mail poured in, asking where to find the UnInstaller," says Wemmers.

And Then in 1995 Came the Really Big Break

Often when a publication is intrigued by new developments or new products that change the way people—or in this case, equipment—do things, they search the industry for what's happening throughout. That's what *The New York Times* did. They produced a news story entirely given to information about UnInstaller, its capabilities, the company, and its president. But it included a sidebar list of the ten "Software Best Sellers," based on a survey of more than 4,000 stores. The UnInstaller placed fourth.

The Times is noted for extensive stories that give immense amounts of information. And they circulate these lengthy pieces to newspapers across this country by way of the *New York Times News Service*. Other newspapers can trim and use the amounts of information they choose to fit space allotments in their publications.

The original story was featured in a 7½ × 10½-inch box (31½ column inches) on page one of the business section, with even more space given to the jump (66 column inches) for a total of almost 100 column inches of prime business section news space . . . in *The New York Times!* Another boxed sidebar featured a story headlined "Minds Behind the Product," which was almost totally about the company's president.

And the photo no eye could miss could easily have been shot for a full-page paid advertisement instead of by one of *The New York Times*'s own news photographers. It showed the company president from the waist up, holding a package with "UnInstaller Cleans Windows" about as prominently displayed as possible. A corner of the company's building appears in the background with the shot arranged so that "MicroHelp" appears on either side of the president's head.

It's not known how many other newspapers used the story, but when it appeared in *The Dallas Morning News*, it had been trimmed to 37½ column inches. But that amounts to one-third of an entire page! Publicity for a company and its product doesn't get much better than this!

First Stories Were More Concise

When publicity first began to appear in 1993 and 1994 in such publications as *Windows* magazine, the stories were perhaps half a magazine-size page. But they contained all the information necessary to spark reader interest and sales.

Why did those initial news releases produce such enormous returns? Because they offered what every editor dreams of when she assigns a reporter to develop a news story: information about something new, something new in a high-tech field, something the public isn't aware of or doesn't understand, and the benefits users want or need—but perhaps didn't realize they wanted or needed until they read the story.

CASE 7: OREGON BFA RESPONSE

This is the type of marketing campaign most businesses won't have to consider—a ballot issue that can vitally affect the business's operation and effectiveness. But, like preparing for a crisis that you never expect to happen, such an issue could pop up for almost any type of enterprise. In this case it was the Oregon Burglar and Fire Alarm Response (OBFAR).

At the heart of this issue was the Portland Police Department's decision to stop responding to monitored burglar alarms, citing high false-alarm statistics, according to Liz Johnson of McKinney Johnson Amato (McK∗J∗A).

So the purpose behind McK∗J∗A's MMMC campaign was to bring this important issue to the attention of those affected, to the benefit of all involved—the commercial businesses, the city's police department, and the public.

It was felt that citizens needed to bring pressure on City Hall directly. But with the city anticipating the first effects of the Measure 5 fallout (the then recently passed property tax limitation measure), there also was a strong belief that public interest would be high.

Research Showed the Way

Liz Johnson describes how the McKinney Johnson Amato agency pulled its MMMC campaign together, the thinking behind it, and the three steps that were taken to get there.

> Our research included re-evaluating the actual circumstances behind the police department's statistics that were being widely quoted. Next, to solidify our position, we polled the various companies comprising the OBFAR's membership, asking them to give us their customers' point of view. Finally, we researched other communities' solutions to similar situations and drew upon our already-established body of research on the crime-fighting effectiveness of monitored alarms.
>
> We were convinced that the police had overstated their alarm burden, so we chose to position the issue as an example of local government wanting to save money at the expense of basic public safety—an action of great disservice to both the business and residential communities. The challenge was to get our point of view out without damaging the OBFAR's long-term relationship with the police department.

Strategy

> Two key issues needed to be communicated if the campaign was to succeed. The first was the importance of monitored alarms in discouraging crime and OBFAR's role as industry representative. Second, were the serious ramifications of the Police Department's proposal.
>
> The "public" we needed to reach was alarm customers who would be most affected and hopefully would bring the most pressure to bear. Beyond that targeted group, the general public needed to know that despite the formidable police statistics, false alarms were dramatically on their way down from a few years earlier. Also, the education campaign developed in cooperation with the police had not been given a chance to work.

Execution

The campaign began with McKinney Johnson Amato preparing and sending out a concise set of materials to give the news media easy access to the story. First, they sent an advisory sheet and background information to both print and broadcast news media. Next, they made a point of being sure that any articles or letters involving the false-alarm issue in the newspaper were immediately responded to with letters to the editor.

Interviews were the next step. OBFAR's executive director was placed on radio and TV talk shows and on news segments for interviews. And with his appearance on more than a dozen news shows, he became the personality for the issue. The final phase of the campaign came with placement of call-to-action ads in the *Oregonian*.

The Results Were Successful

"The campaign was extremely successful," says Johnson. It made the phones ring at City Hall, and the city council determined that the police department *could not* stop responding to monitored alarms and needed to come up with an alternative solution.

Since then, an alternative plan has been implemented with higher fines for chronic false-alarm abusers. And, as promised, the OBFAR has continued to educate alarm users on how to reduce and stop false alarms.

A Testament to the Degree of Success

The effectiveness of the campaign showed with the public's acceptance of McK*J*A's strategies, while a similar campaign, launched by the Fire Department with less thorough planning, encountered much public ridicule, says Liz Johnson with understandable pride.

CASE 9: IT TAKES ALL KINDS

We interrupt this discussion to report a breaking news story. Communicators who are not teens themselves *can* communicate with teens . . . and be *heard!*

When Lindsay, Stone & Briggs was given an assignment by The Madison Advertising Federation to develop a "diversity campaign" that would benefit Madison, Wisconsin, the agency determined it was necessary to choose one aspect of diversity and focus attention on it. Inasmuch as racism has been an issue in the community in spite of its liberal reputation, according to Marsha Lindsay, that was the aspect they agreed on, and teens were the audience to deliver the message to.

Research showed that, in general, teens are so desensitized to messages presented in an authoritative, negative tone that they merely tune them out. The alternative was to put the message into a positive context— a context within which this issue had never been presented to them, Lindsay says. And the result is that the approach used makes it "cool" to be against racism.

Promotion and advertising were substantial parts of the campaign. But since 100 percent of media time and space had to be donated, it was important to get media involved from the beginning. "They appreciated it," says Lindsay, "and endorsed the campaign."

A press conference kicked off the integrated campaign that reached across TV, bus signs, posters, radio, and billboards. It was attended by representatives from the major media, so it received publicity on television and radio news programs as well as coverage in the daily newspaper.

Hopes for the Future

Ultimately, Lindsay, Stone & Briggs hopes the campaign will prompt teens to talk about their cultural differences and to think the conversation is worthwhile and should be continued.

It's apparent the strategy is working. The agency has received teens' requests for teaser posters, interior bus signs, and other materials produced for the campaign to give away at school programs on diversity. Everyone points with pride to the fact that teens are talking about the campaign and quoting phrases used in it . . . and that schools have made their own posters with the smiley face logo and the tagline "It takes all kinds" on them.

The Lesson Is . . .

For marketers this campaign shows how to get messages through to an audience that has its music turned so high it doesn't hear any voice but its own. Teens do listen—and hear—no matter how loud the music or how tuned out they are, when you know how to talk to them. That's a technique worth copycatting!

THE BEGINNING

The last page of a book
is usually considered
The End.

This last page, we hope, is
The Beginning
of a marketing program for
your company that not only moves
it forward but also
successfully moves it upward.

INDEX